HYMNS THAT LIVE

Their Meaning & Message

FRANK COLQUHOUN

InterVarsity Press
Downers Grove
Illinois 60515

InterVarsity Press is the book-publishing division of Inter-Varsity Christian Fellowship, a student movement active on campus at hundreds of universities, colleges and schools of nursing. For information about local and regional activities, write IVCF, 233 Langdon St., Madison, WI 53703.

ISBN 0-87784-473-9

Printed in the United States of America

Library of Congress Cataloging in Publication Data

Colquhoun, Frank.
  Hymns that live.

  Bibliography: p.
  Includes indexes.
  1. Hymns, English–History and criticism.
I. Title.
BV315.C59   1981   264'.2   81-1458
ISBN 0-87784-473-9   AACR2

17	16	15	14	13	12	11	10	9	8	7	6	5	4	3	2	1
95	94	93	92	91	90	89	88	87	86	85	84	83	82	81

I THE CHURCH'S YEAR

II GENERAL HYMNS

PREFACE

HYMN SINGING, so Canon Adam Fox maintained, is by way of
being a national institution in Britain, rather in the same way
as cricket. He was writing over thirty years ago in his admirable little book, *English Hymns and Hymn Writers*, but what
he said then remains broadly true today. Church-going has
markedly declined in the meantime, but hymn singing still has
a wide appeal – to those outside the churches as well as to
those within. Such BBC programmes as 'Songs of Praise' and
'Sunday Half-Hour' are evidence of this. A great many
people who have little interest in institutional Christianity
obviously enjoy singing hymns and listening to them.

This is not altogether surprising, for hymns are the popular
element in religion, the people's part in divine service. They
were written not for parsons or musicians but for the man and
woman in the pew. Let the clergy preach their sermons and
the choirs render their anthems; the people sing their hymns,
and in their hymns they find a medium for expressing their
faith, whether they be church-goers or not.

But while hymn singing is popular, and is a factor still to be
reckoned with in our national life, it is undoubtedly true that
for the most part people do not know much about the hymns
they sing: who wrote them, how they came to be written, or
what some of their language is all about. Many, I am sure,
would like to know more and it is with this in view that I have
put together the short chapters that make up this book.

Admittedly I have not written for the more casual sort of
hymn singers but for those who are prepared to take a
genuine interest in the subject and would like to explore the
fascinating world of hymnody. For this purpose I have
selected for study just over forty representative hymns. They

9

vary considerably as regards their origin, age, authorship, churchmanship and character; but they have one thing in common: they are all hymns that have stood the test of time and are still in constant use. They can therefore rightly be described as hymns that live. For the same reason they are nearly all familiar hymns and include many of the old favourites. My endeavour has been to sketch in their background, examine their structure and language, and interpret their contents and message.

I have concentrated almost entirely on the *words* of the hymns, with only occasional and passing reference to their tunes. It is of course true that hymns cannot be separated from their tunes. They are written to be sung, and a good hymn requires a good tune to make it fully effective. But in the end the words matter most. It is what a hymn says that creates its lasting impression on the heart and mind of the singer. To find out what a hymn really does say, and its value for us today, is the object I have kept in view in writing these studies.

There are one or two other points which have a bearing on what I have written.

First, it is important to remember that hymns belong to the category of *devotional* literature. They are not simply pieces of poetry and cannot be judged as such. Many of them do in fact possess marked poetical qualities, but the aesthetic element in a hymn is not of primary importance. The devotional element counts for more. A hymn has to do with the heart rather than with the intellect. It is an expression of religious feeling as well as of religious faith. For this reason I make no apology for approaching the study of hymns from the spiritual angle and for offering a devotional (not just an academic) commentary on their contents.

The next point is that hymns – certainly the finest of them – are strongly *biblical* in character. Many of them are direct paraphrases of passages of scripture. Others are based on Bible themes and draw freely on its phraseology and imagery. I have no doubt that the close affinity which hymns have with the Bible accounts in large measure for their ecumenical appeal. The Bible is something which all Churches have in common, and hymns which keep close to its language and teaching are likely to be those which Christians in general can sing 'with one voice'. Because I regard the matter as of some importance, I have made a point of drawing attention to the biblical sources of the hymns here surveyed; and this accounts for the large number of scripture references scattered over the pages. Quotations are normally from the Revised Standard Version of the Bible, unless otherwise stated.

Again, no one can write about hymns without being deeply indebted to the work of others in this field. Julian's massive *Dictionary of Hymnology*, though dating from 1892, remains an indispensable source of factual and historical information. The companions to the standard hymnals also provide a lot of useful material. Not many books are currently available dealing with individual hymns in detail. For this reason I am particularly grateful for the assistance I have derived from the writings of G. R. Balleine, Erik Routley, and the American hymnologist Albert Bailey. Details of works quoted, and a list of other books consulted, will be found in the Bibliography at the end. Footnotes have accordingly been kept to the minimum.

It will be seen that the hymns are divided into two parts. In the first they are arranged in the order of the Church's Year; in the second they are in alphabetical order.

On a personal note: some of the studies here presented were originally given (though in a different form) as addresses at the Sunday evening services in Norwich Cathedral during the years I served there as a canon residentiary. The interest then evinced in the subject convinced me that people are interested in hymns and want to know more about them; and that fact has encouraged me in my retirement to write up these studies in a form suitable for publication.

Finally, I gratefully acknowledge the help and advice given me in this undertaking by my friend the Archdeacon of Norwich, Timothy Dudley-Smith – himself one of the leading hymn-writers of our day – who kindly read many of the chapters in manuscript form.

FRANK COLQUHOUN

ABBREVIATIONS

AV	Authorized Version of Bible, 1611
BCP	Book of Common Prayer, 1662
NEB	New English Bible, 1961 and 1970
NIV	New International Version of Bible, 1974
TEV	Today's English Version of Bible

AHB	*Anglican Hymn Book*, 1965
AMR	*Hymns Ancient and Modern Revised*, 1950
BHB	*Baptist Hymn Book*, 1962
CH	*The Church Hymnary*, 3rd edition, 1973
CP	*Congregational Praise*, 1951
EH	*The English Hymnal*, 1906
MHB	*The Methodist Hymn Book*, 1933
SP	*Songs of Praise*, 1931

I

THE CHURCH'S YEAR

1

THE ADVENT ANTIPHONS

O come, O come, Emmanuel

To ANYONE reading it for the first time, 'O come, O come, Emmanuel' must appear to be a very odd kind of Christian hymn. In fact he might well wonder whether it were not a Jewish rather than a Christian composition, for it repeatedly calls upon 'Israel' to rejoice and is full of Jewish phraseology like 'Emmanuel', 'Branch of Jesse', and 'Key of David'. It would be interesting to know what the average church-goer makes of such language. Yet without doubt this is one of the most popular Advent hymns and is in all the main hymnals. One can only conclude that it owes its popularity to its music rather than its message. The tune to which it is invariably set is certainly a fine one and very singable; but if we are to sing the *words* with any understanding we need to know something of the hymn's origin and background.

An interesting story lies behind it.

I

The story takes us back many hundreds of years to the monastic life of the medieval Church. It was customary at certain seasons of the year to sing at the office of Vespers, both before and after the Magnificat, a short versicle known as an 'antiphon' which struck the keynote of the season. During the latter part of Advent a series of seven special antiphons was appointed to be used in preparation for Christmas. Each began with a long drawn-out 'O', expressive of deep yearning for the coming of Christ, and they therefore became known as the 'great O's' of Advent. In each of them Christ was given a particular Old Testament title, and this was followed by a suitable prayer relating to his advent.

A relic of this custom is to be found in the Calendar of the Book of Common Prayer, which inserts after December 16 the cryptic expression *O Sapientia* – the first of the old Latin antiphons, meaning 'O Wisdom'. The other six began with the titles *O Adonay* (O Lord), *O Radix Jesse* (O Root of Jesse), *O Clavis David* (O Key of David), *O Oriens* (O Dayspring), *O Rex gentium* (O King of nations), and *O Emmanuel* (O Emmanuel, 'God with us').

Now we come to the next stage in the story. At some time or other – we do not know when, but Dr Neale thinks it may have been as early as the twelfth century – an unknown poet selected five of these antiphons and turned them into a Latin hymn. In doing so he changed the order, beginning with the last of them (*Veni, veni, Emmanuel*), and at the same time he added a refrain to be sung after each stanza: *Gaude, gaude . . .* ('Rejoice! Rejoice! . . .').

So much for the origin of the hymn. The final stage was reached with the translation of the Latin into English. The first of the English versions was made by Dr J. M. Neale for his *Medieval Hymns*, 1851, and is the basis of the hymn as it appears in the various editions of *Hymns Ancient and Modern*. Another version was made by Canon T. A. Lacey for the *English Hymnal*, 1906. A comparison of these will show the different ways in which the translators have tackled the hymn and interpreted its message.

But what is that message? How is this rather strange hymn to be understood?

We would suggest that there are two keys to the hymn. The first is to recognize that it is written from the stand-point of the Jewish Church, eagerly awaiting the coming of the Christ in accordance with ancient prophecy. The second is to realize that in the hymn two different voices are heard, the first one in the stanzas proper, the other in the refrain. In the stanzas themselves we hear the voice of the People of Israel as they look forward in hope and address their earnest prayer to the promised Messiah: 'O come! O come!' In the refrain we hear an answering voice – we might call it the answer of Faith, or the voice of Revelation – giving comfort and assurance to waiting Israel and saying, 'Rejoice! Rejoice!'

Let us look at the hymn in this light. We shall first follow through the five stanzas and try to unravel their hidden meaning. After that we shall turn to the joyful refrain and note its precise significance.

II

In the stanzas five pictures of Christ are presented, based on the Old Testament scriptures and derived from the original Advent antiphons. It will obviously be helpful if we quote the appropriate antiphon, or at least part of it, as we study each stanza in turn, using one or other of the two versions available.

For *O Emmanuel* the antiphon is: 'O Emmanuel, . . . the Desire of all nations and their Saviour: Come and save us, O Lord our God.' Neale's version of the stanza is:

> O come, O come, Emmanuel,
> And ransom captive Israel,
> That mourns in lonely exile here,
> Until the Son of God appear.

Here *captive Israel* is portrayed as mourning *in lonely exile* in the time of the Babylonian captivity. This sad condition is taken to be a picture of the chosen people patiently waiting *until the Son of God appear*, that is, the coming of the Messiah to save and liberate them. Particularly significant is the use of the word *Emmanuel*, meaning 'God with us'. It comes from

Isaiah 7.14 and is quoted in the first chapter of St Matthew's Gospel with reference to the birth of Jesus: 'Behold, a virgin shall conceive and bear a son, and his name shall be called Emmanuel.' Implicit in that name is the mystery of the Incarnation, God manifest in the flesh.

The second stanza takes up the antiphon beginning *O Radix Jesse*: 'O Root of Jesse, who standest as an ensign of the people, . . . to whom all nations shall seek: Come and deliver us and tarry not.'

> O come, thou Branch of Jesse! draw
> The quarry from the lion's claw;
> From the dread caverns of the grave,
> From nether hell, thy people save.

This is Canon Lacey's translation.

The expression 'Root of Jesse' used in the antiphon comes from the great messianic prophecy of Isaiah 11: 'In that day a root of Jesse shall stand as an ensign to the peoples; him shall the nations seek' (v. 10). But the translators of the stanza take their cue from the opening words of the chapter: 'There shall come forth a shoot from the stump of Jesse; and a branch shall grow out of his roots; and the Spirit of the Lord shall rest upon him . . .' Jesse was the father of David, king of Israel. What the prophet here foresees is that from the defunct royal house of David there would arise a yet greater King, anointed with the Spirit of the Lord, whose empire would embrace all nations. This promised King or Messiah is Jesus. 'Son of David' is the first title given to him in the New Testament (Matthew 1.1). His Davidic descent in fulfilment of prophecy was clearly recognized in the early Church. Thus St Paul describes God's good news as 'the gospel concerning his Son, who was descended from David according to the flesh' (Romans 1.3; see also 2 Timothy 2.8).

Against this background we can understand the words of this stanza, *O come, thou Branch of Jesse!* and the prayer that follows. David, who was renowned for his brave exploits, on one occasion rescued a lamb from the mouth of a lion (1 Samuel 17.34, 35). Hence the prayer that the coming Son of David will save his people *from the dread caverns of the grave*

20

– that is, from the fear of death – and *from nether hell*, the abode of lost souls.

The third stanza is based on the antiphon *O Oriens*: 'O Dayspring from on high, . . . and Sun of righteousness: Come and enlighten those who sit in darkness and the shadow of death.' Canon Lacey's rendering of the stanza is:

> O come, O come, thou Dayspring bright!
> Pour on our souls thy healing light;
> Dispel the long night's lingering gloom,
> And pierce the shadows of the tomb.

Oriens is literally 'East' and refers to dawn or sunrise. *Dayspring* is the old English word for daybreak. The antiphon is based on two Bible passages. The first is in the Old Testament: 'For you who fear my name the sun of righteousness shall arise, with healing in his wings' (Malachi 4.2). The second is from the *Benedictus* or Song of Zechariah: 'The dayspring from on high hath visited us, to give light to them that sit in darkness, and in the shadow of death; and to guide our feet into the way of peace' (BCP). Christ is the *Dayspring bright* whose coming marks the beginning of a new day for mankind. So we pray, in reference to Malachi's prophecy, that the Sun of righteousness may shine upon us and *pour on our souls his healing light*. We also pray, in accordance with the picture at the end of the *Benedictus*, that the 'Dayspring from on high' may *dispel the long night's lingering gloom* and 'death's dark shadows put to flight' (Neale). Christ is both Light-bringer and Life-giver.

The fourth stanza is derived from the antiphon *Clavis David*: 'O Key of David, who openest and no man shutteth, and shuttest and no man openeth: Come and bring forth from the prison house him that is bound.' Here is Neale's version of the stanza:

> O come, thou Key of David, come,
> And open wide our heavenly home;
> Make safe the way that leads on high,
> And close the path to misery.

The figure of the *Key of David* is taken from two passages, again one in the Old Testament and the other in the New. In Isaiah 22.22 the Lord gives authority to Eliakim to serve as the king's chief minister in Jerusalem and Judah, saying, 'I will place on his shoulder the key of the house of David; he shall open, and none shall shut; and he shall shut, and none shall open.' The key represents Eliakim's office and authority. In the book of Revelation this somewhat obscure reference is symbolically applied to Christ: 'The words of the holy one, the true one, who has the key of David, who opens and no one shall shut, who shuts and no one opens' (3.7). The hymn, like the antiphon, employs the symbol in the two ways indicated, of opening and shutting. So first we pray for Christ as the Key of David to *open wide our heavenly home*, for unless he admits us we cannot enter in. At the same time we pray that he will *close the path to misery* – that is, bar the way that leads to eternal death.

So we come to the last stanza and the antiphon *O Adonay*: 'O Lord, who appeared to Moses in the flame of the burning bush, and gave him the law on Sinai: Come and deliver us with an outstretched arm.'

> O come, O come, thou Lord of Might,
> Who to thy tribes, on Sinai's height,
> In ancient times didst give the law
> In cloud and majesty and awe.

Lord of Might: so Neale's version renders the Hebrew *Adonay* used in the antiphon and retained in Lacey's rendering of this stanza. *Adonay*, meaning literally 'my Lord', is the equivalent of *Jahweh* or Jehovah, the name by which God revealed himself to Moses at the burning bush (Exodus 3.15), and also *on Sinai's height* when *in ancient times* he gave Israel *the law* amidst 'thunders and lightnings and thick cloud' (Exodus 19.16f.). The Jews had such a deep reverence for the name Jehovah that they considered it too sacred to be spoken when it occurred in their synagogue worship, so the word *Adonay* was substituted for it. The significance of the word in the hymn, as in the antiphon, is that the name of God, the God of Abraham, Isaac and Jacob, is given to Jesus as the coming Messiah.

III

Such is the fivefold portrait of Christ in the stanzas of the hymn. He is seen as the Incarnate Word, the Son of David, the Light of the world, the Key to heaven's door, the Lord of might.

We now look at the refrain which follows each stanza:

> Rejoice! Rejoice! Emmanuel
> Shall come to thee, O Israel.

Here, as we have pointed out, another voice is heard, responding by way of assurance to Israel's earnest cry, 'O come! O come!' and affirming that Emmanuel shall indeed come. But that is not exactly what the Latin says:

> *Gaude, gaude; Emmanuel*
> *nascetur pro te, Israel.*

Nascetur pro te does not mean 'shall come to thee', as the translators have rendered it, in order to make it fit the tune. It means 'shall *be born* for thee'. This is a small but important point, for it has a bearing on our understanding of the hymn. It makes clear that the reference is not to the Second Coming of Christ but to his lowly birth at Bethlehem. As G. R. Balleine remarks, 'The writer was thinking not of Doomsday but of Christmas.'[1]

It is this fact that makes the hymn so suitable for use in Advent. For a short season we, as Christians, put ourselves in the position of ancient Israel, waiting and preparing for the birth of Christ, the promised Saviour. Of course, we know in fact that the wonderful thing has already happened: it is not a future but a past event. God has fulfilled his promise and the Messiah has come, born of the Virgin Mary. So Israel may rejoice. So too may the Church of Christ, the new Israel, as it makes ready once again to celebrate the feast of the Nativity of our Lord.

NOTE
1 *Sing with the Understanding*, p. 60.

2

THE ENGLISH *DIES IRAE*

Lo, he comes with clouds descending

THE CHURCH'S greatest Advent hymn, it has frequently been claimed in the past, is the *Dies Irae*. This thirteenth-century Latin hymn exists in many different English versions, including a free paraphrase made by Sir Walter Scott (see *EH* 487; *AMR* 228). Probably the best English translation is that by Dr W. J. Irons in 1848, as found in *AMR* 466, beginning:

> Day of wrath! O day of mourning!
> See fulfilled the prophet's warning!
> Heaven and earth to ashes turning!
> O what fear man's bosom rendeth
> When from heaven the Judge descendeth,
> On whose sentence all dependeth!

Undoubtedly this is a most impressive and majestic piece of writing; but no one would suggest that it is a hymn in general use in our churches or is even familiar to the average church-goer. In fact, one might question whether it really is an Advent hymn – or even a hymn at all in the ordinary sense of the word. It is certainly not suitable for congregational singing. In the Latin missal it is in the sequence of All Souls' Day and is obviously designed to be used at a requiem.

I

Of Advent hymns proper in the classical tradition none is finer than Charles Wesley's 'Lo, he comes with clouds descending', which has been called the English *Dies Irae*. Some have suggested that the hymn was prompted by the great medieval sequence, but this is very much open to question.

The hymn has a somewhat curious history. In most hymn books the name of John Cennick (1718–55) is associated with that of Wesley in regard to the hymn's authorship, and to a certain extent this is correct. Cennick, who was one of the early Methodist preachers – and incidentally the author of 'Children of the heavenly King' – did have a part in the hymn. In his *Collection of Sacred Hymns*, 1752, there is a hymn he wrote in six stanzas beginning:

> Lo! he cometh, countless trumpets
> Blow before his bloody sign!
> 'Midst ten thousand saints and angels
> See the Crucifièd shine.
> Alleluia!
> Welcome, welcome, bleeding Lamb!

This hymn would obviously have been known to Charles Wesley, who six years later published his *Hymns of Intercession for all Mankind*. Included in this was his 'Lo, he comes with clouds descending' in four stanzas – inspired no doubt by Cennick's rather crude verses, and written in the same metre, but in reality an almost entirely new composition. To compare the two versions is to reveal how little Wesley was indebted to Cennick. Apart from adopting the general theme of the latter's hymn and borrowing the odd phrase here and there, Wesley showed a masterly independence in producing his majestic verses on the theme of the Lord's coming.

An interesting point which ought to be mentioned is that one of the two stanzas by Cennick which Wesley discarded is that which begins:

26

Now redemption, long expected,
See, in solemn pomp appear.

It is hard to understand why Wesley ignored this stanza, for it is by far the finest in the whole of Cennick's hymn. However, it later attracted the attention of Martin Madan, who edited it and combined it with Wesley's verses, and published it in 1760. It appears as part of the hymn in a number of hymn books, including the *Anglican Hymn Book*.

We come back to consider the hymn as Wesley wrote it. And here at the outset the question must be asked, How are we to understand this hymn, with its extraordinarily vivid language and striking imagery? Does not its extravagant phraseology render it unsuitable for modern use? But let us be fair. The words with which Wesley clothes his hymn are taken from the New Testament, and therefore our understanding of them, and our approach to the hymn, will depend on our interpretation of the apocalyptic language used by our Lord and his apostles.

While on this subject it may be appropriate to quote some words from the report *Doctrine in the Church of England*, 1938, which in dealing with the language of worship states:

> Scriptural phrases and images have peculiar authority in the Church, and their use in worship, especially public worship, has a unique appropriateness. . . . In some cases these phrases and images seem unnatural in the present day. But it is better for us to learn to use them with an interpretation according to our needs than to discard them for others more obviously expressive of present habits of thought.
> . . . It is always to be remembered that the appropriate language of devotion is more nearly akin to poetry than to science and that there are some religious conceptions (such as Heaven) which cannot be expressed by any scientific formulation but only in symbolic language.

The principle thus stated is an important one and has a bearing on many of the hymns to be considered in this book.

II

All Wesley's hymns are steeped in the vocabulary of the Bible. In the case of 'Lo, he comes' the language is largely that of the book of Revelation: poetical, picturesque, sometimes grotesque, but always deeply meaningful. This fact is to be borne in mind as we take a brief look at the stanzas as Wesley himself wrote them, and at the same time note the manner in which he transformed Cennick's doggerel into a great Advent hymn. An exact version of Wesley's original will be found, with only one slight alteration, in the *Methodist Hymn Book* (264); also in *EH* 7, apart from the last two lines of the final verse.

> Lo, he comes with clouds descending,
> Once for favoured sinners slain;
> Thousand thousand saints attending
> Swell the triumph of his train:
> Hallelujah!
> God appears on earth to reign.

Contrast this with Cennick's opening stanza already quoted and it will be evident that Wesley has changed it almost beyond recognition. His first line echoes the words of Revelation 1.7: 'Behold, he cometh with clouds . . .' (AV) and also recalls the words of Jesus himself about 'the Son of man coming on the clouds of heaven' (Matthew 24.30; Mark 14.62). The clouds are the symbol of the divine glory. In this stanza Wesley draws attention to the fact that the Lord who comes in majesty and triumph with *thousand thousand saints attending* (cf. 1 Thessalonians 4.14) is the very one who was *once for favoured sinners slain*: scorned, rejected, crucified.

The next stanza enlarges upon this theme and answers the question, What will the coming of the Lord mean to his enemies?

> Every eye shall now behold him
> Robed in dreadful majesty,
> Those who set at nought and sold him,

> Pierced and nailed him to the tree,
> Deeply wailing
> Shall the true Messiah see.

This corresponds in some measure to Cennick's second verse which ran:

> Now his merits by the harpers
> Through the eternal deeps resounds!
> Now resplendent shine his nail-prints,
> Every eye shall see his wounds!
> They who pierced him
> Shall at his appearing wail.

Clearly Wesley did not find much inspiration here. In fact the only language he has in common with Cennick is that of the scripture passage: '. . . every eye shall see him, and they also which pierced him; and all kindreds of the earth shall wail because of him' (Revelation 1.7 av). By a far more skilful use of these words Wesley builds up a graphic picture of Christ as the Judge of mankind, *robed in dreadful majesty*, whose coming will be a cause of grief and anguish to those who, scorning his messianic claims, *set at nought and sold him* and handed him over to be crucified.

If the coming of Christ be such to his enemies, what will it mean to his own people? Cennick's effort to answer this question was in the words:

> All who love him view his glory,
> Shining in his bruisèd face:
> His dear Person on the rainbow,
> Now his people's head shall raise:
> Happy mourners!
> Now on clouds he comes! he comes!

Wesley vastly improved on this in his third stanza:

> The dear tokens of his passion
> Still his dazzling body bears;
> Cause of endless exultation
> To his ransomed worshippers;
> With what rapture
> Gaze we on those glorious scars!

Wesley here takes up another biblical theme, and one to which in his hymns he returns again and again. The risen, glorified body of the Lord still bears *the dear tokens of his passion*, the marks of the nails and the spear. When he appeared to his disciples after his resurrection he showed them his wounded hands and feet (Luke 24.39) and his pierced side (John 20.27). To St John of the Revelation he appeared as 'a Lamb as though it had been slain', worshipped by the myriad hosts of heaven as worthy to receive 'blessing and honour and glory and might for ever and ever' (Revelation 5.6,11–14).

Against this background we must interpret this stanza with its picture of Jesus in the glory of heaven, *his dazzling body* still bearing the marks of the cross, an object of *endless exultation to his ransomed worshippers*. All down the centuries the Church has cherished in its worship the emblem of Jesus as the slaughtered Lamb, as though newly slain, whose sacrificial death possesses eternal efficacy and whose 'wounds yet visible above, in glory beautified', call forth endless adoration from men and angels.

III

Suitably therefore the final stanza is a call to worship:

> Yea, amen! let all adore thee,
> High on thine eternal throne!
> Saviour, take the power and glory,
> Claim the kingdom for thine own:
> Jah, Jehovah,
> Everlasting God, come down.

The *Yea, amen!* comes again from Revelation 1.7, a double and emphatic affirmation: 'Yes, indeed! So let it be!' Nothing can alter or finally frustrate God's purpose. In the name of Jesus every knee shall bow and do him homage, *high on* his *eternal throne*, for to him belong *the kingdom, the power and* the *glory*. Hence the petition with which the stanza ends is a prayer that the *Saviour* will hasten his advent and establish his rule, in fulfilment of the Church's age-long hope.

There is little in Cennick's final stanza to correspond to Wesley, but it must be quoted if only for its last two lines:

> View him smiling, now determined
> Every evil to destroy!
> All the nations now shall sing him
> Songs of everlasting joy!
> O come quickly!
> Allelujah! come, Lord, come!

Wesley's stanza finished, as we have seen, with the words:

> Jah! Jehovah!

No modern hymnal reproduces the *Jah! Jehovah!* – no doubt because of its obscurity (Jah is the poetic form of Jehovah: see Psalm 68.4 AV). Most hymnals have substituted Cennick's final lines (e.g. *EH* 7; *CP* 160), and it must be granted that they make a fitting end to the hymn. The *Methodist Hymn Book* simply changes the 'Jah Jehovah' to 'Alleluia' and leaves 'Everlasting God, come down' unaltered. Other variants are to be found; but the hymn can scarcely finish better than by echoing the advent prayer of Revelation 22.20: 'Amen. Come, Lord Jesus!'

It only remains to add that this great hymn is matched by a splendid tune, *Helmsley*, which is attributed to Thomas Olivers (1725–99). He is said to have adapted it from an air he heard whistled in the street; but like so many legends associated with hymns, this story should probably be taken with a grain of salt.

3

THE COMING OF CHRIST

Hark the glad sound! the Saviour comes
Ye servants of the Lord

PHILIP DODDRIDGE is probably the least known of the recognized English hymn-writers of the eighteenth century. It is unlikely that in general church-goers are even acquainted with his name, though they sing his hymns: hymns such as 'My God, and is thy table spread', 'O God of Bethel, by whose hand', and 'O happy day, that fixed my choice', in addition to the two hymns listed above.

I

Doddridge (1702–51) was a contemporary of the great Isaac Watts and died only three years after him. The two men had much in common. Both were Dissenting ministers in an age of religious intolerance when not to conform to the Established Church was a costly thing – and both suffered for their convictions. Both were men of considerable learning and scholarship; both were in poor health for a large part of their lives (Doddridge died of consumption at the age of forty-nine); and both possessed poetical gifts and wrote hymns.

In this latter respect Doddridge was considerably overshadowed by Watts. Although he wrote nearly four hundred hymns in all, none of them was published till after his death. In his lifetime he was known for his prose works, and especially as the author of a book called *The Rise and Progress of Religion in the Soul*, 1739, which exercised a wide influence for a great many years. His hymns, on the other hand, were not intended for public use. They were written to be sung by his own congregation, at the end of his sermons in the Independent (Congregational) chapel at Northampton, of which he became the minister in 1729. Eventually his friend and biographer, Job Orton, collected and edited them for publication under the title *Hymns Founded on Various Texts in the Holy Scriptures by the late Philip Doddridge, D.D.,* 1755.

In his preface to this work Orton wrote:

> These hymns being composed to be sung after the Author had been preaching on the texts prefixed to them, it was his design that they should bring over again the leading thoughts in the sermon, and naturally express and warmly enforce those devout sentiments which he hoped were then rising in the minds of his hearers, and help to fix them on the memory and heart.

This not only explains how and why the hymns came to be written. It also accounts for their strongly biblical character. Some of them read like mini-sermons. Many are simply paraphrases of scripture passages. For the most part they were hurriedly written and do not consistently reach a high standard. Less than a score of them have survived; the largest selection (14) will be found, rightly enough, in *Congregational Praise*.

The two hymns at which we are going to look in this chapter serve as admirable examples of Doddridge's hymn-writing at its best. Both are of an Advent character. The first relates to the coming of Christ in history, to be the Saviour of mankind; the second refers to his coming beyond history, to judge and reward his servants.

II

The manuscript of 'Hark the glad sound! the Saviour comes' is still in existence. It is dated December 28, 1735, which indicates that it was sung on the Sunday after Christmas. The heading is 'Christ's Message, from Luke 4.18, 19', so we know what the preacher's text was that morning. The passage tells of our Lord's visit to Nazareth at the beginning of his ministry when 'he went to the synagogue on the sabbath day, and stood up to read'. Handed the book of the prophet Isaiah, he read the passage from chapter 61, verses 1 and 2 (AV):

> The Spirit of the Lord is upon me, because he hath anointed me to preach the gospel to the poor; he hath sent me to heal the broken-hearted, to preach deliverance to the captives, and recovering of sight to the blind, to set at liberty them that are bruised, to preach the acceptable year of the Lord.

Out of these prophetic words the preacher fashioned his hymn. In its original form it consisted of seven verses. Anglican hymn books print only four of them. Other books (e.g. *CP* 74; *BHB* 81) give five. We will take note of the omitted stanzas as we now survey the hymn.

> Hark the glad sound! the Saviour comes,
>   The Saviour promised long:
> Let every heart prepare a throne,
>   And every voice a song.

Isaiah's words were about the coming of the Messiah – the Lord's 'Anointed' – and his mission in the world. After reading the passage Jesus amazed the synagogue congregation by declaring, 'Today this scripture has been fulfilled in your hearing.' Hence the reference in the hymn to Jesus as *the Saviour promised long*. What the prophet had foretold centuries beforehand, Jesus has fulfilled. The stupendous thing has happened. The Christ has come! What then? *Let every heart* enthrone him, let *every voice* sing for joy.

The second stanza is one of those omitted from our hymnals:

> On him the Spirit largely poured
> Exerts its sacred fire;
> Wisdom and might and zeal and love
> His holy breast inspire.

The allusion here is to the opening words of the prophecy: 'The Spirit of the Lord is upon me.' The scene in the synagogue at Nazareth took place, according to Luke's account, soon after the Lord's baptism when the Holy Spirit descended upon him in the form of a dove (3.21, 22). After this, 'Jesus returned to Galilee in the power of the Spirit' (4.14), and thus endued with *wisdom and might and zeal and love* entered upon his Messianic ministry.

The next stanza tells of the purpose of his mission:

> He comes, the prisoners to release
> In Satan's bondage held;
> The gates of brass before him burst,
> The iron fetters yield.

Clearly this links up with the prophetic words, 'He hath sent me to preach deliverance to the captives, . . . to set at liberty them that are bruised'. In the original prophecy the reference was probably to the release of the Jews from their Babylonian captivity. Jesus gives the words a deeper and wider meaning. His mission in the world was not to be a sort of 'freedom-fighter' and rescue his nation from the tyranny of Rome. He deliberately rejected any such conception of Messiahship. As the Lord's Anointed he had come to free mankind from its spiritual imprisonment, to liberate those *in Satan's bondage held*, to break *the iron fetters* of sin.

Doddridge's third stanza, omitted from some of our hymnals, refers to the prophecy, 'He hath sent me to preach recovering of sight to the blind'. As slightly amended by Orton it reads:

> He comes, from thickest films of vice
> To clear the mental ray,
> And on the eyeballs of the blind
> To pour celestial day.

The rather curious wording is largely derived from a couplet in Pope's *Messiah* (1712):

> He from thick films shall purge the visual ray,
> And on the sightless eyeball pour the day.

The mission of Jesus was to bring light to the blind as well as liberty to the bound.

With the next stanza we are back on familiar ground:

> He comes, the broken heart to bind,
>   The bleeding soul to cure,
> And with the treasures of his grace
>   To enrich the humble poor.

'He hath sent me to heal the broken-hearted' is the basis of the first two lines. Another purpose of our Lord's coming was to fulfil a ministry of consolation, to bring healing to troubled hearts and minds. And more: he came, as the opening words of the prophecy declared, 'to preach the gospel to the poor'. These words would have made a particular appeal to Dr Doddridge, for he was a man with a strong social concern and a deep compassion for the poor. Doubtless many in his own congregation at Northampton were numbered among *the humble poor*, and one can well imagine that in his sermon on that Sunday after Christmas in 1735 the preacher did not fail to press home the good news that the Saviour came to *enrich* (not to 'bless', as *AMR*) the poverty-stricken *with the treasures of his grace*.

The next stanza has dropped out of use, and rightly so. No congregation nowadays would be able to make sense of it:

> His silver trumpets publish loud
>   The Jubilee of the Lord;
> Our debts are all remitted now,
>   Our heritage restored.

In these terms Doddridge interpreted the final words of the prophecy, '. . . to preach the acceptable year of the Lord.' For him this became the Jewish year of Jubilee, the joyful fiftieth year, which was heralded by the blowing of trumpets and was the occasion when debts were remitted, slaves released, and

property restored to its original owners. We must assume that
all this had been explained by the learned preacher in his
sermon. In effect what he is saying here is that 'the acceptable
year of the Lord' is the era of salvation inaugurated by the
coming of Christ.

With a splendid final stanza Doddridge rounds off his hymn
on a note of praise in which the Church on earth echoes the
songs of heaven:

> Our glad hosannas, Prince of peace,
>   Thy welcome shall proclaim;
> And heaven's eternal arches ring
>   With thy belovèd name.

III

The other hymn we are looking at, 'Ye servants of the Lord',
is also about the coming of Christ: not the Christ who came to
save mankind but the Christ who is coming to reckon with his
servants and recompense their work. In Doddridge's manuscript it is headed 'The Active Christian' and the scripture
reference is Luke 12.35–38, in which Jesus says:

> Let your loins be girded and your lights burning, and be like
> men who are waiting for their master to come home from the
> marriage feast, so that they may open to him at once when he
> comes and knocks. Blessed are those servants whom the master
> finds awake when he comes; truly, I say to you, he will gird
> himself and have them sit at table, and he will come and serve
> them. If he comes in the second watch, or in the third, and finds
> them so, blessed are those servants!

The hymn is very much a paraphrase of these words and
calls for little comment. Christians are to be ready for the
coming of the Lord, like vigilant servants awaiting their master's return:

> Ye servants of the Lord,
> Each in his office wait,

37

> Observant of his heavenly word,
> And watchful at his gate.

But waiting and watching are not enough. The servant who would be truly prepared for the Lord's coming must have his lamp burning – that is, maintain a clear witness – and his loins girded, ready for active service:

> Let all your lamps be bright,
> And trim the golden flame;
> Gird up your loins as in his sight,
> For aweful is his name.

The hour of his coming is unknown. He may already be on his way. This calls for an attitude of ceaseless vigilance:

> Watch! 'tis your Lord's command,
> And while we speak, he's near;
> Mark the first signal of his hand,
> And ready all appear.

'Blessed are those servants whom the master finds awake when he comes,' said Jesus. Not sleeping in sin, but awake and rejoicing in his praises (as an ancient Gelasian collect puts it) is what he requires of each of us:

> O happy servant he
> In such a posture found!
> He shall his Lord with rapture see,
> And be with honour crowned.

The servant's rich reward will be to share in the heavenly feast, prepared by the Lord himself:

> Christ shall the banquet spread
> With his own royal hand,
> And raise that favoured servant's head
> Amidst the angelic band.

The original third line was, 'And raise that favourite servant's head', the word *favourite* being used in its eighteenth-century sense of 'regarded with especial favour' (*Shorter OED*). We have followed *Congregational Praise* in substituting *favoured* as giving the right meaning. Most other hymnals adopt 'faithful'.

The message of the hymn, like that of the parable on which

it is based, is unmistakably clear. The Lord's coming (*parousia*) is not a subject for theological debate or idle speculation but a call to holy living and dedicated service. The Active Christian, to use Doddridge's phrase, is the one who is ready for Christ's Advent – when ever, or how ever, he may come. None of us knows how much time is left to us. That is why Jesus applied his parable by saying, 'Hold yourselves ready for Christ's Advent – when ever, or how ever, he may expect him' (Luke 12.40 NEB).

4

ADESTE FIDELES

O come, all ye faithful

UNTIL COMPARATIVELY recently the authorship of the hymn *Adeste Fideles* was shrouded in mystery. Scholars were agreed that the Latin original was not of ancient date, as had at one time been assumed. On the evidence available they came to the conclusion that the hymn was probably of French authorship and not earlier than 1700. Hence hymn books published before the middle of this century treated words and music as anonymous and simply assigned it a date in the eighteenth century. And then came a surprising discovery. The hymn, it seemed, instead of being the work of an unknown Frenchman, was actually written by a young Englishman, John Wade, round about the year 1743.

I

This discovery was made when a hitherto unknown manuscript of the Latin hymn came to light in 1946 and was acquired by the hymnologist Maurice Frost, vicar of Deddington, Oxfordshire. The manuscript was carefully examined by Dom Jean Stephens, who after comparing it with other existent manuscripts published his findings in 1949. As a result of his researches he confidently declared that the hymn (words and music) was written by John Francis Wade (*c.*1711–86), a Roman Catholic layman who, while English by birth, lived and worked in Douai, the famous Catholic centre in France where there was an English college. He spent his time in teaching Latin and making beautiful copies of music for use in churches and private chapels.

Dom Stephens concluded that Wade wrote the Latin hymn, comprising the four familiar verses (as in *EH* 28 and *AMR* 59) when he was thirty-two years of age. In all the early manuscript copies it is accompanied by the tune which we know as *Adeste Fideles*, and there is no reason to doubt that this also was Wade's composition. So it comes about that in hymn-books published after 1950 John Wade is usually given the credit for the hymn and its music, though sometimes a cautious 'probably' or 'possibly' is added to the ascription.

What of the three additional stanzas which appear in some hymnals, particularly when the hymn is intended for processional use (*EH* 614; *AMR* 593)? Two of these were the work of the French Abbé, Mgr Etienne Borderies, who having heard the hymn while exiled in England in 1793, wrote the additional verses (in Latin) on his return to France in the following year. As translated into English by W. T. Brooke in the *Altar Hymnal*, 1884, they run:

> See how the shepherds,
> Summoned to his cradle,
> Leaving their flocks, draw nigh with lowly fear;
> We too will thither
> Bend our joyful footsteps:
>
> Child, for us sinners,
> Poor and in the manger,
> Fain we embrace thee, with awe and love;
> Who would not love thee,
> Loving us so dearly?

The remaining stanza, according to Julian, was added by an unknown author (*c.*1868) in order to make provision for the feast of the Epiphany. This we also owe to Brooke's translation:

Lo! star-led chieftains,
Magi, Christ adoring,
Offer him incense, gold, and myrrh;
We to the Christ Child
Bring our hearts' oblations:

In our study of the hymn we are not concerned further with these additions. We shall look at the original four stanzas which in their English version are based on the translation made in 1841 by Canon Frederick Oakeley. At the time he was incumbent of St Margaret's Chapel (now All Saints', Margaret Street), London. His rendering of the hymn was made for use by his own congregation, and keeping close to the Latin text it begins:

Ye faithful, approach ye,
Joyfully triumphant.

Several alterations and improvements were made when the hymn was printed in Murray's *Hymnal*, 1852, and it quickly became one of the most popular Christmas hymns.

It has two unusual features. The first is its irregular metre; all four stanzas are dissimilar in their metrical form. Nevertheless we have little difficulty in accommodating the words to the tune. The other feature is more unusual still – the lack of rhyme. No single line rhymes with any other. There are very few hymns which share this peculiarity; yet strangely enough we are not conscious of it when we sing the hymn at Christmas.

Each of the four stanzas has its distinctive character. They can be summarized as follows: (i) an invitation to Bethlehem; (ii) an affirmation of faith; (iii) an exhortation to worship; and (iv) a salutation to the new-born King.

II

The first stanza is an invitation to Bethlehem, to gaze with adoration on the Holy Child:

42

> O come, all ye faithful,
> Joyful and triumphant,
> O come ye, O come ye to Bethlehem;
> Come and behold him,
> Born the King of angels:
> O come, let us adore him, Christ the Lord.

It is hardly surprising that we are invited to *come to Bethlehem*, for that is where all roads lead at Christmas time. It was the road travelled by Mary and Joseph when they left Nazareth in Galilee and made their way south to Judaea for the enrolment decreed by the Roman authorities. It was the road followed by the shepherds on the night of the Nativity after they had received the staggering tidings of the Messiah's birth. It was the road taken by the Magi when at Herod's injunction they left Jerusalem to seek the infant King in the city of David. It is the road which, in heart and mind and imagination, *all* the *faithful* tread at Christmas as they seek to comprehend more fully the ultimate truth that lies behind the child in the manger – Mary's child, yet *born the King of angels*.

And what is that truth? The next stanza supplies the answer in the form of an affirmation of faith in the mystery of the Incarnation:

> God of God,
> Light of Light,
> Lo! he abhors not the Virgin's womb;
> Very God,
> Begotten, not created:
> O come, let us adore him, Christ the Lord.

Free Church hymnals (e.g. *MHB* 118, *CP* 85, *BHB* 104) tend to follow Godfrey Thring's revision of this verse:

> True God of true God,
> Light of Light eternal,
> Lo, he abhors not the Virgin's womb;
> Son of the Father,
> Begotten, not created.

The alterations were doubtless made to match the words more closely to the tune. Oakley's translation, on the other hand, keeps to the Latin text and echoes the words of the

Nicene Creed, where the incarnate Son is defined as 'God of God, Light of Light, Very God of Very God, begotten, not made'. The meaning, however, in either case is the same. The stanza is a confession of the Church's historic faith that in the person of Jesus God was uniquely present in our humanity's flesh and blood. The child of Mary was also the everlasting Son of the Father.

Admittedly words are inadequate to express such a mystery, and the human mind is incapable of grasping all that it means; but the underlying truth lies at the very heart of the Christian revelation. Without it nothing in the life and teaching, or death and resurrection, of Jesus makes sense in the light of the New Testament records.

III

The Incarnation is not simply a piece of religious dogma. It is a theme for exultant song; and so the third stanza of this hymn takes the form of an exhortation to the angels to sing their *Gloria in excelsis Deo*:

> Sing, choirs of angels,
> Sing in exultation,
> Sing, all ye citizens of heaven above:
> Glory to God
> In the highest:
> O come, let us adore him, Christ the Lord.

The reference to St Luke's story of the first Christmas night is plain enough:

> Suddenly there was with the angel a multitude of the
> heavenly host praising God and saying,
> 'Glory to God in the highest,
> and on earth peace among men with whom he is
> pleased!'
>
> (Luke 2.13,14)

44

Christmas is a time for singing. What would the festival be without our carols and hymns? Yet when Jesus was born at Bethlehem the world was wrapped in silence – a point which Bishop Phillips Brooks makes effectively in his hymn:

> O little town of Bethlehem,
> How still we see thee lie!

But while earth was silent, the *choirs of angels* sang – sang *in exultation*. And the *citizens of heaven above* may well have shared in their song, crying, *Glory to God in the highest!* Certainly the Church has never ceased to echo the angels' song in its worship down the centuries. The *Gloria in Excelsis* – the Angelical Hymn, as it is known in the Eastern Church – is one of the most ancient parts of the liturgy. It serves as a continual reminder that Christianity was born in song, and that glory is due to God supremely because in the coming of Christ to our world he has visited and redeemed his people.

The hymn's final stanza is a salutation or greeting to the Saviour as we joyfully celebrate his nativity.

> Yea, Lord, we greet thee,
> Born this happy morning;
> Jesu, to thee be glory given;
> Word of the Father,
> Now in flesh appearing:
> O come, let us adore him, Christ the Lord.

The line *Born this happy morning* virtually restricts the use of this stanza to Christmas Day. On other occasions it should be omitted (e.g. when used before or after Christmas), or other words substituted for it, such as 'Born for us a Saviour'.

However, on the great feast-day itself the stanza makes a perfect conclusion to the hymn. With hearts full of wonder and gratitude we greet our Lord and give glory to him as the incarnate *Word of the Father*. So here once again we are reminded of what Christmas is all about: 'The Word became flesh, and dwelt among us, full of grace and truth' (John 1.14).

5

ONCE UPON A TIME . . .

Once in royal David's city

How CAN one teach the great doctrines of the Christian faith to little children?

That was the problem confronting the young Irish Sunday school teacher, Fanny Humphreys, in the middle of the last century. She lived in the parish of Strathbane in Northern Ireland, and it was her duty to instruct her class in the Church Catechism. This involved among other things explaining to them the various articles of the Apostles' Creed.

It was a formidable task. To make the deep truths of the creed have some meaning for the small children gathered round her Sunday by Sunday was no easy matter. But happily Fanny found a solution. She was a poet, and she knew that children loved poetry; so she decided to write some simple hymns to illustrate the catechism.

I

Her collection of *Hymns for Little Children* was published in 1848, when she was twenty-five years of age. At her request the Revd John Keble (whom she had met previously in England) wrote a foreword in which he commended the hymns and stated that the profits on the publication would be applied to the support of a school for deaf and dumb children in the north of Ireland. Since the book was an immediate success and went through over a hundred editions the charity school must have benefitted considerably. This would have delighted its author, who throughout her life did everything in her power to help those in poverty, need or sickness.

A year or two after the publication of the book she married a clergyman of about the same age as herself, the Revd William Alexander, who was destined to become Bishop of Derry and eventually Primate of All Ireland. This explains why her name is known to us as Mrs Cecil Frances Alexander. She continued writing verse after her marriage, and among her later hymns which are widely known are 'Jesus calls us' (for St Andrew's Day) and 'I bind unto myself to-day' (for Trinity Sunday).

It is however as a writer of children's hymns that she is chiefly remembered. Three of them from *Hymns for Little Children* are in every hymnal and are familiar to every church-goer. All three come from the second section of the book dealing with the Creed. To illustrate the words *Maker of heaven and earth* is the hymn 'All things bright and beautiful'; for *Who was conceived by the Holy Ghost, born of the Virgin Mary* there is 'Once in royal David's city'; and for *Suffered under Pontius Pilate, was crucified, dead, and buried* the hymn 'There is a green hill far away'. These hymns deal with three cardinal doctrines of the Faith: Creation, the Incarnation, and the Atonement; and they show the way in which the young teacher-poet set about her task.

For one thing, she uses simple language which a child can understand. For another, she writes the sort of poetry which a child can easily learn and remember. Most important of all, she seeks to capture interest by appealing to the imagination. She does not begin a hymn with abstract theology: that would only puzzle or bore a child. She begins by painting a picture, by telling a story, and against that background she develops her teaching.

One of the remarkable facts about these hymns is that, although they were written for children, they are just as suitable for adults and are sung quite normally by adults without any feeling of embarrassment. This is because while they are simple, they are not childish or sentimental. There is another fact, none the less remarkable. Though written well over a century ago, the hymns have lost none of their appeal down the years. Children's hymns usually become dated very soon. Mrs Alexander's are timeless. They are as popular today, with Christians of all traditions, as they ever were; and they require no editing or revising. This is a good thing, for she strongly resented any attempts to tamper with hymns – her own or anyone else's – and regarded it as 'literary sacrilege'.

The hymn we have chosen to look at, 'Once in royal David's city', is a good example of what we have been saying. Inevitably we associate it with Christmas; but we do well to remember that it was not written specifically as a Christmas hymn. It was written to teach children the meaning of the event we celebrate at Christmas, with a view to making clear not only *what* happened but *why* it happened, and some of the implications for ourselves.

Looking at the hymn as a whole, we observe that its six stanzas fall quite naturally into three pairs. The first pair is concerned with our Lord's nativity and what it means; the second deals with the pattern of his childhood; the third points to his heavenly glory which at last we shall see and share.

II

In the first two stanzas Mrs Alexander is dealing not simply with history but with theology. She has to grapple with the profound mystery of the Incarnation. However, she does not make the mistake of starting her hymn with a sermon. She starts it with a story – the most wonderful story in the world, the story of the first Christmas. What is more, knowing that for young children a good story always begins 'Once upon a time . . .' she begins her story in the same way:

> Once in royal David's city
> Stood a lowly cattle shed,
> Where a mother laid her Baby,
> In a manger for his bed.
> Mary was that mother mild,
> Jesus Christ her little Child.

Here in this first stanza the scene is set and the tale unfolds. *Royal David's city* is of course Bethlehem, the birthplace of the shepherd boy who became King of Israel. It was here another King was born many centuries later; but his birth did not take place in the comfort of a house, with all needful help ready to hand. It happened in *a lowly cattle shed*, so that Mary his mother *laid her Baby in a manger* – as St Luke tells us (2.7). But the evangelist does not actually make mention of a stable or a shed. Early tradition, going back as far as Justin Martyr in the second century, states that the birthplace was a cave, and it may well have been so. We cannot be sure. What is certain beyond all doubt is that Jesus was born in conditions of utmost poverty.

The second stanza has something more to say about this; but first it answers the question, What is the real significance of the birth of Jesus?

> He came down to earth from heaven,
>   Who is God and Lord of all,
> And his shelter was a stable,
>   And his cradle was a stall;
> With the poor, and mean, and lowly,
> Lived on earth our Saviour holy.

Here, almost entirely in words of one syllable, the sublime mystery of the Incarnation is stated in the first two lines. Who is this baby in the manger? Incredible as it sounds, he is none other than *God and Lord of all*, who in his amazing love and great humility *came down to earth from heaven*. The Creator took the form of a creature. The Eternal invaded the territory of time. God became Man. This is what is expressed in more profound and philosophical language in the prologue to the

49

fourth Gospel (John 1.1–18). Mrs Alexander puts it in language a child can understand. Then, having stated the fundamental truth, she goes on to contrast the divine and human aspects of this deep mystery. He who is God and Lord of all 'emptied himself' of his glory, 'taking the form of a servant, being born in the likeness of men' (Philippians 2.7). And how humble were the circumstances of his birth! *His shelter* – nothing but *a stable*; *his cradle* – not a cot but *a stall*. And as he *lived on earth* among men it was *with the poor, and mean, and lowly*. Well may St Paul write, 'You know the grace of our Lord Jesus Christ, that though he was rich, yet for your sake he became poor, so that by his poverty you might become rich' (2 Corinthians 8.9).

III

The next pair of verses leads us on from the birth of Jesus to his childhood and the pattern it set.

> And through all his wondrous childhood
>   He would honour and obey,
> Love and watch the lowly maiden
>   In whose gentle arms he lay.
> Christian children all must be
> Mild, obedient, good as he.

The scriptures have little to say about the 'hidden years' and what happened to Jesus *through all his wondrous childhood*. The only explicit glimpse we get of this is in St Luke's account of his visit to the temple with his parents at the age of twelve (2.41–51). The record ends with the words, 'He went down with them to Nazareth, and was obedient to them.' We may therefore be sure that *he would honour and obey* his mother, who is given here the title of *the lowly maiden*. This is an oblique allusion to the virgin birth, and possibly to the Catholic concept of Mary's perpetual virginity. Be that as it may, in this hymn it is the holy Child and not his mother who is in the centre of the picture. Attention is fixed on him as *our childhood's pattern* (verse 4), the one whom *Christian children all must* endeavour to imitate – and so *be mild, obedient, good as he.*

The adjectives used by Mrs Alexander in this last line of the stanza are not those which a modern writer would choose in speaking of the ideals of childhood. They belong very much to the age in which they were written, an age when children were to be seen rather than heard. The language must be judged and understood in this light. In singing the hymn today we need simply to remember that here we are being taught to cultivate the childlike spirit, which is also the Christlike spirit of humility, gentleness, and love.

This theme is continued in the next stanza:

> For he is our childhood's pattern,
>   Day by day like us he grew,
> He was little, weak, and helpless,
>   Tears and smiles like us he knew;
> And he feeleth for our sadness,
> And he shareth in our gladness.

Day by day like us he grew. Twice St Luke refers to the growth of Jesus as a boy. The first is in the words, 'The child grew and became strong, filled with wisdom; and the favour of God was upon him'; the second: 'Jesus increased in wisdom and stature, and in favour with God and man' (2.40, 52). The stress is upon the true humanity of Jesus and his normal development as a child, growing (as all children should) physically, mentally, and spiritually. And because he was fully human, we must accept that in his earliest years *he was little, weak, and helpless*, and knew *tears and smiles* like any other child. The final two lines highlight one of the most beautiful qualities of character as exemplified by Jesus: his ability to sympathize with *our sadness* and participate *in our gladness*.

IV

The last pair of stanzas is concerned with the glory of Jesus in heaven.

> And our eyes at last shall see him,
>   Through his own redeeming love,
> For that Child so dear and gentle
>   Is our Lord in heaven above;
> And he leads his children on
> To the place where he is gone.

In ending her hymn in this sort of way Mrs Alexander was following the conventional pattern of her time. Victorian hymn-writers were very 'heavenly-minded' and customarily finished their hymns with a verse or two about the beatific vision and the life everlasting. This is what we have here in this and the companion stanza. The one born in such lowly circumstances at Bethlehem, *that Child so dear and gentle*, is still the centre of the picture, but now he is *our Lord in heaven above*. There *our eyes at last shall see him* in his divine glory, for he is the forerunner of his people and has entered heaven ahead of us, as he promised: 'I go to prepare a place for you, . . . that where I am, you may be also' (John 14.2, 3). Thither then *he leads his children on*. But how different is *the place where he is gone* from the place where he was born!

> Not in that poor lowly stable,
>   With the oxen standing by,
> We shall see him; but in heaven,
>   Set at God's right hand on high;
> When like stars his children crowned,
> All in white shall wait around.

The *poor lowly stable* in Bethlehem *with the oxen standing by* contrasts strongly with the glory of the heavenly home where Jesus is now, *set at God's right hand on high*. Bethlehem is but the beginning of the good news. Now we are told the ultimate reason why Jesus came to this world of ours and was born of the Virgin Mary. He came to be where *we* are in order that he might take us to be where *he* is. And the hymn ends with a picture of *his children* gathered round him in heaven, shining *like stars, crowned* with glory, and robed *all in white*. For the scriptural allusions, see Daniel 12.3; 1 Peter 5.4; and Revelation 7.9.

A hymn 'for little children' – that is why Mrs Alexander wrote it. Accordingly the *English Hymnal* places it in the Catechism section, but adds a note: *Suitable also for Adults.* So indeed it is. In the end it does not matter very much whether we are children or grown-ups. We all love singing this hymn, and there is something of value in it for us all.

6

CHRISTMAS IN BETHLEHEM

O little town of Bethlehem

TWO POPULAR Christmas hymns have come to us from America, this one and 'It came upon the midnight clear' by Dr Edmund Sears, a Unitarian minister. 'O little town of Bethlehem' was written by Bishop Phillips Brooks (1835–93), one of the giants of the American pulpit in the last century. He was a giant in more ways than one, for he stood six feet six in height and was a most impressive figure in the pulpit. But he was a big man in other ways too. Repeated testimony is borne to his outstanding power as a preacher, his broad sympathies, his strong Christian personality which radiated the love of God. He appealed to people of all kinds of belief, all classes, all ages. Though he was a bachelor, he had a deep love for children, and that love was fully reciprocated by them. He exercised his main ministry as rector of the famous Trinity Church, Boston, from 1869 to 1891. In the latter year he was elected Bishop of Massachusetts, but he died less than two years later.

Such, in briefest outline, is the man who wrote our hymn.

I

The hymn was written in the early days of his ministry when he was rector of a church in Philadelphia. Just turned thirty,

54

he set out on a period of travel overseas, and Christmas 1866 found him in the Holy Land. On Christmas Eve he rode on horseback from Jerusalem to Bethlehem, looked around the village, visited the Field of the Shepherds, and finally joined in the midnight service in the Church of the Nativity.

The experience made a deep impression on him. Having spent Christmas in Bethlehem he had a desire to record something of what he had felt and seen; and on his return to Philadelphia he wrote his hymn, explicitly for the children of his Sunday school. The superintendent of the school, who was also the church organist, composed a suitable tune for it, and the hymn quickly established a place in the worship of the American churches.

Not till some time later did it come into use in England. In fact, it was little known until it appeared in the *English Hymnal*, 1906. Sir Walford Davies did much to popularize it with the appealing tune he wrote for the hymn called *Christmas Carol*. For congregational singing *Forest Green* – an arrangement of a traditional English melody made by Dr Vaughan Williams for *EH* – has proved to be most suitable.

Our concern is to discover what the hymn says to us. In its complete form it consists of five stanzas, as in *EH* 15. A good many books (e.g. *AMR* 65) omit the fourth, for reasons which we shall note in due course. For the moment we must survey the hymn as a whole. As we do so we soon discover that each stanza has a character of its own. The first is descriptive and sets the scene in the sleeping town of Bethlehem. The second takes the form of a poetic narrative of the Christmas event. The third is a reflection on the way in which God comes to men in Christ. The fourth develops this in a little homily on Christmas and the human situation. The fifth is a personal prayer that the holy Child of Bethlehem may be born in us and abide with us always.

All this is worth looking at in a little more detail.

II

We begin with Bethlehem on Christmas night. All is peaceful and normal – or at least, so it seems:

> O little town of Bethlehem,
>   How still we see thee lie!
> Above thy deep and dreamless sleep
>   The silent stars go by:
> Yet in thy dark streets shineth
>   The everlasting Light;
> The hopes and fears of all the years
>   Are met in thee to-night.

Little town of Bethlehem – little indeed, for Bethlehem was not much more than a village, situated some six miles south of Jerusalem. But small though it may have been, Bethlehem was by no means insignificant. It was known as 'the city of David' (Luke 2.11), being the place where he was born. It had another significance as well, for it figured in an important messianic prophecy: 'You, O Bethlehem Ephrathah, who are little to be among the clans of Judah, from you shall come forth for me one who is to be ruler in Israel, whose origin is from of old, from ancient days' (Micah 5.2).

On Christmas night little Bethlehem seems no different from usual. It is sleeping peacefully under *the silent stars*. To all appearances – *How still we see thee lie!* But there is more here than meets the eye. God is working his purpose out, and all unknown to its people this is an historic night for Bethlehem. In its *dark streets* there is shining *the everlasting Light*, the light of Christ; for 'the true light that enlightens every man was coming into the world' (John 1.9). *The hopes and fears of all the years met* in that climactic moment. 'The world's only true Hope came, and by coming conquered all the fears to which mankind, whether in the first or the twentieth century, is a prey' (G. F. S. Gray).

What happened that night is related in poetical language in the next stanza.

CHRISTMAS IN BETHLEHEM

O morning stars, together
  Proclaim the holy birth,
And praises sing to God the King,
  And peace to men on earth;
For Christ is born of Mary;
  And, gathered all above,
While mortals sleep, the angels keep
  Their watch of wondering love.

Christ is born of Mary. Such is the great fact of Christmas: the heart of the whole matter and the central affirmation of this stanza. But surrounding the event itself the hymn-writer discerns much activity in the spiritual world. The angels were busy when Jesus was born. They are referred to both at the beginning and at the end of the stanza. The *morning stars* which are called upon to *proclaim the holy birth* are in fact the 'Christmas angels' of the fifth stanza, the same 'morning stars' that sang together at creation (Job 38.7). It was to the shepherds that they made their proclamation and sang their anthem, ascribing glory to God in the highest and announcing *peace to men on earth* (Luke 2.14). Again, *while mortals sleep*, they are pictured as *gathered all above* and keeping *their watch of wondering love* over the holy Child and his mother – like the two cherubim overshadowing the mercy-seat (Exodus 25.20). There is probably also a reference here to 1 Peter 1.12, where the apostle describes the gospel mysteries as 'things into which angels desire to look'. His words indicate the angels' intense interest in the salvation of sinful men (*cf.* Luke 15.10) while at the same time implying that the work of redemption is ultimately beyond their comprehension. The words of one of Charles Wesley's hymns conveys the meaning:

The first-born sons of light
Desire in vain its depths to see,
They cannot reach the mystery,
  The length and breadth and height.

III

It happened so strangely, the writer reflects, this amazing thing, this coming of God into his world in our human flesh and blood.

> How silently, how silently,
>   The wondrous gift is given!
> So God imparts to human hearts
>   The blessings of his heaven.
> No ear may hear his coming;
>   But in this world of sin,
> Where meek souls will receive him, still
>   The dear Christ enters in.

The miracle of the Incarnation takes place so quietly. There is no pomp and show. No fanfare announces the event. *How silently* God comes! *How silently the wondrous gift is given!* Who would have dreamt that the phenomenon of God-become-Man would have taken place in so obscure a fashion? In the words of Dr J. Paterson Smyth:

> Simply, ordinarily as the coming of the dawn, happened this tremendous thing in the history of the universe, the coming of the Lord of Glory into human life. On the earthly side just a stable, a manger, the cattle in the stalls, a woman wrapping her baby in swaddling clothes. Nothing of wonder in it. Nothing of awe. Until the world from which he came flashes in upon the scene, where high over the stable, outside in the starlight, was the heavenly host, stirred to its depths at the coming of the Christ-child.

God moves in a mysterious way, as the poet William Cowper reminds us, his wonders to perform. And it was so in the supreme wonder of the Word made flesh. In similar manner he fulfils his purpose in human lives today and imparts to us *the blessings of his heaven*; and though *no ear may hear his coming*, Christ still *enters in* wherever *meek souls will receive him* (Revelation 3.20).

It is this truth that lies behind the fourth stanza, which is omitted from many hymnals. No doubt it can be argued that the hymn is complete without it, and becomes unduly long with it. Nevertheless it does convey a message and adds something other than length to the hymn.

> Where children pure and happy
>   Pray to the blessèd Child,
> Where misery cries out to thee,
>   Son of the mother mild;
> Where charity stands watching
>   And faith holds wide the door,
> The dark night wakes, the glory breaks,
>   And Christmas comes once more.

The key to these words is in the last two lines: *the glory breaks, and Christmas comes once more.* Where does the glory of Christmas break into human life? In a number of situations, the stanza suggests. It comes where, in their happiness, *children pray to the blessèd Child* of Bethlehem; *where* in its *misery* humanity *cries out* for help to the compassionate *Son of the mother mild*; *where charity stands watching* over the needs of the poor and under-privileged, *and faith holds wide the door* to welcome them in. Christmas comes again, so to speak, in all these situations, for at such times Christ himself draws near to listen, to succour and to bless.

So we make our own prayer to him:

> O holy Child of Bethlehem,
>   Descend to us, we pray;
> Cast out our sin, and enter in,
>   Be born in us today.
> We hear the Christmas angels
>   The great glad tidings tell:
> O come to us, abide with us,
>   Our Lord Emmanuel.

The hymn begins with Christmas in Bethlehem; it ends with Christmas in the heart. It begins with Christ being born of Mary; it ends with Christ being born in us. The mystical poet of the seventeenth century, Angelus Silesius, wrote:

> Should Christ be born a thousand times anew,
> Despair, O man, unless he's born in you.

59

This spiritual birth happens when, *our sin* having been *cast out*, we allow Christ to *enter in* and take possession of our lives.

Christmas thus has for each of us a contemporary message and a personal meaning. Amid its festivities we must take time to pause and listen to *the great glad tidings* of the *Christmas angels* as if they were speaking directly to us, and then ask *our Lord Emmanuel* to *come to us* and *abide with us* – 'God with us' for ever.

7

THE MAGI

As with gladness men of old

OF THE half-dozen or so hymns regularly sung at the Epiphany season none has a more popular appeal than Chatterton Dix's 'As with gladness men of old'. This is probably due to the direct and straightforward way in which it interprets the story of the Magi and the star of Bethlehem. Bishop Heber's approach in his 'Brightest and best of the sons of the morning' is more sophisticated, as well as more poetical. Much the same is true of Monsell's 'O worship the Lord in the beauty of holiness'. Dix does not indulge in any fanciful flights or attempt to write fine poetry. He is content to take the story as it stands and interpret its teaching in simple terms, and in a spirit of prayer and devotion.

I

William Chatterton Dix (1837–98) belongs to the small and select company of laymen (*men* as distinct from women) who have contributed to the Church's hymnody. He was the son of a Bristol surgeon and educated at the city's grammar school, before embarking upon a commercial career. For a large part of his life he was manager of a maritime insurance company in

Glasgow. He was an Anglican in the High Church tradition, a fact which is reflected at times in his hymns.

In the course of his life he published four volumes of sacred verse, and it is from these that his hymns are derived. His eucharistic hymn, 'Alleluia, sing to Jesus', is familiar to all church people, and so is his hymn for harvest thanksgiving, 'To thee, O Lord, our hearts we raise'; but best known of all is this hymn for the feast of the Epiphany. He wrote it at the age of twenty-one while recovering from a serious illness. The words came into his mind, he said, as he was reflecting on the Epiphany Gospel (Matthew 2.1–12), and the hymn was quickly completed. It was first printed in a small collection of hymns for private circulation. Not long afterwards it found its way into the first edition of *Hymns Ancient and Modern*, 1860, and won immediate acclaim.

Its structure is quite simple. In each of the first three stanzas the writer draws out a lesson from the story of the wise men: their joyful quest for the one who had been 'born king of the Jews'; the humble worship they offered him as they bowed in his presence; and the costly gifts they presented to him in token of his royalty. Each of these verses ends with an appropriate prayer. The last two are a meditation on the theme of the Christian life as a journey to the heavenly country, of which Jesus himself is the everlasting light.

II

The first stanza portrays the Magi pursuing their journey in search of the King.

> As with gladness men of old
> Did the guiding star behold,
> As with joy they hailed its light,
> Leading onward, beaming bright,
> So, most gracious Lord, may we
> Evermore be led to thee.

The picture here is derived from Matthew 2.9, 10 (NEB): 'The

star which they had seen at its rising went ahead of them . . .
At the sight of the star they were overjoyed.' Joy is one of the
keynotes of this hymn. The note is struck in four of its five
stanzas. Kingship is another dominant theme. The story of the
wise men is the story of two kings: Jesus and Herod.

The note of joy is heard in the opening line: *As with
gladness men of old* . . . The gladness of the Magi arose from
their conviction that the star they had seen 'at its rising' in
their eastern land – and which now appeared to them again in
the land of Judah – was leading them to the new-born King of
the Jews. It was a *guiding star*. So *with joy they hailed its light*
as they pressed onwards in their quest. They were men with a
purpose. They were looking for a king and were resolved not
to rest until they found him. Fittingly, then, attached to this
opening stanza is the prayer that we in like manner *may
evermore be led to* Jesus, our *most gracious Lord*. There are
many roads that lead to him, but they all point in the same
direction; for he is the goal of Everyman's search for truth, for
peace, for freedom, for life abundant.

The second stanza portrays the Magi's arrival in Bethlehem
and links up with the words in the Gospel: 'Going into the
house they saw the child with Mary his mother, and they fell
down and worshipped him' (v.11).

> As with joyful steps they sped,
> Saviour, to thy lowly bed,
> There to bend the knee before
> Thee whom heaven and earth adore,
> So may we with willing feet
> Ever seek thy mercy-seat.

The stanza as quoted differs slightly from the form in which
Dix originally wrote it, and as it appears in *EH* 39, where the
second line runs, 'To that lowly manger-bed'. The amended
version dates back to the revised edition of *Hymns Ancient
and Modern*, 1875. The editors pointed out to the author that
the reference to the *manger-bed* implied that the Magi found
the infant Jesus in the stable of Bethlehem, whereas the
scripture record states that they came to 'the house', not to a
stable. Their visit is envisaged as having taken place some

while after the Nativity. Accordingly the stanza was recast in the above form, and one or two other minor alterations were made in the hymn for the sake of consistency. Dix not only approved of these changes but expressed the wish that in future the hymn should be printed in this form.

The worship of the Magi, as they *bend the knee before* the infant King, is an impressive part of the story. It represents the Gentile world acknowledging the God of Israel, who is the Lord of all nations. The story also reveals that the Magi were indeed 'wise men'; for 'the fear of the Lord is the beginning of wisdom' – or, as the marginal reading puts it, the 'chief part' of wisdom (Psalm 111.10). It is the fool who says there is no God. Those who are wise reverence and adore him. Hence the stanza concludes with the prayer that we may willingly and constantly *seek* the *mercy-seat* – that is, the throne of God's heavenly grace – and bow in worship before him.

The third stanza carries the story to its final phase as the Magi opened their treasures and 'offered him gifts, gold and frankincense and myrrh'.

> As they offered gifts most rare
> At thy cradle rude and bare,
> So may we with holy joy,
> Pure and free from sin's alloy,
> All our costliest treasures bring,
> Christ, to thee our heavenly King.

The allusion in the second line to the *cradle* as *rude and bare* must strike anyone who thinks about it as somewhat odd. The explanation, of course, is that the original reading was not 'cradle' but 'manger'. To describe a manger as rude and bare is appropriate enough. The words are scarcely applicable to a cradle; but perhaps we can regard them as a reminder of the poor and humble circumstances in which the Lord of glory entered our world (2 Corinthians 8.9).

Various symbolical values have been attached to the *gifts most rare* presented to Jesus. Epiphanius in the fourth century said the Magi offered 'gold because he is a king, incense because he is God, and myrrh because he is mortal'. Hence in a hymn of the same period Prudentius (b. 348) identified the gifts thus:

> Solemn things of mystic meaning:
> Incense doth the God disclose,
> Gold a royal child proclaimeth,
> Myrrh a future tomb foreshows.[1]

Monsell in his Epiphany hymn suggests other meanings and invites us to worship the Lord 'with gold of obedience, and incense of lowliness'.

Dix does not pursue any of these ideas. He is content to recognize the supreme worth of the Magi's offerings, which were doubtless the choicest products of their eastern lands and gifts worthy of a king (*cf.*Psalm 72.10; Isaiah 60.6). As for ourselves, the prayer we offer here is that we may *with holy joy* bring to Christ *all our costliest treasures* – that is, the treasures that cost us most. What are they? Surely things of spiritual rather than material value: the surrender of our wills, the devotion of our hearts, and the service of our lives.

III

The two final stanzas, while not abandoning the Epiphany story, look at it in a different way. The quest of the Magi is now viewed as a picture of the Christian's pilgrimage through this world to the celestial city, and its message is developed in the form of a prayer:

> Holy Jesus, every day
> Keep us in the narrow way;
> And, when earthly things are past,
> Bring our ransomed souls at last
> Where they need no star to guide,
> Where no clouds thy glory hide.

It was Jesus himself who warned us that the road that leads to life is a *narrow way* and that those who find it are few (Matthew 7.13,14). It is fitting, then, that we should ask the

65

Lord to *keep us* – and keep us *every day* – as we journey on amid the darkness of this present world, till we come to the unfading light and unclouded glory of the heavenly life. The line *Where they need no star to guide* is a glance back to the Epiphany Gospel. It also points us forward to the final stanza:

> In the heavenly country bright
> Need they no created light;
> Thou its light, its joy, its crown,
> Thou its sun which goes not down;
> There for ever may we sing
> Alleluias to our King.

It is typical of this nineteenth-century hymn that it should conclude with a lyrical allusion to *the heavenly country* of which Christ is *its light, its joy, its crown*. The Victorian Church is often criticized for having been too heavenly minded, and perhaps it was. But at least it took the prospect of heaven more seriously than we do and regarded it not as a form of escapism or a pious extra tacked on to the gospel but as an integral part of the Christian faith.

Today the situation is different. The Church's outlook has changed. This is illustrated by a comment on the hymn by the American scholar Albert Bailey: 'In our day a first-class hymn writer would be less likely to utilize two stanzas in describing a symbolic heaven, and more likely to bring the actual sinful world, wise men and all, to realize the necessity of laying its heart at the feet of Christ.' In Dix's day, he asserts, the social implications of the gospel had not assumed wide acceptance.[2]

We can sympathize with what Professor Bailey says, but how far we defer to his judgment will depend on our view of the 'social gospel' and its adequacy as a remedy for the ills of 'the actual sinful world'. A Church which is so engrossed in serving the present age that it loses its vision of heaven is not likely in the end to accomplish much of eternal worth in this world. Indeed, the story of the Victorian Church itself has something to teach us here. Those who were foremost in the work of social reform were men and women who believed intensely in the reality of the world to come and who found in the heavenly hope a powerful incentive to fulfil Christ's commission to serve and save mankind.

NOTES
1 Trans. E. Caswall, as in *EH* 40.
2 *The Gospel in Hymns*, p.360.

8

CHRIST'S UNIVERSAL KINGDOM

Jesus shall reign where'er the sun

A LITTLE man, five feet high; a large head, made bigger with a huge wig; small piercing eyes; a frail and sickly body; the whole combination looking more like an embryo than a fully developed organism. Who, you may well ask, is the poor, pathetic specimen of humanity answering to such a description? The answer is: none other than the great Dr Isaac Watts, the distinguished eighteenth-century divine, renowned as scholar, preacher and poet, the man to whom we owe the birth of the English hymn.

Our concern in this book is not with the details of his life or with his scholarly achievements but with his notable contribution to hymnody. And the writing of his hymns all began in a very simple way. Returning from morning chapel at Southampton one Sunday morning, the young Isaac – then a student, twenty years of age, training for the Dissenting ministry – complained about the wretched quality of the metrical psalms used in their worship that day. His father, who had probably heard the same sort of thing many times before, exclaimed somewhat impatiently, 'Then give us something better, young man!' Isaac accepted the challenge, and before the day was out he had produced a hymn which was sung at the chapel the following Sunday. It was the first of about six hundred and fifty hymns which he wrote in the course of his life. He died in 1748 at the age of seventy-four.

I

Isaac Watts's contribution to English hymnody was twofold. His supreme achievement was to break free from the tyranny of the metrical psalms, which since the Reformation had virtually constituted the sole element of congregational praise in the churches of England and Scotland. At their best the metrical psalms were good, and some of them are still in use today (e.g. 'The Lord's my shepherd', Ps. 23; 'Through all the changing scenes of life', Ps. 34; 'All people that on earth do dwell', Ps. 100). But all too often, in their efforts to adhere strictly to the words of scripture, within fixed verse-forms, they degenerated into mere doggerel.

Watts not only recognized their unfitness for divine service: he saw no reason why Christian praise should be confined, as Calvin had insisted, to the actual language of the Bible. He argued that there was a place for hymns which were not simply biblical paraphrases but free expressions of Christian truth in poetical form. And by his efforts and example he won his case. 'To Watts more than to any other man,' said Bernard Manning, 'is due the triumph of the hymn in English worship.' Among his own best known hymns are 'O God, our help in ages past', 'There is a land of pure delight', 'Come let us join our cheerful songs,' 'How bright those glorious spirits shine', 'Give me the wings of faith to rise' – and finest of all, 'When I survey the wondrous cross'.[1]

Watts's other achievement was to adopt a new approach to the use of the psalms in Christian worship. His aim here, in effect, was to baptize the psalms in the name of the Holy Trinity and to infuse them with the Spirit of Christ. So it was that, rejecting those psalms which he considered unsuitable, and carefully adapting others to his purpose, he published in 1719 a book entitled *The Psalms of David Imitated in the Language of the New Testament, and Applied to the Christian State and Worship*. He declared his design to be to 'compose a psalm book for Christians after the manner of the Jewish

69

psalter'; and accordingly he rendered the psalms 'as I may suppose David would have done had he lived in the days of Christianity'.

The hymn we have chosen to study provides a very good example. 'Jesus shall reign' is a paraphrase and adaptation of parts of Psalm 72, one of the proper psalms appointed for the feast of the Epiphany. The psalm itself – which scholars think may originally have been a coronation anthem – presents a vision of an ideal king and his reign of righteousness extending throughout the earth. Clearly no such king as is here portrayed existed in history when the psalm was written. Accordingly, the Jews came to see in it a foreshadowing of the great messianic King foretold by the prophets (the language has similarities to Isaiah 11.1–5 and chapters 60–2).

Watts accepts the psalm in this sense and gives it a fully Christian interpretation. Borrowing not so much its language as its imagery and leading ideas, he builds up a picture of Christ's universal kingdom in harmony with New Testament teaching. As he originally wrote it, the hymn consisted of eight stanzas and was entitled 'Christ's kingdom among the Gentiles'. The particular verses of the psalm (in AV) on which the stanzas are based will be noted as we look at them in turn.

II

The hymn opens with a panoramic view of Christ's coming kingdom, a kingdom without boundaries of space or time:

> Jesus shall reign where'er the sun
> Does his successive journeys run;
> His kingdom stretch from shore to shore,
> Till moons shall wax and wane no more.

The psalm begins with the words, 'Give the king thy judgements, O God'; but the writer does not name the king, for he did not know his name. He was writing of a perfect sovereign whose reign was yet to be established. Watts, however, knows who this king is and identifies him most emphatically in the opening word of the hymn: *Jesus shall reign*. In him, and in him alone, does the exalted language of the psalm find fulfilment. His reign, it is there said, shall be 'as long as the sun and moon endure, throughout all generations' (v. 5), and 'he shall have dominion from sea to sea . . . unto the ends of the earth' (v. 8). So Watts asserts that the reign of Jesus shall extend wherever *the sun* runs *his successive journeys*, and *his kingdom stretch from shore to shore*.

The theme of Christ's universal empire is enlarged upon in the next two stanzas, which are omitted from all the hymn books:

> Behold the islands with their kings,
> And Europe her best tribute brings;
> From north to south the princes meet,
> To pay their homage at his feet.

> There Persia, glorious to behold,
> There India shines in eastern gold;
> And barbarous nations at his word
> Submit, and bow, and own their Lord.

These words interpret verses 10 and 11 of the psalm:

> The kings of Tarshish and of the isles shall bring presents; the kings of Sheba and Seba shall offer gifts.
> Yea, all kings shall bow down before him: all nations shall serve him.

The psalmist's knowledge of distant lands was limited, and having mentioned Tarshish (in Spain) and Sheba and Seba (in South Arabia), he falls back on generalities: 'all kings' and 'all nations' shall serve the Messiah. Watts had a wider knowledge of geography and chose other parts of the world to designate the range of Christ's boundless realm. He sees it embracing nearby *Europe*, far-off *Persia* and *India*, as well as *barbarous nations*, all of which would *submit* to the claims of Jesus, *bow* in worship before him, and thus *own their Lord*.

In employing such language Watts was not simply drawing upon his imagination. He was asserting his faith in the Church's ultimate obedience to the Lord's commission to

71

spread the gospel throughout the world and make disciples of all nations. At the time he wrote, the modern missionary movement had not even been thought of. More than seventy years were to elapse before William Carey set sail for India. In this, as in other respects, Watts was a man ahead of his times. His hymn speaks with a prophetic note. It also speaks with a note of challenge, for it constantly recalls the Church to fulfil its divine mission in the world.

Prayer and praise constitute the theme of the fourth stanza:

> For him shall endless prayer be made,
> And praises throng to crown his head;
> His name like sweet perfume shall rise
> With every morning sacrifice.

'Prayer shall be made for him continually,' says the psalm; 'and daily shall he be praised' (v.15). Hence: *For him shall endless prayer be made.* Some hymnals retain the *For him*, which can be interpreted as meaning 'for his sake' or 'for his cause'; others change it to *To him*, as giving a better sense. *And praises* ascend to Jesus with his people's prayers. This, their morning sacrifice of worship, is offered in *his name*, which is likened to *sweet perfume*. In using this latter expression, was Watts thinking of the text, 'Thy name is as ointment poured forth' (Song of Songs 1.3)? Or had he in mind the words of Revelation 5.8: 'golden bowls full of incense, which are the prayers of the saints'? *Ancient and Modern Revised* adopts this view and renders the third line, 'His name like incense shall arise'. As a convinced Dissenter Watts would hardly have approved of incense in worship, but he might have accepted it as a symbol of prayer rising to the Father in the fragrant name of Jesus.

In this offering of prayer and praise all partake, whatever their language, whatever their age:

> People and realms of every tongue
> Dwell on his love with sweetest song;
> And infant voices shall proclaim
> Their early blessings on his name.

Christ, the King of all, is worthy of the praise of all.

III

The hymn continues by dwelling on the beneficence of Christ's compassionate rule:

> Blessings abound where'er he reigns,
> The prisoner leaps to lose his chains;
> The weary find eternal rest,
> And all the sons of want are blest.

The part of the psalm here under review is that which says:

> He shall deliver the needy when he crieth; the poor also, and him that hath no helper.
> He shall spare the poor and needy . . .
> He shall redeem their soul from deceit and violence: and precious shall their blood be in his sight.

> (vv. 12–14)

The promised King is the merciful Redeemer of the 'poor and needy' – the victims of human injustice and oppression, those who are unable to help themselves. So it is in the kingdom of Christ: *Blessings abound where'er he reigns*, that is, wherever his rule is acknowledged and his will obeyed. *The prisoner* obtains release from his chains, *the weary* find rest from their burdens, *and all the sons of want are blest*. The expression 'the sons of want' is a biblical usage and simply means those in want. Whatever their need, it is met out of the abundance of Christ's blessings.

There follows a striking stanza in which the writer, departing from the language of the psalm, dwells still further on the beneficence of Christ's kingdom:

> Where he displays his healing power
> Death and the curse are known no more;
> In him the tribes of Adam boast
> More blessings than their father lost.

Christ's kingdom is now defined as *where he displays his healing power*, for wherever his gentle rule is accepted, sin-sick humanity is made whole. As a result, *death and the curse are known no more.* The background to this is the story of the Fall in Genesis 3, as interpreted by St Paul in Romans 5.12f. Through Adam's disobedience, 'sin entered into the world, and death by sin; and so death passed upon all men, for that all have sinned'; and 'judgment came upon all men to condemnation' (vv. 12, 18). But Christ, the second Adam, by his perfect obedience and redeeming work, ends the reign of sin and freely offers us life in place of death, and righteousness in place of condemnation. As Paul puts it elsewhere, Christ has both 'abolished death' and 'redeemed us from the curse of the law' (2 Timothy 1.10; Galatians 3.13). This is the truth that Watts is asserting here. And he even goes a step further than the apostle. He declares not only that Christ restores sinful man's lost fortunes. He asserts that in Christ redeemed humanity can actually *boast more blessings than* Adam enjoyed before the Fall.

In this exultant faith he issues a great call to praise, based on the doxology which rounds off the psalm (vv. 18, 19) and marks the end of the Second Book of the Psalter:

> Let every creature rise and bring
> Peculiar honours to our King;
> Angels descend with songs again,
> And earth repeat the long Amen.

The call to render homage to Jesus is addressed to *every creature*, to all humanity. In the psalm we read of the nations and their rulers paying tribute to the messianic King and offering him their gifts (vv. 10, 15). So with ourselves and Jesus. Every one of us, acknowledging our indebtedness, must *bring peculiar honours to our King.* By 'peculiar honours' is meant those honours which are peculiar to us as individuals, the homage and service and praise which are distinctively our own. *Angels* are also called upon to pay their tribute: to *descend with songs again* – meaning, in all probability, as they did on the first Christmas night. Finally, *earth* adds its own *long Amen*, as in the psalm: 'Let the whole earth be filled with his glory; Amen and Amen.' In some books the long Amen becomes the *loud* Amen, but this is not what

Watts intended. The double Amen at the end of the psalm indicates that earth is to repeat it again and again – that in fact it is to be prolonged continually, like the praise which is offered by angels and men.

NOTE
1 For a study of this hymn see chapter 9.

9

IN DEBT TO CHRIST

When I survey the wondrous cross

PROBABLY NOT many people who sing 'When I survey the wondrous cross' are aware that it was written as a communion hymn. Yet Isaac Watts in his *Hymns and Spiritual Songs*, 1707, included it in the last section of the book containing hymns 'Prepared for the Holy Ordinance of the Lord's Supper'. Admittedly the hymn makes no specific reference to the sacrament, as do the other hymns in this section; so that while the passion theme renders it eminently suitable for the eucharist, it is equally suitable for use on other occasions.

I

Matthew Arnold considered 'When I survey' to be the finest hymn in the English language. It is certainly the finest of the six hundred and more hymns written by Isaac Watts. Julian placed it as 'one of the four which stand at the head of all hymns in the English language'. Robert Bridges judged it to be the best of the few English hymns which can be held to compare with the greatest of the old Latin hymns of the same measure. Erik Routley describes it as 'the most penetrating of all hymns, the most demanding, the most imaginative', and says that it is these things because of its restrained style. 'It is drawn throughout in strong, clear, simple lines and colours.'[1]

The title Watts gave the hymn was 'Crucifixion to the world by the cross of Christ'. He based it on the text in Galatians 6.14: 'God forbid that I should glory, save in the cross of our Lord Jesus Christ, by whom the world is crucified to me, and I to the world.'

In the five stanzas which make up the hymn he invites us to look at the cross and he tells us how to do so. The Methodist preacher Dr Dinsdale T. Young once remarked, 'If you look critically at the wondrous cross you will see in it nothing but common wood. The cross is best discerned through penitential tears.' It is possible to look at the cross and see in it nothing but a ghastly tragedy. But if we look with the eyes of a penitent and humble faith we may see in the cross some profound and piercing truths – about ourselves and our personal need, but most of all about Christ and his amazing love.

II

To look at the cross in this way is a humbling experience:

> When I survey the wondrous cross,
>   On which the Prince of glory died,
> My richest gain I count but loss,
>   And pour contempt on all my pride.

Watts calls upon us to *survey* the cross. It is an arresting and unusual word in this connection. But is it not, as has been suggested, a rather cold and formal word to use of a sinner looking at his crucified Saviour? The answer is that it is thoroughly characteristic of Watts, who was a man of a philosophical and scientific turn of mind.[2] In asking us to 'survey' the cross he is urging us not to be content with a brief and hasty glance but to look at the cross in a contemplative mood: the mood of the devout communicant as he prepares to receive the sacrament of the body and blood of Christ, and in doing so seeks to penetrate more deeply into the meaning of the Lord's passion.

In Watts's original version of the hymn the second line was *Where the young Prince of glory died.* He altered it to the present form when the hymn was republished a couple of years later (1709). It was done apparently in response to the criticism of certain friends who pointed out that in the New Testament no particular significance is attached to the age of Jesus when he died. That may be so. All the same, many will agree that the change was regrettable and unnecessary. It is worth remembering that when the hymn was first published Watts himself was a young man of thirty-three, the same age as Jesus at the time of the crucifixion. It may have been this that brought home to him the fact that the Prince of glory laid down his life in the bloom and vigour of his manhood. It is also a point which we ourselves should bear in mind when faced with the seeming tragedy of a human life cut short in the service of God. Why should it happen? we ask. Let us remember that it happened to the young Prince of glory. The value of life is measured not in length of years but in terms of achievement.

When I look at the crucified Son of God and recognize that he died for my sins I reassess my scale of values: *My richest gain I count but loss* – and I am robbed of every bit of self-esteem and self-satisfaction. There is an obvious reference here to St Paul's words in Philippians 3.7–9, where after looking back on his old life as a self-righteous Pharisee and his proud endeavours to win God's approval by his own religious works, he wrote:

> Whatever gain I had, I counted as loss for the sake of Christ. Indeed I count everything as loss because of the surpassing worth of knowing Christ Jesus my Lord. For his sake I have suffered the loss of all things, and count them as refuse, in order that I may gain Christ and be found in him, not having a righteousness of my own, based on law, but that which is through faith in Christ.

In the light of the cross Paul saw that he had to write off as sheer loss his own righteousness. It simply was not good

78

enough for God. Instead he had to humble himself and accept by faith God's gift of righteousness in Christ crucified. *I pour contempt on all my pride* – that was now his confession. It has been said that there are three insidious forms of pride: pride of face, pride of race, and pride of grace. The last is the most insidious of all – spiritual pride. When we look at the cross we see just how contemptible and worthless it is. We glory not in what we have done but only in what Christ has done for us:

> Forbid it, Lord, that I should boast
> Save in the death of Christ my God;
> All the vain things that charm me most,
> I sacrifice them to his blood.

This second stanza directs us back to the words which inspired the hymn: 'God forbid that I should glory save in the cross of our Lord Jesus Christ.' We see in the cross the one thing we may boast about, the thing of supreme worth: God's saving act, accomplished once and for all *in the death of Christ my God.* Compared with this, all other things are secondary. They are but *vain things*, empty, futile, worthless, even the things *that charm me most.* All must be abandoned if they come between me and my Lord: *I sacrifice them to his blood.* That is *my* sacrifice; but what is it compared with his? In the words of C. T. Studd, 'If Jesus Christ be God, and he died for me, no sacrifice can be too great for me to make for him.' The cross enables us to sort out our priorities and rethink our scale of values.

III

We look at the cross again and see in it an unveiling of the heart of God:

> See, from his head, his hands, his feet,
> Sorrow and love flow mingled down;
> Did e'er such love and sorrow meet,
> Or thorns compose so rich a crown?

Duncan Campbell wrote: 'For tender solemn beauty, for a reverent setting forth of what the inner vision discerns as it looks upon the Crucified, we know no verse in the whole range of hymnology to touch the stanza beginning, *See, from his head, his hands, his feet.*'[3]

The imagery of the stanza is derived from St John's Gospel where we are told that a soldier, to prove that Jesus was really dead, 'pierced his side with a spear, and at once there came out blood and water'. Watts, with a touch of poetic imagination, perhaps a flash of spiritual genius, gazes at the terrible scene and sees not blood and water, but *sorrow and love flow mingled down*. What is the significance of that?

We can hardly be mistaken in discerning in the sorrow of the Saviour on the cross his sorrow for *sin*: the sin of the world for which he suffered and died. He was a 'man of sorrows and acquainted with grief' because 'he was wounded for our transgressions' and 'the Lord laid on him the iniquity of us all' (Isaiah 53.3, 5, 6). So equally we see in the love of the Saviour on the cross his love for the *sinner*; for 'God shows his love for us in that while we were yet sinners Christ died for us' (Romans 5.8). It was our sin which took Jesus to the cross, but it was his love for us that held him there, not the nails of the Roman soldiers.

Did e'er such love and sorrow meet? No, never! Nor will they meet again on such a scale through all the ages to come. Or again, did ever *thorns compose so rich a crown?* It is an astonishing suggestion! To the believer gazing with reverent adoration on the crucified Saviour, the cruel wreath of thorns which encircled his brow is transfigured into a glittering diadem, a monarch's crown. The Man of Sorrows is the King of Love.

The fourth stanza of Watts's hymn is commonly omitted from our hymnals as being, presumably, too vivid, too terrifying for the susceptibilities of the modern worshipper:

> His dying crimson, like a robe,
> Spreads o'er his body on the tree;
> Then am I dead to all the globe,
> And all the globe is dead to me.

The picture of Jesus bathed in his blood which, *like a robe, spreads o'er his body on the tree*, is striking and startling, indeed almost revolting. But plainly Watts intends it to be so. He wants to shock and disturb us, to jolt us out of our complacency and make us see in the crucifixion of Jesus the fearful and horrible thing it is – not simply to stir our emotions but to move us to a decisive act of committal to Christ and renunciation of the world. For – to put it in personal terms – if this is what Christ has suffered for me, if this is how the world treated my Lord, *then am I dead to all the globe, and all the globe is dead to me.* The words are a further reference to the text which heads the hymn: 'By the cross the world has been crucified to me, and I to the world.'

The cross not only changes our relationship to God. It also radically alters our relationship to the world. In reconciling us to God it alienates us to the world: not to the people of the world, but to the world's evil and corruption, its empty pomp and show, its false values and standards. In this sense we die with Christ to the world, and similarly the world is dead to us. Henceforth life has a new centre, a new purpose, a new ambition, a new love. Above all it has a new Master to whom I owe everything. To him therefore I must give everything:

> Were the whole realm of nature mine,
>   That were a present far too small;
> Love so amazing, so divine,
>   Demands my soul, my life, my all.

Here set plainly before us is the ultimate challenge of the cross and the demand it makes upon us.

Were the whole realm of nature mine, says Watts, and the expression is typical of his way of thinking. He was a man with a cosmic outlook, deeply interested in the world of nature, the earth and the sky, the sun, the moon and the stars. But here he recognizes that even if it were his to give, the whole realm of nature would be an inadequate return for all that Christ had done for him, *a present far too small.*

The same is true of us, such is the measure of our indebtedness to our Lord. In the greatness of his love he gave all for us;

and *love so amazing, so divine, demands* – what? Ourselves, and the whole of ourselves: *my soul, my life, my all.*

My *soul* is what I am, as an individual, my essential personality. My *life* is what I do, my daily work and activities. My *all* is what I have, my gifts and talents, my wealth and possessions.

Total love demands total surrender.

NOTES
1 *Hymns and the Faith*, p.112.
2 See B. Manning, *The Hymns of Wesley and Watts*, p. 83.
3 *Hymns and Hymn Makers*, p. 39.

10

THE SECOND ADAM

Praise to the Holiest in the height

CARDINAL NEWMAN'S 'Praise to the Holiest in the height' comes from his *Dream of Gerontius*, 1865, set to memorable music by Sir Edward Elgar. The verses which make up the hymn are part of a much longer poem, consisting of thirty-five verses in all, divided into five sections. We are concerned only with the final section; but in looking at it we need to keep in mind that the work as a whole is about the journey of the Christian soul from this world to the next through the gate of death. The section which constitutes the hymn is sung by a choir of angels as the soul enters the presence-chamber of Emmanuel. In their song they celebrate Christ's redemptive work by virtue of which the believer is enabled to face death without fear.

Although frequently sung in our churches, this is not a 'popular' type of hymn which readily yields up its meaning. It is essentially theological in character. It contains some difficult language, such as 'a second Adam', 'a higher gift than grace', and 'the double agony in Man'. It is therefore a hymn which demands thoughtful study and needs to be carefully interpreted. It has a great deal to teach about our Lord's passion and its meaning for ourselves, in life and in death.

I

The opening stanza, with its magnificent outburst of praise, is a sort of refrain which runs through the entire poem. Each of the five sections, like this last, begins with it, and it therefore sets the tone of the whole work.

> Praise to the Holiest in the height,
>   And in the depth be praise,
> In all his words most wonderful,
>   Most sure in all his ways.

One cannot but be impressed by the fact that a poem which is so much occupied with the death of man and his passing from earth to Paradise should be so full of praise. Yet it is not strange in the light of New Testament teaching. The Christian believer looks at death in a very different way from the unbeliever. He is able to view it calmly and confidently in the light of Christ's redeeming work and Easter victory. So here in this hymn, face to face with the mystery of death, he ascribes *praise to the Holiest*, both *in the height* of heaven and *in the depth* of earth; for in Christ the Church in heaven and on earth is one.

In the context of praise the verse has something to say about God's *words*, which are *most wonderful*, and about *his ways*, which are *most sure*. God the all-holy has not hidden himself from us. He has revealed himself, both in what he has spoken and in what he has done. His 'words' embrace his promises, commands, counsels – and supremely his gospel, the good news of Jesus Christ. His 'ways' are his works, his love in action, the things he has done for us men and for our salvation. What are they?

The next stanza supplies the answer.

> O loving wisdom of our God!
>   When all was sin and shame,
> A second Adam to the fight
>   And to the rescue came.

What God has done, to put it simply, is to *rescue* man from his *sin and shame*. This is the meaning of redemption. It spells deliverance, emancipation, freedom. And our Christian redemption springs from the *loving wisdom of our God*. Here is a phrase to ponder. We often dwell upon the love of God in the work of salvation, and rightly so, for it all begins with that fact. But we should also reflect upon the wisdom of God as seen in what the older divines spoke of as 'the plan of salvation' (*cf.* 1 Corinthians 1.18–25). There is divine wisdom as well as divine love in the manner in which our redemption has been achieved, and this hymn unfolds that loving wisdom in biblical terms. Newman's words can only be understood in the light of scripture.

Take, for example, the reference to the *second Adam*. St Paul supplies the key to this in the following passages (it must be remembered that Adam simply means 'man'):

> As one man's trespass led to condemnation for all men, so one man's act of righteousness leads to acquittal and life for all men. For as by one man's disobedience many were made sinners, so by one man's obedience many will be made righteous.
>
> (Romans 5.18,19)

> As in Adam all die, so also in Christ shall all be made alive. The first man was from the earth, a man of dust; the second man is from heaven. As was the man of dust, so are those who are of the dust; and as is the man of heaven, so are those who are of heaven.
>
> (1 Corinthians 15.22,47,48)

What the apostle is saying here is that there are two representative men, two Adams, with whom the destiny of all humanity is bound up. The first Adam, the Adam of the Genesis story, represents the whole of sinful mankind; and by nature we, as fallen sinners, are related to him and are therefore under judgment. The second Adam is Jesus, 'the man from heaven', who came to do battle with sin and rescue us from its condemnation and power. By God's grace all believers are united to him and receive his gift of righteousness and eternal life.

It is to this great theological truth that Newman is giving poetical expression in the second stanza. Christ came to save men from their sins.

In what manner did he come? The next stanza supplies the answer:

> O wisest love! that flesh and blood
> Which did in Adam fail,
> Should strive afresh against their foe,
> Should strive and should prevail;

O wisest love! cries the poet. And now we can see why the wisdom of the divine love is especially stressed. The Son of God, the heavenly man, came to us in the form of *flesh and blood* – the same flesh and blood of the first Adam, the flesh and blood in which he failed, the flesh and blood of which we all partake. And the marvellous thing is, as Erik Routley put it, that 'God should use flesh and blood to redeem flesh and blood'.[1] In coming to earth Christ identified himself fully with the sons of men, sharing their very nature so that as their representative he might *strive afresh against their foe* – and this time not strive and fail, as did the first Adam, but *strive . . . and prevail.*

II

But that is not the whole picture. The flesh-and-blood Jesus is only one side of it, as Newman knew well enough; and so in the next stanza – which, it should be noted, is continuous with the present one and follows straight on without a break – he presents the other side. God's wisest love revealed itself in something yet more wonderful than the perfect manhood of Jesus:

> And that a higher gift than grace
> Should flesh and blood refine,
> God's presence and his very Self,
> And essence all-divine.

What is the *higher gift than grace*? The phrase is not, as

some Protestant critics have mistakenly supposed, a subtle reference to the Roman doctrine of transubstantiation. It is a reference to the Incarnation. An examination of Newman's language makes this unmistakably plain. What he is saying is that the man Christ Jesus who took our flesh and blood and shared our human life was not simply a man in whom the grace of God dwelt in a superlative degree. There have always been those who in their estimate of Jesus of Nazareth have not been prepared to go further than that. There are those in our own day who stop short at that point. But such is not the New Testament view, nor is it the teaching of the historic Catholic Faith. Nor is it the teaching of this hymn. In the coming of Jesus to share and *refine* our humanity God gave *a higher gift than grace.* He gave himself. In the person of Jesus was embodied, enfleshed, *God's presence and his very Self and essence all-divine.*

Admittedly this is strong language, but it is no stronger than that of St Paul when he declares, 'It is in Christ that the complete being of the Godhead dwells embodied' (Colossians 2.9 NEB), or the declaration concerning Jesus in the prologue to the fourth Gospel: 'In the beginning was the Word, and the Word was with God, and the Word was God. . . . And the Word became flesh and dwelt among us' (John 1.1,14). This is the fundamental Christian belief: that in the person of Jesus, the incarnate Son, God himself, without ceasing to be God, became truly man and lived our human life. Apart from this faith it is impossible to make sense of the New Testament teaching about what Jesus Christ has achieved for us by his cross and passion.

To that subject the hymn next turns our attention:

> O generous love! that he who smote
>   In Man for man the foe,
> The double agony in Man
>   For man should undergo;

O generous love! God's love is wise, as we have already seen. It is also generous, because it has done something at infinite cost for mankind. How are we to explain it? How can our minds comprehend it?

Newman found it difficult to put so unfathomable a truth as the Atonement into human language, and we may well be puzzled by the way he attempts to express it. But let us be clear that at this point in the hymn he is bringing us to the cross: that here he is grappling with the doctrine of the Atonement, as in the previous stanza he came to grips with the Incarnation. Four times in this one verse the word 'man' occurs, or to be more precise, twice the word is *Man* and twice it is *man*. Man with the capital letter denotes Jesus Christ, the second Adam, the Man from heaven. The word without the capital denotes mankind, the human race, ourselves included. So what the verse declares is this, that when God in his generous love smote the foe in the Man Christ Jesus – and did this for the sake of mankind – he himself endured *the double agony* in all that Christ suffered for our salvation.

By the 'double agony' is meant the physical and the spiritual sufferings of Jesus. This is made clear by an earlier couplet in the poem:

A double agony awaits
His body and his soul.

In thinking of the cross we tend to concentrate on the physical anguish which Jesus endured, since that is the element we can most readily understand. We must not forget, however, that the deepest agony Jesus suffered was within his own soul when, as the sin-bearer, he entered into the darkness of spiritual desolation and at last cried out, 'My God, my God, why hast thou forsaken me?' Into the mystery of that suffering we cannot penetrate with our finite minds. But we know the price he paid: he gave his life as a ransom for many.

III

This is the ultimate meaning of the death of Christ. It is his unique work for the redemption of sinful humanity. But it has another meaning as well, and it is to this that the hymn points us in the sixth (and final) stanza:

And in the garden secretly,
 And on the cross on high,
Should teach his brethren, and inspire
 To suffer and to die.

To some, this represents a disappointing and unsatisfactory finish to the hymn. No less a critic than Bernard Manning described it as 'a perfect anticlimax' after all the massive theology that has gone before. Is the sacrifice of God himself on the cross, he asks, merely to teach us to bear suffering and death? And he goes as far as to suggest that Newman ends his passion hymn as a Unitarian might have done.[2]

At first sight this stricture may appear to carry some weight. In fact, it is quite unjustified and is due to a misunderstanding of the hymn as a whole. Much of the difficulty is removed once we recognize that this sixth stanza and the previous one are continuous (like the third and fourth) and follow on without a break. Both the stanzas in question have the same subject: the generous love of God revealed in the passion of our Lord; and they link together what the cross has *done* for us, in securing our salvation, and what the cross *teaches* us, in showing us how to live and die.

Newman, most emphatically, is not saying that Jesus suffered and died 'merely to teach us to bear suffering and death'. He is adamant that the cross possesses, first and foremost, a redemptive value. The body of the hymn puts that as strongly as possible. What he is saying now, in this final verse, is that the cross also possesses an exemplary value; and this is in complete accord with New Testament teaching. To see in the Christ of Calvary our example as well as our Redeemer is not to turn Unitarian. The two ideas are brought together by the apostle Peter in the counsel he offers to Christian slaves who were suffering unjust punishment:

If when you do right and suffer for it you take it patiently, you have God's approval. For to this you have been called, because Christ also suffered for you, leaving you an example, that you should follow in his steps. He committed no sin; no guile was found on his lips. When he was reviled, he did not revile in return; when he suffered, he did not threaten; but he trusted to him who judges justly. He himself bore our sins in his body on the tree, that we might die to sin and live to righteousness. By his wounds you have been healed.

(1 Peter 2.20–4)

Against this background we can take a correct view of what Newman is saying in this hymn. Christ as the second Adam, the incarnate Son, suffered the double agony for man and thereby achieved the work of rescue and defeated the foe. But more: by what he endured *secretly in the garden* of Gethsemane, and openly *on the cross* lifted *high* before the world, he provided for *his brethren* in their afflictions a pattern of patient and victorious suffering. Hence the value of the final stanza is that it relates the theology of the cross to the realities of life here and now, and more especially to the supreme realities of suffering and death. Jesus has experienced both for us, and by the way he has done so he is able to *teach* and *inspire* us *to suffer and to die*.

Looking at it in this way – the way Newman doubtless intended – we must agree that the hymn ends not with an anticlimax but on a note of triumph. And because that is so, it is not inappropriate in singing the hymn to repeat the opening verse, as is ordered by our hymn-books, as a final act of praise.

NOTES
1 *Hymns and the Faith*, p. 286.
2 *The hymns of Wesley and Watts*, p. 40.

11

GLORYING IN THE CROSS

We sing the praise of him who died

THOMAS KELLY, the author of this hymn, was an unusual man. Just possibly the fact that he was an Irishman had something to do with it. Some might be tempted to dismiss him as a religious fanatic. Others would revere him as a gifted preacher, poet and musician. None could deny that he was a most generous benefactor, especially of the poor. Add to that the fact that he was a biblical scholar, well versed in oriental languages, and it must be agreed that he was somebody out of the ordinary, worthy to be remembered apart from his hymns.

I

Born in 1769, the son of an Irish judge, Thomas Kelly was educated at Trinity College, Dublin, and studied for the Bar. But in his early twenties he experienced a deep evangelical conversion, as a result of which he dedicated his life to the service of Christ. In due course he was ordained to the Anglican ministry. However, his fervent preaching of the gospel was too much for the Archbishop of Dublin (Dr Fowler), who disapproved of his 'methodistical' ways and inhibited him from preaching in his diocese. Thereupon Kelly parted com-

91

pany not only with the archbishop but with the Church of Ireland and turned Dissenter. Being a man of ample means he built chapels in a number of places where he and his friends (including Rowland Hill) were free to preach and conduct divine service. His own magnetic preaching always drew large congregations.

Kelly, however, not only *preached* the gospel. He also practised it. He was the friend of all benevolent causes, and during the grim years of famine in Ireland he gave liberal help to the poverty-stricken population of Dublin. The story is told of how one man cheered his wife in time of desperate need by saying, 'Hould up, Bridget! Bedad, there's always Misther Kelly to pull us out of the bog afther we've sunk for the last time!'

Throughout his ministry he expressed his evangelical faith in a third direction: he turned the gospel into poetry and song. His first collection of hymns appeared in 1802; his last in 1853, a year before he died. In all he wrote well over seven hundred hymns. The vast majority of them are of little value, but they include a handful of gems. Among those still in use the best known are: 'Look, ye saints, the sight is glorious' (Advent); 'The Lord is risen indeed' (Easter); and 'The head that once was crowned with thorns' (Ascension) – together of course with 'We sing the praise of him who died' (Passiontide). The four hymns listed justify the comment made in Julian's *Dictionary* that Kelly's strength is seen chiefly in hymns of praise.

II

'We sing the praise of him who died' was published in 1815. It very much took the fancy of Lord Selborne, the Victorian hymnologist, who quoted it at the York Church Congress in 1866 and declared, 'I doubt whether Montgomery ever wrote anything quite equal to this.'

When Kelly published the hymn he headed it with the

words from Galatians 6.14: 'God forbid that I should glory,
save in the cross of our Lord Jesus Christ' – the same words
that inspired Isaac Watts's 'When I survey the wondrous
cross'.[1] The opening stanza introduces the theme in the light
of those words.

> We sing the praise of him who died,
> Of him who died upon the cross;
> The sinner's hope let men deride,
> For this we count the world but loss.

Thomas Kelly, like the apostle Paul, gloried in the cross. But
it is noteworthy that here in this hymn he is praising not the
cross itself, as a mere sign or symbol, but *him who died upon
the cross*. He gloried in the cross only because it was the cross
of Jesus, knowing only too well that the cross possesses no
value or merit apart from the Crucified. Moreover, he gloried
in the cross because he recognized in the Crucified *the sinner's
hope* – the sinner's only hope of salvation, let *men deride* or
deny it as they will. He was not concerned with the world's
opinion: *For this we count the world but loss.*

These words are a further echo of what the apostle wrote in
Galatians 6.14, where in reference to the cross of our Lord
Jesus Christ he added, 'by whom the world has been crucified
to me, and I to the world'. The death of the Son of God
establishes a new relationship between the believer and the
'world' – that is, unregenerate humanity and society organized apart from the word and will of God. This is the point that
Watts makes in the fearsome fourth stanza of his 'When I
survey'. Professor G. G. Findlay, commenting on the Gala-
tian text in the *Expositor's Bible*, wrote:

> A whole world was crucified for Paul when his Lord died upon
> the cross. The world that slew Him put an end to itself, so far as
> he is concerned. He can never believe in it, never take pride in
> it, never do homage to it any more.

In the next stanza we take another look at the cross and
catch a new glimpse of its glory:

> Inscribed upon the cross we see
> In shining letters, 'God is Love';

He bears our sins upon the tree,
He brings us mercy from above.

In the gospel records we are told that by order of the Roman governor the charge against Jesus was inscribed over his head: 'This is Jesus the King of the Jews'. That is what the passers-by saw and read as they gazed at the cross on the first Good Friday. It was a pronouncement of doom. To the eye of faith the cross of Jesus bears a very different inscription – a message of hope. *In shining letters* we read the gospel word, *'God is Love'*. There, in the crucified Redeemer, we see a glowing revelation of what God is, and what God has done. We discover, in objective reality, the meaning of the words 'God so loved the world'. We comprehend what the apostle had in mind when he wrote, 'God has shown us how much he loves us: it was while we were still sinners that Christ died for us!' (Romans 5.8 TEV). Yes, it was for us he died: *he bears our sins upon the tree*, for his death was a vicarious sacrifice. God was in Christ reconciling the world to himself. All is of God, and all is of grace: *he brings us mercy from above*. What we could not do for ourselves, and what we did not deserve to have done, God has done for us.

III

There is no end to God's mercy and grace:

> The cross! it takes our guilt away;
> It holds the fainting spirit up;
> It cheers with hope the gloomy day,
> And sweetens every bitter cup.

This stanza reads almost like a sermon outline on 'The Cross in Christian experience'. Just possibly Kelly may have used it in that way. At any rate four 'points' are clearly laid out.

In the cross of Jesus we find, first, pardon for our sins: *it takes our guilt away*; second, support in time of weakness: *it holds the fainting spirit up*; third, assurance when everything seems dark: *it cheers with hope the gloomy day*; and fourth, consolation amid life's sorrows and disappointments: it *sweetens every bitter cup.*

Here the cross is set before us not as a piece of abstract theology but as a vital truth which impinges on our everyday life. In those moments when we are conscious of guilt, aware of our own weakness, tempted to despair, weighed down with sickness or sorrow, the cross speaks to our condition; for there we learn, in the words of Dr James S. Stewart, 'that God in his sovereign love still leads captivity captive, still transforms the wrecking circumstances of life into means of grace, the dark places into a Holy of Holies, and the thorns that pierce into a crown of glory.'[2]

Again, in the cross we find the courage we need, both in life and in death.

> It makes the coward spirit brave,
>   And nerves the feeble arm for fight;
> It takes its terror from the grave,
>   And gilds the bed of death with light.

How are we to face the battle of life? It is not easy. The first two lines of this stanza remind us of the *coward spirit* which is in us all, of *the feeble arm* of the flesh which fails us again and again. Can the cross help us here? Can it really make us brave and nerve us for the fight?

The answer is Yes, once we recognize that as Christians we are called upon to identify ourselves with the Christ of the cross and find in his passion not only the ground of our faith but the pattern of our life. Some words in Hebrews chapter 12 may help us here. The writer, after recalling the heroes of the old covenant who triumphed through their faith in God, bids us 'run with perseverance the race that is set before us, looking to Jesus the pioneer and perfecter of our faith, who for the joy that was set before him endured the cross, despising the shame, and is seated at the right hand of the throne of God' (vv. 1, 2). In his example of patient endurance we find both a challenge and an inspiration in our own conflicts, sufferings and griefs.

The cross gives us the courage to live. It also gives us the courage to die. *It takes its terror from the grave*, says the hymn, *and gilds the bed of death with light.* The first of these statements is negative in character. The Christian's faith in the crucified and risen Saviour robs the grave of all dread, so that he can face death without fear. The second statement has a positive ring. Death for the believer, far from being a leap in the dark, is a passing into the glory of heaven. It is the gate to everlasting life. There is light at eventide.

The final stanza is a continuation of the previous one and sums up all that has gone before. In the cross we find

> The balm of life, the cure of woe,
> The measure and the pledge of love,
> The sinner's refuge here below,
> The angels' theme in heaven above.

Here are brought together various contrasts: life's weal and woe; sinners and angels; earth and heaven. Most important of all, here we return to the glorious theme of the love of God, inscribed in shining letters upon the cross. The cross is the *measure* of that love, the expression in time and history of its length and breadth, its height and depth – immeasurable though it be. And the cross is also the *pledge* of God's love, the assurance that as his love is without beginning or end he will never cease to love us, and love us to the utmost limit.

In this redeeming love is *the sinner's refuge here below*, his hiding place from sin and shame. It is also *the angels' theme in heaven above.* With us they sing the praise of him who died, saying, 'Worthy is the Lamb who was slain, to receive power and wealth and wisdom and might and honour and glory and blessing!' (Revelation 5.12).

IV

By way of postscript, and as an exception to our normal rule, we add a word about the tune to which this hymn should be sung. In the Standard edition of *Hymns Ancient and Modern* it was set to *Breslau*, and the same tune is also used in *Songs of Praise* and *Congregational Praise*.

To the present writer this is rather a dreary tune. Somehow it does not seem to match the spirit of Kelly's inspiring words. Sir Sidney Nicholson's *Bow Brickhill* (written for the words) in *A. & M. Revised* is a vast improvement and brings the hymn to life. The *BBC Hymn Book* and the *Church Hymnary* both use *Fulda*; the *Methodist Hymn Book* has *Church Triumphant*; and the *Baptist Hymn Book* provides *Warrington*. All of these surely are more suitable than *Breslau* for this particular hymn.

NOTES
1 For this hymn see chapter 9.
2 *Herald of God* (Hodder & Stoughton, 1946), p. 78.

12

THE CLEFT ROCK

Rock of ages, cleft for me

LEGENDS ABOUT hymns and how they came to be written continue to circulate long after their credibility has been disproved. 'Rock of ages' provides a case in point. The familiar story is still around of how Augustus Toplady, curate of Blagdon in Somerset, was overtaken by a sudden storm in Burrington Combe and sought shelter in the cleft of a rock, and then and there – or maybe shortly afterwards – wrote the hymn as a direct result of that experience.

I

It is an attractive story, and sounds plausible, but unfortunately it is not true. The evidence is all against it. The hymn did not make its appearance until twelve years after Toplady had left Blagdon; and the legend about his sheltering in the cleft rock was not heard of until seventy years after his death. Of course, it is true that Toplady was curate of Blagdon, 1762–64, and that there is a rock in Burrington Combe with an opening large enough for a man to hide in – and which still attracts many sightseers. But we must accept the fact that there is no historical connection between the cleft rock and Toplady's immortal hymn.

This raises the question as to how the hymn came to be written. Is there any evidence at all? The answer is that there is at least one clue, and an accurate clue at that. Augustus Toplady (1740–78) was a contemporary of the Wesleys, though unhappily, on account of his strong Calvinistic views, he was not on very good terms with them. In their day there was a well-known manual dealing with the Holy Communion written by Dr Daniel Brevint, later Dean of Lincoln. John Wesley thought highly of it and included long extracts from it in the Wesleys' *Hymns on the Lord's Supper*. Among the quotations is this prayer:

O Rock of Israel, Rock of Salvation, Rock struck and cleft for me, let those two streams of blood and water which once gushed out of thy side, bring down pardon and holiness into my soul. And let me thirst after them now, as if I stood upon the mount whence sprung this water, and near the cleft of that Rock, the wounds of my Lord, whence gushed this sacred blood.

Toplady, as an Anglican clergyman, would certainly have been familiar with Brevint's manual; and it seems equally certain that it was there, in the words quoted, that he found the inspiration for his hymn. The parallels are too close to be mere coincidence.

In his prayer Brevint addressed our Lord as 'Rock of Israel, Rock of Salvation'. Toplady changed that to 'Rock of ages'. He got the title from the Bible, from a marginal reading of Isaiah 26.5 in the Authorized Version: 'in the Lord Jehovah is the rock of ages'. He took hold of that striking phrase and made it the beginning and end of the hymn. Having found so good a theme, he searched the scriptures and discovered other references to a cleft rock – in particular two passages in the book of Exodus. The first is in chapter 17. It tells of how, when the Israelites were dying of thirst in the wilderness, Moses with his rod struck a rock and, as it were, clave it in two, so that from the rock water gushed out. St Paul refers to this incident in 1 Corinthians 10.4 and says that the cleft rock is a picture of Christ. The other passage is in Exodus 33.17–23 and records how Moses hid himself in the cleft of a rock while the glory of the Lord passed by.

Those passages provide the Old Testament background to Toplady's hymn. Clearly he also had in mind a New Testament passage, part of the Passion story in St John's Gospel which tells of how, after Jesus had died on the cross, 'one of the soldiers pierced his side with a spear, and at once there came out blood and water' (19.34).

The hymn was published in 1776 in the *Gospel Magazine* of which Toplady was then the editor. It was headed with the words, 'A Living and Dying Prayer for the Holiest Believer in the World'. In using that curious title Toplady was hitting at the doctrine of 'sinless perfection' which he mistakenly believed was taught by the Wesleys. As against that notion he was asserting that, however good and holy a Christian may be, he is still a sinner until he dies and therefore is always in need of God's mercy and forgiveness. Accordingly the prayer that followed was one suitable for the greatest saint as well as the greatest sinner.

Toplady wrote many other hymns in the course of his short life, one or two of which will be found in *Congregational Praise*; but it is for 'Rock of ages' alone that he is now remembered. It is odd to reflect that this hymn, written by a narrow-minded Calvinistic clergyman – and one who could be very cantankerous, as his correspondence with the Wesleys proves – should have found its way more than two hundred years later into almost every hymn-book and should be sung by Christians of every persuasion throughout the world.

II

There is no doubt about the hymn's message. It is a hymn about sin and salvation; or to put it in personal terms, about the sinner in his helpless need and Jesus Christ in the all-sufficiency of his atoning sacrifice. This is clear from the very beginning:

> Rock of ages, cleft for me,
> Let me hide myself in thee;

> Let the water and the blood,
> From thy riven side which flowed,
> Be of sin the double cure:
> Cleanse me from its guilt and power.

The personal note is predominant throughout the hymn. There is no thought of corporate salvation, no mention of the Church, no word of intercession for others. Christ the *Rock of ages* was *cleft for me*, an an individual. Therefore I pray, *Let me hide myself in thee*, as Moses hid himself in the rock on Mount Sinai as the Lord passed by. But the same Moses also smote the rock in the desert and caused the water to flow out to meet the need of the dying Israelites. So from the *riven side* of the smitten and crucified Saviour there flowed water and blood; and this reference to *the water and the blood* causes Toplady to think of sin's *double cure* and to pray, *Cleanse me from its guilt and power.*

This prayer echoes Brevint's words, already quoted: 'let those two streams of blood and water . . . bring down pardon and holiness into my soul.' Sin does two things to us. On the one hand it condemns us and involves us in guilt, with the result that we need God's forgiveness. But sin not only condemns: it also enslaves us and we need to be rescued from its power. In Christ's saving work both these needs are met. Through his death and resurrection he offers us pardon *and* holiness: salvation from the guilt *and* from the power of sin.

What is our part in this matter? What have we to do? In a word – nothing:

> Not the labours of my hands
> Can fulfil thy law's demands;
> Could my zeal no respite know,
> Could my tears for ever flow,
> All for sin could not atone:
> Thou must save, and thou alone.

Most of the stanza is negative in character. It is concerned with sweeping away every prop we might be inclined to lean upon to make us acceptable to God. To put it in personal terms, as Toplady does, it is no use relying on *the labours of my hands*: they cannot meet the requirements of God's *law*.

Nor can *my zeal*, however fervent, or *my tears*, *flow* as they may, make atonement for sin. I am totally unable to contribute anything to my own salvation. That is the first thing I must grasp. But having grasped that, I am in a position to accept the great positive truth which rings out in the last line of this stanza: *Thou must save, and thou alone.*

In writing like this Toplady is not simply giving expression to his own evangelical convictions. He is putting into picture form the theology of salvation as taught by the apostle Paul in Ephesians 2.8–10 (NEB):

> It is by God's grace you are saved, through trusting him; it is not your own doing. It is God's gift, not a reward for work done. There is nothing for anyone to boast of. For we are God's handiwork, created in Christ Jesus to devote ourselves to the good deeds for which God has designed us.

The question of boasting does not come into it, since salvation is not a matter of merit. It is not our work at all but God's. It springs from his sheer unmerited love (his 'grace'). It is offered us as a gift for our free acceptance in Christ. The taking of the gift is what is meant by 'faith' or trust.

The next stanza puts this faith into words:

> Nothing in my hand I bring,
> Simply to thy cross I cling;
> Naked, come to thee for dress;
> Helpless, look to thee for grace;
> Foul, I to the fountain fly:
> Wash me, Saviour, or I die.

The stanza is remarkable for its varied figures of speech, all of them illustrating what faith in Christ is and how he meets our every need.

Faith is clinging to Christ crucified, laying hold of him with empty hand and renouncing all our own endeavours.

Faith is coming to Christ in the nakedness of our guilt and shame, to be clothed in the garment of his righteousness.

Faith is looking to Christ in our utter helplessness and casting ourselves on his grace.

Faith is fleeing to Christ, foul and filthy as we are, to be washed in the fountain opened for sin and uncleanness.

If the second stanza presents the dark side of the picture, stressing the futility of our feeble efforts to save ourselves, the third shines with the glory of God's grace. What the sinner cannot do for himself, God can do for him; and Christ is sufficient for everyone who trusts in him.

III

The final stanza looks beyond time to eternity.

> While I draw this fleeting breath,
> When my eyelids close in death,
> When I soar through tracts unknown,
> See thee on thy judgment throne:
> Rock of ages, cleft for me,
> Let me hide myself in thee.

Toplady's own form of the second line was 'When my eye-strings break in death'. The change to the wording given above was made by Thomas Cotterill in his selection of hymns published in 1815. Another slight variation, found in some hymnals (including *EH*), is 'When mine eyes are closed in death' – a change made on the ground that in death eyelids do not close but have to be closed.

Apart from this, the stanza calls for little comment. Percy Dearmer spoke of its 'growing exultation, and the quiet return at the end, in a changed tone of gentle confidence, to the opening words'. What it affirms is the timeless nature of Christ's sacrificial death. It avails in every moment of life: *while I draw this fleeting breath*. It avails in the hour of our departure from the world: *when mine eyes are closed in death*. And it avails in the day of final reckoning: when I *see thee on thy judgment throne*.

In view of what he says here about death, it is good to know that Toplady's own end, at the age of thirty-eight, was jubilant and triumphant. 'I enjoy heaven already in my soul,' he said as he lay dying; 'my prayers are all converted into praises.'

One question remains, and it is worth considering. What is the secret of this hymn's astonishing popularity? On several grounds it is open to criticism. Its theology is old-fashioned, with a strong emphasis on sin. Its imagery is obscure in places and its metaphors are mixed. And its whole tone is intensely subjective in character. Nevertheless, down the years it has laid a firm hold on all kinds of people, high and low alike, including people of widely different brands of churchmanship.

The secret lies partly, no doubt, in the hymn's vivid and passionate language. The bold opening phrase 'Rock of ages, cleft for me' at once arrests attention and gets the hymn off to a splendid start. But ultimately the answer to our question is to be found in the hymn's spiritual qualities and penetrating message. It speaks to our condition. Just because it has so much to say about sin it makes an appeal to every man who knows his own heart, whether he be the holiest believer in the world or the most deeply-dyed sinner. 'The facts of Sin and Grace,' comments H. A. L. Jefferson, 'are not transient modes of theological thought; they are abiding, inescapable verities.'[1] Never mind the mixed metaphors. As Duncan Campbell says, 'When men are conscious of deep need, when heart condemns and conscience accuses, these very metaphors, with their combined suggestion of shelter and cleansing, are strangely restful.'[2]

NOTES
1 *Hymns in Christian Worship*, p.91.
2 *Hymns and Hymn Makers*, p.57.

13

CRUCIFIED AND RISEN

Jesus Christ is risen to-day

I

I<small>T IS</small> strange that the best known of all Easter hymns – at least as far as Anglicans are concerned[1] – is entirely anonymous. No one knows who wrote the original fourteenth-century Latin carol beginning *Surrexit Christus hodie* on which the hymn is based, or who translated it into English, or who composed the magnificent tune *Easter Hymn* with which it is always associated. Both the English translation and the tune first appeared in a book called *Lyra Davidica*, published in 1708; but only the first stanza assumed a form familiar to us to-day:

> Jesus Christ is risen to-day, Halle-Halle-lujah.
> Our triumphant Holyday
> Who so lately on the Cross
> Suffered to redeem our loss.

The two verses that followed were based on a later part of the Latin text, the first of them being an address to the women at the tomb, the second consisting of a call to praise:

> Haste ye females from your fright
> Take to Galilee your flight
> To his sad disciples say
> Jesus Christ is risen to-day.

In our paschal joy and feast
Let the Lord of life be blest
Let the Holy Trine be praised
And thankful heart to heaven be raised.

Perhaps it is hardly surprising that these stanzas were dropped when the hymn next made its appearance some seventy years later in Arnold's *Compleat Psalmodist*, 1779. In their place were two new stanzas, written without any reference to the original Latin carol. The hymn now differed only in detail from the form in which we sing it to-day. In fact, what we have in our hymnals is the version which was printed in the *Supplement* (1816) to Tate and Brady's *New Version* of the psalms: a small collection of hymns for various occasions which included 'While shepherds watched their flocks by night'. Under the heading 'For Easter Day' the text of the hymn was as follows.

> Jesus Christ is risen to-day,
> Our triumphant holy day;
> Who did once, upon the cross,
> Suffer to redeem our loss.
>
> Hallelujah.

> Hymns of praise then let us sing
> Unto Christ our heavenly King;
> Who endured the cross and grave,
> Sinners to redeem and save.
>
> Hallelujah.

> But the pains which he endured
> Our salvation hath procured;
> Now above the sky he's King,
> Where the angels ever sing.
>
> Hallelujah.

II

A glance at these verses reveals that they make no pretentions to greatness. In fact at first sight the hymn lacks any distinction as far as the words are concerned. It is not too much to say that the hymn would scarcely have survived apart from its famous tune. And yet obviously the words have a certain appeal. Their very simplicity and directness are part of their attraction; and of course they do keep closely to the Easter theme.

That brings us to the heart of the matter. This is an Easter hymn, and the Easter message, as it makes clear, is not simply the Lord's triumphant resurrection. It is also his bitter cross and passion, the sufferings he bore for our redemption. In the hymn the two themes are closely interwoven, and it is worth noting the way in which this is done.

A close look at the hymn shows that the four lines in each of the three stanzas consist of two couplets, and that in each case one couplet refers directly to the resurrection, the other to the passion. Take the resurrection theme first. In the first stanza it is expressed in the opening couplet:

> Jesus Christ is risen to-day,
> Our triumphant holy day.

So also in the second stanza:

> Hymns of praise then let us sing
> Unto Christ, our heavenly King.

In the third stanza the theme occurs in the final couplet:

> Now above the sky he's King,
> Where the angels ever sing.

As the complement to these lines are the three couplets which refer to Christ's passion. In the first stanza:

> Who did once, upon the cross,
> Suffer to redeem our loss.

In the next stanza this is repeated in the lines:

> Who endured the cross and grave,
> Sinners to redeem and save.

Finally in the third stanza we have:

> But the pains which he endured,
> Our salvation hath procured.

This device, simple as it is and also somewhat repetitive, is worth observing. It not only indicates the pattern on which the hymn is built; it means that the hymn has the merit of presenting the *whole* Easter message – the Paschal sacrifice *and* the Paschal victory – and presenting it in a way that is easy to understand. Two pictures of Jesus emerge which must always be viewed together. We see him as the crucified Saviour who by his death accomplished our redemption. We see him also as the risen, reigning Lord enthroned in heaven to whom we lift up our hearts in joyful adoration. This is the gospel, the good news – Jesus crucified and risen (1 Corinthians 15.1–4).

No comment has been offered as yet on the *Alleluia* at the end of every line of the hymn. Its use is significant and represents an old Christian tradition. 'Alleluia' – the Greek equivalent of the Hebrew *Hallelujah*, 'Praise the Lord!' – had an important place in Christian worship from the beginning. However, in the Middle Ages its use was forbidden during Lent (from Septuagesima Sunday onwards), to mark the penitential character of the season. A reference to this is found in the ancient Latin hymn *Alleluia, dulce carmen*, 'Alleluia, song of sweetness' (*EH* 63; *AMR* 82), which is marked in the hymnals 'For the week before Septuagesima'. The hymn, after acknowledging that Alleluia is the normal note of joy to be sounded in the Church's worship, goes on to say that for a season we must forgo its use,

> For the solemn time is coming
> When our tears for sin must flow.

Hence it was a question of farewell to Alleluia between Septuagesima and Easter. Holy Saturday, or Easter Even, was sometimes named 'Alleluia Saturday', as it greeted the return of Alleluia after its long absence. Then, on Easter Day, Alleluia burst forth once more in the Church's worship and every opportunity was taken to sing it again and again.

This accounts for the multiplication of Alleluias in the Easter hymns, as in the one we have been looking at. A glance at the Easter section of any hymnal will furnish plenty of other examples. Eastertide is supremely the season of Alleluia, of praise to the risen Lord.

III

In some hymn books a fourth stanza is added to our hymn in the form of a doxology. In this case there is no mystery regarding its authorship. It was written by Charles Wesley to provide the hymn with a Trinitarian ending. It will be found as the last verse of the hymn in the *Methodist Hymn Book* (205):

> Sing we to our God above,
> Praise eternal as his love;
> Praise him, all ye heavenly host,
> Father, Son, and Holy Ghost!

The first line may be said to link up with the last line of the previous verse, 'Where the angels ever sing'. We join our voices with the angels in celebration of the resurrection of Christ. Even so, it may be questioned whether the doxology adds anything of value to the hymn as a whole.

Charles Wesley's own fine Easter hymn, 'Christ the Lord is risen to-day' (*MHB* 204) was probably inspired by the hymn we have been considering, for it begins in much the same way, is written in the same metre, and like it links together the cross and the resurrection. But it also goes a stage further: it sees in Christ's resurrection the pattern and pledge of our own. Published in 1739, the hymn originally consisted of eleven verses. Martin Madan later shortened and edited it for the use of the Methodists, and this is the form it takes in *MHB*. In another version it is now familiar to many Anglican worshippers in the cento beginning with Wesley's second stanza, 'Love's redeeming work is done' (*EH* 135; *AMR* 141).

No one would deny that both poetically and theologically Wesley's hymn is superior to 'Jesus Christ is risen to-day'. For all that, it is safe to say that the latter will long remain the hymn *par excellence* for Easter worship in most of our churches.

NOTE
1 The hymn is not included in *Congregational Praise*, so it may not be as familiar in Free Church circles.

14

EASTER VICTORY

The day of Resurrection!

JOHN MASON Neale describes St John of Damascus as the greatest poet of the Greek Church. He lived in the eighth century, but few details are known of his life. Most of it was spent in the monastery of St Sabas, some ten miles south-east of Jerusalem, not far from the Dead Sea; and there in that lonely spot he engaged in artistic and musical studies, wrote his theology and composed his poetry.

I

In his day St John Damascene gave a great impetus to Greek hymnody and music. His own most important contributions were the 'Canons' he wrote for the chief festivals of the Church, and it is from one of these – the 'Golden Canon' for Easter, the Queen of Festivals – that the hymn 'The day of Resurrection' comes.

The canon was a form of hymn consisting normally of nine odes or subdivisions in a set pattern, sung in the monasteries at the office of Lauds. The design of the odes which make up the Golden Canon, according to Julian's *Dictionary of Hymnology*, 'is to set forth the fact of the Resurrection, its fulfilment of ancient types and figures and prophecies, and the benefits which it has brought to mankind; out of which arises the call for praise and thanksgiving.'

Several of these elements are to be found in the first of the odes, the hymn which now concerns us. The translation comes from Dr Neale's *Hymns of the Eastern Church*, 1862, where it begins

> 'Tis the Day of Resurrection:
> Earth! tell it out abroad!

The only other significant alteration in our hymn-books is in the final stanza, where the original fifth and sixth lines ran

> Invisible and visible
> Their notes let all things blend.

As amended the lines are an improvement, being easier to sing while conveying the same meaning.

II

The hymn has an arresting beginning.

> The day of Resurrection!
>   Earth, tell it out abroad;
> The Passover of gladness,
>   The Passover of God!
> From death to life eternal,
>   From earth unto the sky,
> Our God hath brought us over
>   With hymns of victory.

The day of Resurrection! Yes, it is Easter morning and dawn is breaking. The faithful women are already at the tomb. They have come to anoint a dead body, but to their astonishment the body is not there. The tomb is empty. *'Tis the day of Resurrection!* The Lord is risen! So the trumpet note rings out – *Earth, tell it out abroad!* For this is good news for a world without hope, and all the world must hear it.

112

But what precisely is this good news, this gospel of the resurrection? The remainder of the stanza supplies the answer. It interprets the message and meaning of Easter in terms of victory, and it does this by drawing on the analogy of the Jewish Passover: *The Passover of gladness, the Passover of God!*

From the very beginning the Christian Church saw in the story of the Passover a picture of Christ's redemptive work. Thus St Paul: 'Christ, our paschal lamb, has been sacrificed' (1 Corinthians 5.7). The apostle Peter likewise recalls the Passover ritual when he says that we have been redeemed 'with the precious blood of Christ, like that of a lamb without blemish' (1 Peter 1.19; *cf.* Exodus 12.5). Again, in St John's record of the Passion we find an oblique reference to the paschal lamb in relation to the crucified Saviour (John 19.36; *cf.* Exodus 12.46).

For the Israelites the Passover had two distinct meanings: first, deliverance from death by the slaying of the paschal lamb and the sprinkling of its blood on their houses; second, emancipation from bondage by their triumphant exodus from Egypt and their crossing of the Red Sea, thereby passing from the old life of slavery to the new life of freedom.

It is small wonder that the early Christians, with their Jewish background, came to see in the blood of the paschal lamb a foreshadowing of the death of Christ, and in the Red Sea crossing a striking picture of his resurrection victory. These are the figures employed in our hymn to interpret the message of the risen Lord. Easter is the Christian Passover, celebrated not once a year (like the Jewish Passover) but perpetually; for Christ is alive for evermore and it is Easter all the year round. By his cross and his resurrection God has *brought us over from death to life eternal*, and we celebrate our deliverance *with hymns of victory*.

The Passover symbolism is expressed more fully in another Easter hymn by St John of Damascus, written for St Thomas's Sunday, the Sunday after Easter, beginning:

> Come, ye faithful, raise the strain
> Of triumphant gladness;

113

God hath brought his Israel
Into joy from sadness;
Loosed from Pharaoh's bitter yoke
Jacob's sons and daughters;
Led them with unmoistened foot
Through the Red Sea waters.

III

The second stanza moves from the Old Testament into the New. We leave behind the dramatic symbolism of the Passover story – and suddenly it is, in very truth, the day of Resurrection.

Our hearts be pure from evil,
That we may see aright
The Lord in rays eternal
Of resurrection-light;
And, listening to his accents,
May hear so calm and plain
His own 'All hail,' and hearing,
May raise the victor strain.

Now, provided *our hearts be pure from evil*, so that our spiritual vision is unclouded, we may see *the Lord in rays eternal of resurrection-light*. This dazzling picture of the risen Christ is derived from St John's vision in Revelation 1.14–16:

His head and his hair were white as wool, white as snow; his eyes were like a flame of fire; his feet were like burnished bronze, refined as in a furnace, . . . and his face was like the sun shining in full strength.

Perhaps there is also here a recollection of the Lord's transfiguration on the mount when his face shone like the sun and his garments became white as light (Matthew 17.2).

After that breath-taking vision we are brought back to the gospel record. Again it is early on Easter morning and we join the little group of women returning from the tomb 'with fear and great joy' to tell the disciples what they had seen. 'And behold, Jesus met them, saying, All hail. And they came and ... worshipped him' (Matthew 28.9 AV).

Easter is not complete unless we too encounter the risen Lord Jesus and, *listening to his accents*, hear him greet us as his friends. Commentators on St Matthew's Gospel point out that the greeting Jesus gave the women was not something special or formal, as 'All hail' tends to suggest, but the ordinary Jewish salutation between friends. 'Peace be with you' (as in TEV) would be a more satisfactory rendering. As we thus meet with him and listen to him we, like the women, worship him and *raise the victor strain*.

The final stanza is a call to universal praise because of Christ's Easter victory.

> Now let the heavens be joyful
>   And earth her song begin,
> The round world keep high triumph
>   And all that is therein;
> Let all things seen and unseen
>   Their notes of gladness blend,
> For Christ the Lord hath risen,
>   Our Joy that hath no end.

The whole of creation is summoned to join in a song of celebration. Here we catch the spirit of the Benedicite: 'O all ye works of the Lord, bless ye the Lord!' and of St Francis of Assisi's *Canticle of the Sun*: 'All creatures of our God and King'. The language of the hymn contains echoes of many passages of scripture where the same call rings out, especially in some of the later psalms. Take as an example Psalm 96.11–13, or the whole of Psalm 148. A fine instance is also found in Isaiah 49, which proclaims the living God not only as the Lord of the nations but also as the King of creation:

> Sing, O heavens, for the Lord has done it:
>   Shout, O depths of the earth!
> Break forth into singing, O mountains,
>   O forest, and every tree in it!
> For the Lord has redeemed Jacob,
>   And will be glorified in Israel. (v. 13)

115

And from the New Testament here is the Song of Creation in Revelation 5.13 (NEB):

> Then I heard every created thing in heaven and on earth and under the earth and in the sea, all that is in them, crying,
>
>> 'Praise and honour, glory and might, to him who sits on the throne and to the Lamb for ever and ever!'

In keeping with all this the hymn bids *the heavens and earth* to be joyful with song, *the round world* to *keep high triumph*, and *all things seen and unseen* to blend *their notes of gladness*. And why? Because of the resurrection victory of the Lord Christ, *our Joy that hath no end.* Nor is he *our* joy alone. The Church's joy is also Creation's joy, for both partake of the same hope.

Is this mere fantasy? Not if in any way we share St Paul's cosmic view of redemption set out in Colossians 1.19, 20 and Romans 8.18–21. God's purpose in the incarnate Christ was 'to reconcile to himself all things, whether on earth or in heaven, making peace by the blood of his cross'. The whole created order was involved at the beginning in Adam's disobedience and sin; and in some mysterious way, beyond our human comprehension, it will also be involved at the end in the second Adam's conquest of death and evil. So the apostle sets before us the ultimate hope that the material universe will be liberated from the bondage of decay and enjoy the glory and freedom of the children of God. The same Bible which asserts a cosmic Fall also promises a cosmic redemption.

'Behold, I create new heavens and a new earth.'

15

LIVING LORD

Jesus lives! thy terrors now

THIS FINE Easter hymn introduces us to one of the noble army of women hymn-writers of the last century. Frances Elizabeth Cox (1812–97) did not compose original hymns, but under the guidance of Baron Bunsen she translated many of the finest German hymns into English. She was in fact one of the pioneers in this particular field. Her *Sacred Hymns from the German* was published in 1841, and included in this was 'Jesus lives!' – the best known of all her work. Among her other translations which are still in use are 'Sleepers, wake! the watch-cry pealeth' (Advent), 'Who are these like stars appearing?' (Saints' Days), and 'Sing praise to God who reigns above'.

We need not give further attention here to Miss Cox, apart from acknowledging the valuable contribution she made to our hymnody; but something must certainly be said about the exceptionally fine man who wrote the German original of this hymn in the middle of the eighteenth century.

I

Christian Gellert (1715–69) was the son of a German pastor. He entered the University of Leipzig in 1734 to study theology, and in due course was ordained to the ministry of the Lutheran Church. But it soon became clear to him that this was not his true vocation, and he later returned to Leipzig to pursue other studies. Eventually he was appointed lecturer in poetry, and later Professor of Philosophy, in the University. A man of deep Christian piety, he exercised a profound influence over his students on account of the unselfish and saintly quality of his life. He was generous to the point of recklessness and was careless of his own comfort. When Prince Henry of Prussia sought him out, he was found to be living in one empty room without food or fire. Among his students was the poet Goethe, who testified: 'The reverence and affection which Gellert received from all the young men was extraordinary. His lecture room was always crowded to the utmost, and his beautiful soul, purity of will, his admonitions, warnings and entreaties . . . produced a deep impression.' He undertook the writing of his hymns in a spirit of prayer and regarded it as a task to be done for the glory of God. Published in 1757, the hymns became popular throughout Germany and remain among the classics of German hymnody.

Theologian, philosopher, poet, saint – such was the man who wrote *Jesus lebt, mit ihm auch ich*, the hymn we sing as 'Jesus lives!' Gellert's strong and vigorous Christian faith is reflected in every line. In the form in which he wrote the hymn each verse ended with the triumphant words, 'This shall be my confidence!' In the English translation *Alleluia!* becomes the equivalent of this.

But perhaps the most striking feature of the hymn is the ringing affirmation with which every stanza begins: *Jesus lives!* It is the keynote of the entire composition. Gellert teaches us to celebrate Easter not by contemplating the empty tomb, as a past event, but by coming face to face with the living Lord as a present reality.

This is the heart of the resurrection faith. It was the conviction that Jesus was alive that gripped the apostles, scattered their doubts, changed their lives, and gave them a gospel to preach. The resurrection is more than a fact. It is a faith and a force. It is not simply something that happened long ago. It is something that happens now. The resurrection belongs to the present as much as to the past. The Lord rose. The Lord is risen. Easter has an eternal significance. Jesus lives!

The fabric of the hymn is woven out of this theme. In affirming the Easter faith it faces the question, What difference does it make to us that Jesus lives? How does it affect our lives? The five stanzas in turn supply the answers.

II

In the first place, the living Lord robs death of its power, and therefore releases us from its fear.

> Jesus lives! thy terrors now
> Can, O death, no more appal us;
> Jesus lives! by this we know
> Thou, O grave, canst not enthral us.
> Alleluia!

In Miss Cox's original version of the hymn the opening lines were

> Jesus lives! no longer now
> Can thy terrors, death, appal us.

With her consent they were altered to their present form to avoid confusion when the first line alone was quoted. The hymn as a whole underwent a good deal of revision at her own and other hands during the last century, but the details of this need not detain us here. We are concerned with the hymn in its now familiar form.

The opening stanza affirms that because *Jesus lives*, the *terrors* of *death* can no longer *appal* or terrify us. Nor can the *grave enthral us* – that is, enslave us. The believer can face the last great enemy calmly, fearlessly, hopefully. Gellert headed the hymn when he wrote it with the words of Jesus, 'Because I live, you shall live also' (John 14.19). Just as by his death he has destroyed death, so by his rising to life again he has restored to us everlasting life. The apostle boldly asserts that

119

Christ has 'abolished death' (2 Timothy 1.10) – abolished its tyranny, annihilated its power, ended its reign. In the risen Lord death has met its master. He has destroyed death in so far as it is something that can harm us, something to be feared (see 1 Corinthians 15.55–7; Hebrews 2.14,15). Certainly death had no terrors for the man who wrote this hymn. When Christian Gellert was dying and was told that he had about an hour more to live, he lifted his hands and cried, 'Now God be praised, only an hour!'

For Christ's victory over the grave let us raise our *Alleluia!*

The next stanza takes us a stage further. The living Lord opens to us the gate of life:

> Jesus lives! henceforth is death
> But the gate of life immortal;
> This shall calm our trembling breath,
> When we pass its gloomy portal.
> Alleluia!

This is the positive side of the truth affirmed in the previous stanza. Christ has not only abolished death but has brought life and immortality to light through the gospel (2 Timothy 1.10). Death is not the finish, the end of everything, as the world supposes. Far from being an end it is an entrance: *henceforth is death but the gate of life immortal.* The language is similar to that in the collect of Easter Even, in which we pray that 'through the gate of death we may pass to our joyful resurrection'. The risen Christ has the keys of that gate, the keys of death and of the unseen world (Revelation 1.18).

This is our comfort now, when we think about death, as indeed we ought to do from time to time. It will be our strong consolation *when we pass its gloomy portal*, as inevitably we shall have to do when our time comes. At that moment death, the enemy, will fulfil the office of a friend, for it will usher us into the nearer presence of our Lord. 'For the Christian,' it has been said, 'the King of Terrors has become a slave. He is clad indeed in black, but he is sent to draw back the curtains of mystery and to lead the follower of Christ into the spacious chambers of the Father's house' (Charles R. Erdman). For this assurance let us sing another *Alleluia!*

But more. The living Lord claims our love and our lives:

> Jesus lives! for us he died;
>> Then, alone to Jesus living,
> Pure in heart may we abide,
>> Glory to our Saviour giving.
>>> Alleluia!

Some words of St Paul are the best commentary on these lines:

> The love of Christ controls us, because we are convinced that one has died for all; therefore all have died. And he died for all, that those who live might live no longer for themselves but for him who for their sake died and was raised.
>
> (2 Corinthians 5.14,15)

The motivating power of the Christian life derives from the love of Christ exhibited supremely in his death and resurrection. *For us he died*, and therefore he has a total claim upon us. We have been bought with a price. Once we have been grasped by the love of Christ and recognize our indebtedness to him, our life can never be an egocentric affair. We belong to another. What then? *Then, alone to Jesus living.* This must be the new pattern of things. He who gave all for us deserves all from us. *Pure in heart* as *we abide* in him, we yield ourselves wholly to his service, *glory to our Saviour giving*. And in that spirit we raise another *Alleluia!*

III

The next stanza rings with the note of assurance. The living Lord guarantees our eternal security:

> Jesus lives! our hearts know well
>> Nought from us his love shall sever;
> Life, nor death, nor powers of hell
>> Tear us from his keeping ever.
>>> Alleluia!

'Who shall separate us from the love of Christ?' asks St Paul. The answer of the hymn is, *Naught from us his love shall sever*. The apostle gives the same answer in a different form, ending his inquiry with the words:

> I am convinced that there is nothing in death or life, in the realm of spirits or superhuman powers, in the world as it is or the world as it shall be, in the forces of the universe, in heights or depths – nothing in all creation that can separate us from the love of God in Christ Jesus our Lord.
>
> (Romans 8.38, 39 NEB)

Life cannot separate us from the love of Christ, not even life's harshest experiences, such as those detailed by the apostle – tribulation, persecution, hunger, nakedness, peril, and the rest. Nor can *death* come between Christ's love and his people. Far from separating them, death unites them, as we have already seen, so that for the believer to die is not loss but gain (Philippians 1.21–3). And *powers of hell*, however powerful they be – those spiritual forces of evil rampant in the life of society in our own day, no less than of old – not even they can separate us from the living Christ or *tear us from his keeping ever*. On the contrary, in all things we are more than conquerors through him who loves us, and his is the love that will not let us go. However feeble our hold of Christ, his hold of us is secure. And because that is so, let us again sing *Alleluia!*

The final stanza gives to the resurrection of Jesus a wider and grander dimension. The living Lord is King of the universe:

> Jesus lives! to him the throne
> Over all the world is given;
> May we go where he is gone,
> Rest and reign with him in heaven.
> Alleluia!

The risen Christ is the reigning Christ. *To him the throne over all the world is given.*

The sovereignty of Jesus is an exhilarating and triumphant note on which to end an Easter hymn. He is not only Lord of the Church. His kingdom rules over all. When in his risen power he gave his disciples their world-wide commission, he declared, 'All authority in heaven and on earth has been committed to me' (Matthew 28.18–20). It was with that conviction they went forth to make disciples of all nations. The Resurrection of Jesus has a cosmic significance. In the words of Dr James Stewart, the Resurrection is 'the one fact which vitally concerns not only the life of the individual Christian, but the entire human scene and the destiny of the race. It is the breakthrough of the eternal order into this world of suffering and confusion and sin and death . . . It is the kingdom of God made visible.'[1]

The exalted Lord has entered heaven both as the King of the universe and as the Forerunner of his people (see Hebrews 6.19,20). This gives us a hope that is 'a sure and steadfast anchor of the soul'; and that is why we can pray with confidence that *we may go where he is gone* – and not only go there, but *rest and reign with him in heaven.* We shall not only behold his glory (John 17.24). We shall share his throne (2 Timothy 2.12; Revelation 3.21). What a prospect! Gellert wrote, 'This shall be my confidence!' We can only respond, *Alleluia!*

NOTE
1 *Heralds of God* (Hodder & Stoughton, 1946), p.89.

16

CHRIST THE KING

All hail the power of Jesus' name

THE ESSENTIAL meaning of the Church's feast of the Ascension is the Kingship of Christ. His exaltation to the right hand of God can be described as his coronation in the courts of heaven. Hence among the hymns we sing at Ascensiontide are those which recognize and proclaim what the old divines called 'the crown rights of the Redeemer', his royalty and his reign. One such hymn is Charles Wesley's 'Rejoice, the Lord is King'. Another is Thomas Kelly's 'The head that once was crowned with thorns'. Yet another, obviously enough, is Matthew Bridge's 'Crown him with many crowns'. All these celebrate the sovereignty of him who is 'crowned with glory and honour' and who claims the allegiance and homage of his people. None does it better than the hymn we are going to consider in this chapter.

I

'All hail the power of Jesus' name' was written by Edward Perronet (1726–92), a protégé of John Wesley and one of his early itinerant preachers. His father, the saintly Vincent Perronet, for over fifty years vicar of the village of Shoreham in

Kent, was an intimate friend of both the Wesleys. Edward Perronet, a deeply earnest evangelical with no mean poetical talent, was a somewhat hot-headed character who found it difficult to work with others and was highly critical of the Church of England. Eventually he parted company with the Methodists, turned Dissenter, and ended his days as minister of a small Independent chapel in Canterbury. Evidently his Anglican origins were not forgotten at the end, for he was buried in the cloisters of the cathedral.

Of the many hymns he wrote only this one is now remembered; but the fact that it has survived for two hundred years is testimony to its undoubted worth. The hymn has a rather strange history. The first verse alone was printed in the *Gospel Magazine* for November 1779, together with the tune *Miles Lane* with which it has been associated from the first. Some months later, in the spring of 1780, the hymn in its complete form appeared in the same magazine under the title 'On the Resurrection, the Lord is King'. It consisted then of eight stanzas. The second of them has long dropped out of use and is found in no modern hymnal. One writer calls it a 'delicious quatrain'. It is certainly quaint and deserves to be quoted:

> Let high-born seraphs tune the lyre,
>   And as they tune it, fall
> Before his face, who tunes their choir,
>   And crown him Lord of all.

Several changes were made to the hymn by Dr John Rippon, a Baptist minister, when he included it in his *Selection of Hymns from the Best Authors*, 1787. Not only did he rewrite some of the stanzas. He omitted three of them altogether, and added two of his own, to make up a hymn of seven stanzas. To each of these he gave a suitable title, such as 'Angels', 'Martyrs', and so on, and the whole hymn was headed 'The Spiritual Coronation'. One of the stanzas Rippon himself contributed ('Sinners of every age') has long since disappeared and is not worthy of the hymn; but his final verse, headed 'Ourselves', still finds a place in several hymn books in the following form:

O that with yonder sacred throng
    We at his feet may fall,
Join in the everlasting song,
    And crown him Lord of all.

Editors in modern times have found it difficult to decide which version of the hymn to print in their hymnals. The result is somewhat bewildering, for it appears in a different form in almost every book in current use. Some, such as *EH* and *AMR*, keep as close as possible to Perronet's original verses. Others make considerable use of Rippon's revision. In every case there is some measure of compromise. However, whatever version we follow, the grand design of the hymn is not affected, which is to affirm in the most positive terms the Kingship of Christ and to call upon different companies of people to ascribe royal honours to his name as they 'crown him Lord of all'.

A word may be added about the tune *Miles Lane* which, as we have noted, was published at the same time that the hymn made its appearance. It was written by a former chorister of Canterbury Cathedral, William Shrubsole, who was born in 1760. This means that he wrote the celebrated tune when he was only nineteen years of age. Elgar pronounced it the finest tune in English hymnody – high praise indeed. Shrubsole, who was later appointed organist of Bangor Cathedral, is remembered for this single musical composition: his solitary but worthy memorial.

II

We turn now to the words of the hymn. We shall give the text as Perronet wrote it but shall omit the second stanza (the one about the high-born seraphs tuning their lyres) since this is no longer part of the hymn as we know it. We shall also take note of the more important variations made to the text in the various hymnals.

All hail the power of Jesus' name!
Let angels prostrate fall;
Bring forth the royal diadem,
To crown him Lord of all.

All hail the power of Jesus' name! – a magnificent and arresting opening line for a hymn of this character. We must observe that what we are called upon to 'hail' – that is, to honour and exalt – is not simply the name of Jesus but the *power* of his name. That power belongs to him by virtue of his resurrection victory and heavenly enthronement. To him, the living and reigning Christ, all authority has been given in heaven and on earth (Matthew 28.18). He is King of kings and Lord of lords (Revelation 19.16). Therefore *let angels prostrate fall*, bowing before him in homage and adoration. Angels are the first of the spiritual companies summoned to share in the coronation of the King of glory; and it is they, seemingly, who are invited to *bring forth the royal diadem* for the ceremonial act. The imagery is clearly borrowed from the book of Revelation, where the glorified Son of Man is represented as wearing a crown of gold (14.14). In a later vision (19.11–13) he is given the name of 'The Word of God', and 'on his head are many diadems' – the 'many' indicating that his sovereignty extends over all rulers and nations.

The lordship of Jesus is not only acknowledged in the heavenly sphere but also in the world of nature.

Crown him, ye morning stars of light,
Who fixed this floating ball;
Now hail the Strength of Israel's might,
And crown him Lord of all.

The *morning stars of light* (*cf.* Job 38.7; Psalm 148.3) represent the created order, the material universe. Hence in this stanza creation is called upon to acknowledge Christ in his capacity as Creator, the one *who fixed this floating ball.* 'In him all things were created, in heaven and on earth' (Colossians 1.16; *cf.* John 1.3; Hebrews 1.2). The poetical description of our planet as a 'floating ball' which nevertheless the Lord has 'fixed' is probably derived from the Prayer Book version of Psalm 96.10: 'The Lord is King, and hath made the

127

round world so fast that it cannot be moved'. The Lord is also *the Strength of Israel's might*: a biblical expression which can be traced to 1 Samuel 15.29 (AV).

III

We pass from the company of angels and the order of creation to redeemed humanity, the People of God.

> Crown him, ye martyrs of your God,
>   Who from his altar call;
> Extol the stem of Jesse's rod,
>   And crown him Lord of all.

The noble army of martyrs has always been highly honoured in the Church on account of their courageous 'witness' (the meaning of the Greek word *martus*) – a witness sealed by their blood. The modern Church is not without its martyrs, and those who have thus died for the faith of Christ in our own time are as worthy of honour as those of any other age. Here the picture of those who gave their lives as *martyrs of* their *God* and who *call* to him *from his altar* is borrowed from Revelation 6.9,10:

> I saw under the altar the souls of those who had been slain for the word of God and for the witness they had borne; they cried out with a loud voice, 'O Sovereign Lord, holy and true, how long before thou wilt judge and avenge our blood on those who dwell upon the earth?'

Perronet's third line, *Extol the stem of Jesse's rod* – which is a reference to Jesus as the promised Messiah, drawn from Isaiah 11.1 – is changed in many hymn books to something like 'Praise him whose way of pain ye trod' (as in *EH*). This is a justifiable alteration. Not only does it remove the obscurity of 'the stem of Jesse's rod'; it also associates the martyrs' path of suffering with our Lord's own passion and death (*cf.* Mark 8.31–5; Romans 8.17; 1 Peter 4.13).

The next company addressed is not so easy to identify:

Ye seed of Israel's chosen race,
Ye ransomed of the fall,
Hail him who saves you by his grace,
And crown him Lord of all.

Whom are we to understand by the *seed of Israel's chosen
race*, the *ransomed of the fall*? The words could, of course, be
interpreted with reference to the Christian Church as the new
Israel, the true seed of Abraham, in accordance with St Paul's
teaching in Galatians 3.29. However, the Church appears to
be specifically designated in the next stanza; and it is noteworthy that Dr Rippon in his version of the hymn headed this
stanza 'Converted Jews'. Probably this is what Perronet had
in mind. Rippon actually altered the first two lines in order to
make this meaning clear:

Ye chosen seed of Israel's race,
A remnant weak and small.

The Jewish people who embrace the Christian faith and in
baptism acknowledge Jesus as Messiah and Lord are indeed a
small remnant, 'a remnant chosen by grace', as the apostle
says. 'But,' he adds, 'if it is by grace, it is no longer on the basis
of works' (Romans 11.5,6). In keeping with this, the hymn
bids the 'ransomed' Israelites to magnify the Lord Jesus as the
one *who saves* them *by his grace*, not by their fulfilment of the
works of the law (Acts 15.11).

The next stanza also requires a bit of sorting out:

Hail him, ye heirs of David's line,
Whom David Lord did call;
The God incarnate, Man divine,
And crown him Lord of all.

Here the *heirs of David's line* are bidden to *hail him . . . whom
David Lord did call*. David, as we know, was the king of
Israel. His 'line' therefore consists of those who are in the
royal succession. In the first instance this would indicate Jesus
himself, who, as the promised Messiah, 'was descended from
David according to the flesh' (Romans 1.3; see Psalm 132.11;
Matthew 1.1) and is therefore given the messianic title of Son
of David. But the royal succession does not end with Christ. It

is perpetuated in a succession of grace in the people of Christ, who partake of his royal character and are members of a royal priesthood (1 Peter 2.9).

However, the attention here is focused not on ourselves as the heirs of David's line but on him whom David called 'Lord' (Psalm 110.1). The stanza thus reaches its climax in the tremendous third line and builds up to this in the following way. He whom David called Lord is the Messiah. The Messiah is in fact Jesus of Nazareth. Jesus of Nazareth is none other than *the God incarnate, Man divine.* It is him that we, as Christians, worship and enthrone, the Word made flesh, *vere deus*, *vere homo*, truly God and truly Man.

IV

The first five stanzas have called upon specific companies to join in the coronation anthem: the angels, the created order, the martyrs, converted Jews, the Church of Christ. The last two stanzas are of a more general and inclusive character. The first of them is addressed simply to 'sinners':

> Sinners, whose love can ne'er forget
> The wormwood and the gall,
> Go, spread your trophies at his feet,
> And crown him Lord of all.

It would be interesting to know precisely what *sinners* Perronet had in mind when he wrote these lines. Dr Rippon in his version of the hymn gave to this stanza the title 'Gentile sinners' and changed the first line to 'Ye Gentile sinners, ne'er forget'. But his amendment has not found acceptance, and it seems unlikely that at this point a distinction is intended between Jewish and Gentile believers. It is better to regard these words as addressed to redeemed sinners of every kind who acknowledge their indebtedness to Christ and *whose love can ne'er forget the wormwood and the gall* – that is, the bitter price paid for their redemption (*cf.* Lamentations 3.19). They love much because they have been forgiven much (Luke 7.47); and they show their love in service to their Lord, so that they have *trophies* of grace to *spread at his feet.*

The final summons is to all mankind:

> Let every tribe and every tongue
> That bound creation's call,
> Now shout in universal song
> The crownèd Lord of all.

Such is Perronet's original ending. The second line is obscure and invites some revision. Rippon rewrote the stanza in the following form:

> Let every kindred, every tribe,
> On this terrestrial ball,
> To him all majesty ascribe,
> And crown him Lord of all.

This is adopted by *CP* among others. Many hymnals are content to leave the first line unaltered and change the second line to, for example, 'Before him prostrate fall' (as *AMR*) or 'To him their hearts enthral' (*EH*). Whatever version we choose to follow – or, more likely, is chosen for us – the meaning of the stanza remains the same. It is a call to the whole of humanity to acknowledge the Kingship of Jesus, so that *every tribe and every tongue* may *shout in universal song* the praises of *the crownèd Lord of all.* This is in accordance with God's cosmic purpose 'that at the name of Jesus every knee should bow ... and every tongue confess that Jesus Christ is Lord' (Philippians 2.10, 11); and it finds apocalyptic expression in the vision of Revelation 7.9, 10:

> I looked, and behold, a great multitude which no man could number, from every nation, from all tribes and peoples and tongues, standing before the throne and before the Lamb, clothed in white robes, with palm branches in their hands, and crying out with a loud voice, 'Salvation belongs to our God who sits upon the throne, and to the Lamb!'

131

17

VENI, CREATOR SPIRITUS

Come, Holy Ghost, our souls inspire

THE ANCIENT Latin hymn *Veni, Creator Spiritus*, best known to us in the translation beginning 'Come, Holy Ghost, our souls inspire', has the distinction of being the only metrical hymn to be found in the Book of Common Prayer. It also has the distinction of having been in unbroken use in the English Church – in one form or another – for a thousand years, for it was retained after the Reformation and incorporated in an English translation into the Ordinal of 1550. This gives it a place of peculiar honour in Christian history and devotion.

I

The authorship of the Latin original, which consisted of six four-line verses, is unknown. Many distinguished names have been suggested as possible writers, including most commonly Rhabanus Maurus, who in 847 became Archbishop of Mainz in Germany. But nothing certain is known on the subject, and speculation is unprofitable. What is certain is that the hymn dates from at least the tenth century, for by then it was already in use in the monastic services at the feast of Pentecost. In the next century it found its place in the Roman *Pontifical* and so formed part of the Ordination service. Through the centuries its use has been widened. It has associations with many of the great occasions in Church and State, including coronations, consecrations, church councils and synods; but to the average churchgoer it is pre-eminently a Whitsuntide hymn.

Numerous English translations exist. The earliest is the lengthy and unsatisfactory one which was made for the first English Ordinal. This was improved somewhat when the Prayer Book was revised a century and more later (1662); but at the same time another version was added as an alternative – our 'Come, Holy Ghost, our souls inspire'. This translation was the work of John Cosin, Bishop of Durham, one of the revisers of the 1662 book. He had actually written it thirty-five years earlier for his *Collection of Private Devotions in the Practice of the Ancient Church*. This book, which was intended simply for personal use, not for public worship, contained a hymn for each of the canonical hours. The translation of the *Veni Creator* was appointed for use at the third hour (9 a.m.), the hour of the outpouring of the Holy Spirit on the day of Pentecost (Acts 2.15).

The merit of Cosin's version is its conciseness. Its weakness results from this, for it is not a complete translation and ignores parts of the Latin text. From this point of view a more satisfactory rendering of the original hymn is the excellent translation made by Robert Bridges (1844–1930) for his *Yattendon Hymnal*, 1899, beginning 'Come, O Creator Spirit, come'. A third version, found in many hymn books, is that by the seventeenth-century poet John Dryden, 'Creator Spirit, by whose aid'; but this is more of a paraphrase than a translation and does not reflect the true character of the original. Whatever its faults, Cosin's rendering remains the most popular and is the form the hymn takes when it is sung on big and solemn occasions.

II

The key to the hymn lies in the title given to the Holy Spirit in the opening line. He is the *Creator* Spirit; and the hymn accordingly stresses his creative activity. Cosin does not actually use the title Creator, as do Bridges and Dryden; but his version does faithfully reveal the various aspects of the Spirit's energetic work in the life of the people of God.

The hymn begins with an invocation:

> Come, Holy Ghost, our souls inspire,
> And lighten with celestial fire;
> Thou the anointing Spirit art,
> Who dost thy sevenfold gifts impart.

Come is the opening word of this invocation. From the original it is clear that this is an invitation to the Holy Spirit to visit our hearts and minds and to fill them with his heavenly grace. Cosin sums up this activity of the Spirit in the phrase *our souls inspire.* In the seventeenth century the word 'inspire' bore its original meaning of to breathe-in, and the Holy Spirit is thought of as the Breath of God, quickening our souls with life divine. With this we may compare Edwin Hatch's hymn, 'Breathe on me, Breath of God', in *AMR* 236. But the Holy Spirit is the source of light as well as life: *And lighten with celestial fire.* There is a further and fuller reference to the illumination of the Spirit in the next stanza. The reference to 'celestial fire' is particularly apt when the hymn is used at an ordination, for it recalls St Paul's exhoration to Timothy 'to stir into flame the gift of God which is within you through the laying on of my hands' (2 Timothy 1.6 NEB; *cf.* 1 Timothy 4.14).

Thou the anointing Spirit art. Another symbol of the Spirit is now introduced, that of unction or anointing with oil. It is employed again in the second and third stanzas. Here, by his anointing, the Spirit is said to *impart* his *sevenfold gifts.* These gifts are those enumerated in the bishop's prayer for the candidates before the laying on of hands in the Prayer Book order of Confirmation: 'Daily increase in them thy manifold gifts of grace: the spirit of wisdom and understanding; the spirit of counsel and ghostly strength; the spirit of knowledge and true godliness; and . . . the spirit of thy holy fear.' These titles are derived in the main from Isaiah 11.2. In scripture seven is the number of completeness or perfection. This is the significance of the expression in Revelation 1.4, 'the seven spirits before his throne', which is simply a way of designating the Holy Spirit in the plenitude of his grace and power. The 'sevenfold Spirit' might be a more suitable translation.

III

Thy blessèd unction from above
Is comfort, life, and fire of love;
Enable with perpetual light
The dullness of our blinded sight.

Thy blessèd unction from above. Here again is the 'anointing Spirit', bestowing further gifts on the people of God. There are two references to this divine unction or chrism in the First Epistle of St John, chapter 2, where the apostle tells his readers, threatened as they were by false teachers, 'You have an anointing from the Holy One, and all of you know the truth'; and again: 'the anointing you received from him remains in you, and you do not need anyone to teach you' (vv. 20, 27). The anointing Spirit reveals the truth of God, as Jesus promised (John 16.13), and is the ultimate source of knowledge.

This line of thought is developed in the final stanza of the hymn. Meanwhile in this second stanza we are assured that the Spirit's unction *is comfort, life, and fire of love.* The word *comfort* here is derived from the Latin of the hymn, which refers to the Holy Spirit as the promised *Parakletos* (Greek), translated in the Authorized Version as the 'Comforter'. Hence Bridges' rendering:

O Comforter, that name is thine,
Of God most high the gift divine.

When the AV was made, the word 'comfort' meant not to console but to fortify, to make strong; so part of the 'blessed unction from above' is the gift of spiritual strength. Another is the gift of spiritual *life*; for as the Nicene Creed affirms, the Holy Spirit is the Giver of life, through whose agency we are

135

born anew (John 3.1–8). Yet a further gift he bestows is *fire of love*: a phrase which forcefully reminds us that the love which the Spirit gives – the love we owe to God, our brother, and our neighbour – is not something tepid or half-hearted, but warm and strong and glowing.

Again, the Spirit is the source of spiritual vision. We ask him to *enable with perpetual light* our inner blindness. The word 'enable' here has the older meaning of to assist, so as to render able. By the Spirit's enabling the eyes of our hearts are enlightened (Ephesians 1.18), so that we can walk as children of light and learn what is pleasing to the Lord (Ephesians 5.8, 10).

The prayer continues:

> Anoint and cheer our soilèd face,
> With the abundance of thy grace:
> Keep far our foes, give peace at home;
> Where thou art guide no ill can come.

Anoint and cheer our soilèd face. What are we asking for here? Simply to be anointed with 'the oil of gladness' (Psalm 45.7), so that we may have a cheerful countenance? Possibly; but there may be more to it than that. In scripture anointing with oil is connected with the healing of bodily ills, as in James 5.14, 15. The Latin of the hymn includes a specific prayer for the strengthening of our physical infirmities (see the fourth stanza of Bridges' version), and it may be that Cosin had this in mind in speaking of our 'soilèd face'. He was almost certainly thinking of the words in the 23rd Psalm, 'Thou anointest my head with oil'. Since our bodies are temples of the Holy Spirit (1 Corinthians 6.19), it is not difficult to believe that he sanctifies and strengthens us in body as well as in soul *with the abundance of (his) grace.*

The stanza concludes with a threefold prayer. First, there is a request for protection against our spiritual enemies: *Keep far our foes* – that is, repel them, drive them back. This is coupled with the petition, *Give peace at home*, meaning, Give us peace now, in our present circumstances. And third is a prayer for the Spirit to lead us in the way ahead, so that we may escape all evil; for *where thou art guide no ill can come.*

IV

The last part of the *Veni Creator* is a prayer that the Spirit of truth may impart to us the knowledge of God in the mystery of his Being; and this is suitably followed by an ascription of praise to the Holy Trinity.

> Teach us to know the Father, Son,
> And thee, of Both, to be but One;
> That through the ages all along
> This may be our endless song,
> Praise to thy eternal merit,
> Father, Son, and Holy Spirit.

The Whitsun collect in the Prayer Book states that God taught the hearts of his faithful people by the sending to them the light of his Holy Spirit. So now the Spirit is addressed in his office as Teacher, in accordance with our Lord's promise:

> These things I have spoken to you, while I am still with you. But the Counsellor, the Holy Spirit, whom the Father will send in my name, he will teach you all things, and will bring to your remembrance all that I have said to you.
>
> I have many things to say to you, but you cannot bear them now. When the Spirit of truth comes, he will guide you into all the truth; for he will not speak on his own authority, but whatever he hears he will speak, and he will declare to you the things that are coming.
>
> (John 14.25,26; 16.12,13)

Teach us to know the Father, Son. To know God is our highest wisdom. To know the Father and the Son is eternal life (John 17.3). Such knowledge far excels all other; but it cannot be attained by our own unaided learning or searching, as St Paul declares in 1 Corinthians 3.10–16. The Spirit searches the deep things of God and enables us to comprehend the thoughts of God. So we pray that he will teach us to know God: the Father, the Son – and also himself: *thee, of Both, to be but One.*

137

Especially significant – though doubtless the ordinary worshipper fails to recognize the significance – are the two little words *of Both* in defining the relation of the Holy Spirit to the Father and the Son. They affirm the faith of the Western Church, as declared in the Nicene Creed, that the Holy Spirit 'proceedeth from the Father and the Son'. The Eastern Church, on the other hand, objects to what is called the *filioque* clause ('and from the Son') and insists that the Holy Spirit proceeds from the Father alone. This seemingly small difference of opinion was, tragically, one of the factors which in the eleventh century caused the schism between the Greek and the Roman Church. It would be out of place here to enter into this sad controversy; but it can be claimed that the *filioque* clause is of value in associating the Holy Spirit in the closest possible way with God the Son and helps us to think of him, as doubtless we should, as the Spirit of Christ, as Christ in us (Romans 8.9, 10).

Knowing God, as we are thus taught by the Spirit through the scriptures, and acknowledging the glory of the eternal Trinity, we respond in an act of worship. *Through the ages* we raise to him *our endless song*, ascribing *praise to Father, Son, and Holy Spirit.* Dryden in his rendering of the hymn considerably expands the doxology in the florid style of his age:

> Immortal honour, endless fame,
> Attend the almighty Father's name;
> The Saviour Son be glorified,
> Who for lost man's redemption died;
> And equal adoration be,
> Eternal Paraclete, to thee.

18

THE HOLY GUEST

Our blest Redeemer, ere he breathed

THE WHITSUN hymn to which we now turn contrasts in many ways with the one we looked at in the previous chapter. Though the essential theme of both is the same, the two hymns are very different from one another in their origin, their style, their appeal, and in their treatment of the subject. 'Come, Holy Ghost, our souls inspire' is one of the great classical hymns of the Christian Church. 'Our blest Redeemer' has not the same claims to greatness, but for all that it is a good hymn. Writers have spoken of its 'exquisite words' and described it as a 'beautiful and timeless lyric'. The fact that it is still immensely popular and in constant use well over a century after it was written is evidence that it possesses some very positive values.

I

Little need be said about the author of the hymn. Harriet Auber (1773–1862) lived a quiet and secluded life, most of it in the Hertfordshire villages of Broxbourne and Hoddesdon. Her hymns were published in 1829 in a book called *The Spirit of the Psalms*. Her aim, like that of Henry Francis Lyte in a

139

book of the same title which came out a few years later, was to provide versions of selected psalms in a more poetical form than the metrical psalms still in use at that time. Miss Auber's efforts in this direction were not as successful as Lyte's, for none of her psalm-paraphrases has survived. But included in her volume were some hymns of a more general character, one of them being 'Our blest Redeemer', written for Whitsuntide. It is by this composition alone that her name is now remembered.

For long a curious story was in circulation – and is still sometimes related – to the effect that Miss Auber wrote her hymn with her diamond ring on one of the window panes of her house at Hoddesdon. The reason given for her doing this is that the words came to her in a sudden flash of inspiration as she sat in her bedroom and she had no writing materials ready to hand at the time. And confirmation has been given to the story by those who claim to have seen the pane with the writing on it, several years after her death.

That such a pane actually existed at one time in a bedroom window of the house seems reasonably certain, but there is no evidence that the words scratched on it were done by Miss Auber herself. The story must be dismissed as pure legend.

In its complete form the hymn consists of seven stanzas. As it now appears in our hymn books only five or six are normally used. It will be found in its entirety in the *Baptist Hymn Book* (236).

II

The opening stanza has as its theme the promise of the Spirit, interpreted as Christ's legacy to his Church:

> Our blest Redeemer, ere he breathed
>   His tender last farewell,
> A Guide, a Comforter, bequeathed
>   With us to dwell.

In thought we are now with Jesus and his disciples in the upper room on the night before he died. He is meeting with them for the last time, preparing them for what lies immediately ahead: his approaching passion and his departure to the Father. This is his farewell to them – *his tender last farewell*, as the hymn calls it. But before he leaves them he gives them the assurance that though they will no longer have his physical companionship in the days ahead, they are not, in the deepest sense, to be deprived of his presence. These are his words (John 14.15–18):

> If you love me, you will keep my commandments. And I will pray the Father, and he will give you another Counsellor, to be with you for ever, even the Spirit of truth, whom the world cannot receive, because it neither sees him nor knows him; but you know him, for he dwells with you, and will be in you.
>
> I will not leave you desolate; I will come to you.

The Spirit would be theirs, *with them to dwell*, not to compensate for Christ's absence but to ensure his presence. He would be their *Guide*, to lead them to a fuller knowledge of Jesus and his truth. He would be their *Comforter*, the one who would stand by them to encourage, strengthen and counsel them in their Lord's service.

The second stanza is not included in most hymn books:

> He came in semblance of a dove,
> With sheltering wings outspread,
> The holy balm of peace and love
> On earth to shed.

The allusion is to the coming of the Holy Spirit *in semblance of a dove* at our Lord's baptism, when 'the heaven was opened, and the Holy Spirit descended upon him in bodily form, as a dove' (Luke 3.21,22). The stanza certainly does not lack poetical beauty, and ought not to be excluded on that ground. But it appears to be out of place at this point of the hymn. It breaks the sequence of thought. In the previous stanza Jesus is saying farewell to the disciples at the end of his ministry, whereas the reference to his baptism takes us back to the beginning of the ministry. For this reason the verse, for all its merits, is better omitted. When this is done, the third stanza follows the first quite naturally, in terms of promise and fulfilment:

> He came in tongues of living flame,
>   To teach, convince, subdue;
> All-powerful as the wind he came,
>   As viewless too.

The Lord's farewell to the disciples took place at the Passover festival. Now, fifty days later, it is the feast of Pentecost, and the disciples are gathered together in one place, possibly the same upper room as before.

> And suddenly a sound came from heaven like the rush of a mighty wind, and it filled all the house where they were sitting. And there appeared to them tongues as of fire, distributed and resting on each one of them. And they were all filled with the Holy Spirit and began to speak in other tongues, as the Spirit gave them utterance. (Acts 2.2–4)

The two symbols of the Spirit, wind and fire, are brought together in the stanza, but in the reverse order. *He came in tongues of living flame.* Fire was the visible token of the Spirit's presence. But the fire took a particular form – 'tongues of fire'. The tongue is the organ of speech, and accordingly we are reminded that those in whom the Spirit dwells are enabled to speak for God: *to teach* those who know not the gospel, to *convince* those who doubt it, and to *subdue* those who oppose it. It is significant that the first act of the Church at Pentecost was to bear witness to Christ, and to do so in such a way that people of many nations heard in their own speech the mighty works of God (v. 11).

The Spirit also came *all-powerful as the wind*, and *as viewless too*. The wind is the audible token of the Spirit's presence, heard but not seen – or seen only by its effects (John 3.8). The Greek word for 'spirit' (*pneuma*) also means wind or breath. It represents the Holy Spirit's powerful but invisible energy as the Life-giver at work in the believer, in the Church, and in creation. A striking Old Testament illustration of this is seen in Ezekiel's vision of the valley of dry bones (37.1–10).

The next stanza touches on another aspect of the Spirit's work:

The Holy Guest

> He came sweet influence to impart,
>> A gracious, willing Guest,
> While he can find one humble heart
>> Wherein to rest.

This stanza is in direct contrast to the former and supplements its teaching. The Holy Spirit's operations are not only like the mighty forces of wind and fire. He works in quieter and gentler ways, for *he came sweet influence to impart.* If we inquire into the meaning of that phrase, the answer is supplied by what St Paul says about the fruit of the Spirit: 'love, joy, peace, patience, kindness, goodness, faithfulness, gentleness, self-control' (Galatians 5.22). Where the Church's life manifests these spiritual qualities, it is exercising a 'sweet influence' amid all the bitterness, hatred and violence of human society. Such fruit is the outward evidence that the Spirit is dwelling within. He is *a gracious, willing Guest* – willing indeed to make his abode with us. But he will not force his way into anyone's life. He awaits the response of personal faith; he seeks *one humble heart wherein to rest.* In his promise of the Spirit Jesus said, 'If a man loves me, he will keep my word, and my Father will love him, and we will come to him and make our home with him' (John 14.23). For those who love Jesus, the Holy Ghost is the Holy Guest.

III

The second part of the hymn is a reflection on what the Holy Spirit means in Christian experience. He speaks to us:

> And his that gentle voice we hear,
>> Soft as the breath of even,
> That checks each fault, that calms each fear,
>> And speaks of heaven.

The Spirit came on the day of Pentecost with a sound 'like the rush of a mighty wind'; but when he speaks to our hearts now it is with a *gentle voice, soft as the breath of even* – like the

143

'still small voice' that Elijah heard when he stood before the Lord on the mount (1 Kings 19.11,12). This means that we have to be quiet and cultivate the grace of silence if we are to hear what he says. If we do that, we shall find that he *checks each fault* when we are tempted to do wrong; that he *calms each fear* when we are anxious, and restores our peace; and that he *speaks of heaven* when we are weighed down by the things of this transitory life. Not only does the Holy Spirit lift our hearts above: he is himself 'the earnest of our inheritance' (Ephesians 1.14), the pledge that we shall at last possess the heavenly heritage when our redemption is complete.

> And every virtue we possess,
>   And every victory won,
> And every thought of holiness,
>   Are his alone.

With the three 'everys' of this stanza we reflect further on the Holy Spirit's work in our daily life. *Every virtue we possess* we owe to him. Scholars have a way of classifying the Christian virtues, dividing them between the four cardinal virtues – prudence, temperance, fortitude, and justice – and the three theological virtues of faith, hope, and love. All of them, of whatever kind or class, are kindled and deepened within us by the Spirit of Christ. *And every victory won* over the world, the flesh and the devil is achieved by his grace; for in all our struggles and temptations 'the Spirit comes to the aid of our weakness,' and 'in everything he co-operates for good with those who love God' (Romans 8.26,28 NEB). Again, *every thought of holiness* is *his alone*. We constantly pray that God may cleanse the thoughts of our hearts by the inspiration (or 'in-breathing') of his Holy Spirit. This prayer is our preparation for worship. It is also a good preparation for life. Only by the sanctifying work of the Holy Spirit in us day by day can we be holy, not only in thought but also in word and deed. So we pray further:

> Spirit of purity and grace,
>   Our weakness pitying see:
> O make our hearts thy dwelling-place,
>   And worthier thee.

We could hardly find a better prayer than this for our personal use at Whitsuntide. In it we recognize that the Holy Spirit is the source and giver *of purity and grace*; we confess *our weakness* and our need to be strengthened with might through the Spirit in our inner being (Ephesians 3.16); and accordingly we ask him not only to *make our hearts* his *dwelling-place*, but at the same time to make them *worthier* of his presence.

19

HOLY TRINITY

Holy, Holy, Holy! Lord God Almighty!

THERE ARE three hymns which are popularly associated with Trinity Sunday. One of them is 'Bright the vision that delighted', written by Bishop Richard Mant and based on the Old Testament lesson for the Sunday, Isaiah 6.1–8. Another is Mrs C. F. Alexander's translation of the Irish hymn known as St Patrick's Breastplate, beginning

> I bind unto myself to-day
>> The strong name of the Trinity,
> By invocation of the same,
>> The Three in One, and One in Three.

The third, and undoubtedly the best known, is Bishop Heber's 'Holy, Holy, Holy! Lord God Almighty!', inseparably associated in most of our minds with Dyke's great tune, *Nicaea*, though the twentieth-century tune *Tersanctus*, by Gordon Hartless, has also gained acceptance in many quarters.

I

Reginald Heber (1783–1826) was one of the outstanding Anglican clergymen at the beginning of the nineteenth century. At Oxford he showed brilliant gifts, was awarded the Newdigate prize for poetry, and won a fellowship at All Souls. Ordained in 1807, he became incumbent of the family living of Hodnet in Shropshire. Here he proved himself to be a devoted pastor and was greatly beloved by his people; and it was during this time as a country rector that he wrote his hymns. After serving other appointments in the church, including that of Bampton Lecturer in 1815, he was offered the bishopric of Calcutta. Reluctantly, and against the advice of his friends, he at length accepted. It was an impossible assignment. The diocese included the whole of British India and the work involved incessant travel and activity. The whole thing put him under enormous strain, and after three years his health broke. He died suddenly at the age of forty-three.

Short as his life was, Heber profoundly influenced the development of hymnody in the Church of England. Before his time hymn singing was regarded almost exclusively as part of the Nonconformist heritage and found little favour in the Established Church as a whole. Heber was convinced of the value of hymns in worship and wished to see them used in the parish churches of the land. At the same time he was far from happy about the standard of many of the hymns emanating from Dissenting and evangelical circles of the previous century. They tended to be too subjective in character, too narrow in outlook, of poor literary quality, and to have little relation to the Church's year. He conceived the idea of producing, with the aid of some of his poet friends, a collection of suitable hymns for church use which might receive episcopal sanction; but his call to India and his death so soon afterwards prevented this project being carried into effect. However, in 1827, the year after he died, his own hymns (fifty-seven in all) were published under the title *Hymns written and adapted to the Weekly Church Service of the Year.* They were designed to be sung 'between the Nicene Creed and the sermon'.

These hymns, which prepared the way for the work of those who later in the century followed in his steps, entitle him to be regarded as the first of the modern Anglican hymn-writers. He was at once a pioneer and a reformer: as much concerned about the standard as about the status of hymns in the church of his day. He was mistaken in too closely identifying hymnody with poetry; but he was right in his desire to ensure that the hymns sung in church were worthy of divine service. Among his best known hymns, apart from the one we are about to consider, are 'Brightest and best of the sons of the morning' (Epiphany), 'The Son of God goes forth to war' (St Stephen's Day), the communion hymn, 'Bread of the world, in mercy broken', and the once popular missionary hymn, 'From Greenland's icy mountains'.

II

Without doubt, 'Holy, Holy, Holy' is the finest as well as the most famous of Heber's hymns. Written for Trinity Sunday, it is a metrical paraphrase of the passage of scripture which forms the Epistle for the day, Revelation chapter 4. As through an open door the seer catches a glimpse of the glory of heaven:

> At once I was in the Spirit, and lo, a throne stood in heaven, with one seated on the throne! . . . Round the throne were twenty-four thrones, and seated on the thrones were twenty-four elders, clad in white garments, with golden crowns upon their heads . . . and before the throne there is as it were a sea of glass, like crystal.
>
> And round the throne, on each side of the throne, are four living creatures, . . . and the four living creatures, each of them with six wings, are full of eyes all round and within, and day and night they never cease to sing,
>
> 'Holy, holy, holy, is the Lord God Almighty, who was and is and is to come!' (vv. 2, 4, 6, 8)

The symbolic language of the whole passage accounts for the distinctive vocabulary of the hymn. The solemn and sonorous 'Holy, Holy, Holy' with which each stanza begins sets the keynote of the entire work and focuses our attention on what God is in the essence of his being. Everywhere in

148

scripture, alike in the Old Testament and in the New, God is revealed in his holiness. The basic idea of the word 'holy', alike in Hebrew and Greek, is that of separation; and when it is applied to God it denotes his separateness from the created order, from false deities, and from all evil. Hence positively it expresses his transcendence, his uniqueness, his moral perfection. The holiness of God is his 'wholly otherness', that which sets him apart from everything else – the sheer incommensurate 'God-ness' of God, to use Dr H. H. Farmer's phrase.

It is this God who is the theme of Bishop Heber's majestic hymn for Trinity Sunday. With its firm biblical and theological basis the hymn is wholly objective in character. It is pure adoration from start to finish, awakening in the worshipper a spirit of reverence, awe, wonder and praise. A closer look at it will serve to make this clear.

> Holy, Holy, Holy! Lord God Almighty!
> Early in the morning our song shall rise to thee;
> Holy, Holy, Holy! Merciful and mighty!
> God in three Persons, blessed Trinity!

Holy, Holy, Holy! Lord God Almighty! The words are a direct echo of the song of the four living creatures in the Revelation passage. The thrice repeated 'Holy' is also found in Isaiah 6.3 ('Holy, holy, holy is the Lord of hosts; the whole earth is full of his glory'); and from this is derived the *Sanctus* in the eucharist. Hence it is 'with angels and archangels and all the company of heaven' that we lift up our voices in praise to God. *Early in the morning our song shall rise to thee.* Why early in the morning? The answer, presumably, is that Heber conceived of his hymn as essentially a morning act of praise. But this creates a problem when it is desired to use the hymn at other times of the day. In the past various changes were made to this second line in order to adapt the hymn to any hour, such as 'Gratefully adoring our song shall rise to thee'; but modern hymnals are content to adhere to the original wording.

Holy, Holy, Holy! Merciful and mighty! As it unfolds, the hymn builds up a magnificent picture of God in his manifold glory. Here we are reminded again of his holiness and power,

149

but a new element is introduced. He who is all-holy and all-mighty is also all-merciful. In keeping with this the Prayer Book collect of the eleventh Sunday after Trinity begins, 'O God, who declarest thy almighty power most chiefly in shewing mercy and pity'; and the same note is struck in Ecclesiasticus 2.18: 'as his majesty is, so also is his mercy'. Such is the God we worship and adore: *God in three Persons, blessèd Trinity*. Here, stated but not argued, is the Christian doctrine of God in the mystery of his being as the Three in One and One in Three; and so, in the words of the Trinity Sunday collect, we 'acknowledge the glory of the eternal Trinity, and in the power of the Divine Majesty . . . worship the Unity'.

III

Holy, Holy, Holy! all the saints adore thee,
  Casting down their golden crowns around the glassy sea;
Cherubim and seraphim falling down before thee,
  Which wert, and art, and evermore shalt be.

With this stanza the vision of God in his majesty, adored by the citizens of heaven, is set before us in the symbolic language of Revelation 4. These citizens form two groups. First, there are *all the saints* who are seen *casting down their golden crowns around the glassy sea*. These 'saints', as they are called in the hymn, are the 'twenty-four elders, clad in white garments, with golden crowns upon their heads', gathered round the throne of God; and 'before the throne there is as it were a sea of glass, like crystal'; and as they bow in worship before the living God 'they cast their crowns before the throne' (vv. 4,6,10). The twenty-four elders are generally taken to represent the whole church of God in its unbroken continuity under the old and new covenants. The Jewish Church is symbolized by 'the twelve tribes of the sons of Israel', the Christian Church by 'the twelve apostles of the Lamb' (see Revelation 21.12–14). In the persons of the elders the entire people of God, both before and after Christ, are seen as a worshipping community in the presence of the holy God.

The other group consists of *cherubim and seraphim falling down before* the Lord. These correspond to the 'four living creatures', with their six wings apiece and with faces like a lion, an ox, a man, and an eagle (Revelation 4.6–8). It can be taken that they 'represent the powers of creation in the service of the Creator' (F. F. Bruce). Heber in his hymn identifies them with the six-winged seraphim of Isaiah 6.2 and the cherubim of Ezekiel 10.20. It is they who day and night ceaselessly sing, 'Holy, holy, holy, is the Lord God Almighty, who was and is and is to come!' The latter words are reproduced in the final line of this second stanza: *Which wert, and art, and evermore shalt be.* God is the Eternal One, the great I AM of Exodus 3.14, who exists outside the sphere of time and is unchanging and unchangeable.

> Holy, Holy, Holy! though the darkness hide thee,
>> Though the eye of sinful man thy glory may not see,
> Only thou art holy, there is none beside thee
>> Perfect in power, in love, and purity.

Holy, Holy, Holy! though the darkness hide thee. What is this darkness? Certainly to the Jews of old God was hidden from human view in the utter darkness of the Holy of Holies in the temple; but equally certainly the darkness does not pertain to God himself, for 'God is light, and in him is no darkness at all' (1 John 1.5). The darkness is of our own making: it is *the eye of sinful man* – man in his fallen state – that *may not see* God's *glory*. Yet admittedly there is an element of paradox here. On the one hand it is true, 'No one has ever seen God'; on the other hand, 'the only Son, who is in the bosom of the Father, he has made him known' (John 1.18). In his pure essence God is beyond our sight: no direct vision of him is possible. But Christ the incarnate Son is the disclosure of the invisible God, and in his person God can be seen (John 14.9). 'The light of the knowledge of the glory of God' shines for us 'in the face of Christ' (2 Corinthians 4.6).

Only thou art holy. Here we affirm not only the sanctity but the unity of the Godhead. Our faith in the Trinity does not by

151

one iota diminish our conviction that God is one. It must be so. Because God *is* God, the First Cause, the Ultimate Reality, he can have no equal and will brook no rival. 'You shall have no other gods before me' is the first of the Ten Commandments (Exodus 20.3). That being so, 'Who shall not fear and glorify thy name, O Lord? For thou alone art holy' (Revelation 15.4). And this one and holy God is *perfect in power, in love, and purity.* All that God is and does is perfect; and perfection belongs to him alone. So the power he exercises, the love he bestows, the purity he demands, are all alike perfect.

IV

The final stanza is a repetition of the first, with one line altered:

> Holy, Holy, Holy! Lord God Almighty!
> All thy works shall praise thy name, in earth,
>   and sky, and sea;
> Holy, Holy, Holy! Merciful and mighty!
> God in three Persons, blessed Trinity!

The altered line is the second: *All thy works shall praise thy name, in earth, and sky, and sea.* This gives expression to the anthem of praise addressed to God (at the end of Revelation 4) by the twenty-four elders in harmony with the four living creatures. It represents the voice of creation glorifying its Creator:

> Worthy art thou, our Lord and God,
> to receive glory and honour and power;
> for thou didst create all things,
> and by thy will they existed and were created.

God as Creator is worthy of universal and eternal praise. Before they were made all things existed in his mind and purpose; by his will and power they were created and brought into being; and to his glory and honour they continue to exist.

We ourselves as part of his creation recognize this when in the *Te Deum* we join our praise with angels round the throne and sing:

> All the earth doth worship thee,
> the Father everlasting.
> To thee all angels cry aloud,
> the heavens and all the powers therein.
> To thee cherubim and seraphim continually do cry,
> Holy, holy, holy, Lord God of hosts!
> Heaven and earth are full of thy glory!

20

THE COMMUNION OF SAINTS

For all the saints who from their labours rest

SAINTS' DAYS are no longer as widely observed in church life as they used to be; and this probably accounts for the fact that very few hymns written for particular 'saints' are at all well known. Mrs Alexander's hymn for St Andrew's Day, 'Jesus calls us', is the one great exception. On the other hand, the festival of All Saints on November 1st still retains a firm hold on the affections of church people, and many of the hymns associated with it have a popular appeal. Among these are Isaac Watts's 'Give me the wings of faith to rise', Bishop Wordsworth's 'Hark the sound of holy voices', and Dean Alford's 'Ten thousand times ten thousand'. But without question the outstanding hymn for this great festival, and the best known, is Bishop How's 'For all the saints who from their labours rest'.

I

William Walsham How (1823–97) was certainly one of the most loved bishops in the Church of England during the last century. A simple, single-hearted man, he had no interest in gaining preferment in the church and spent the first part of his ministry in comparative obscurity. Then for nearly ten years he served as suffragan bishop of what was virtually East London, an area marked by great poverty and wretched social conditions. Here, by his warm-hearted humanity as well as his pastoral devotion, he earned for himself such titles as 'the people's bishop', 'the poor man's bishop', and 'the children's bishop'. It was the last title that delighted him most. He was always at home in the company of children. Inscribed on his pastoral staff were the words of St Bernard, *Pasce verbo, Pasce vita*: 'Feed with the Word, Feed with the life'. It was his life as much as his preaching that commended the gospel and drew people to Christ. After declining a number of important bishoprics, including that of Durham, he eventually at the age of sixty-five agreed to leave his East Londoners and become bishop of the newly formed diocese of Wakefield, where he spent the remaining years of his life.

Bishop How was a great hymn lover. In the course of his life he collaborated with others in editing two hymn books, and in 1886 he published a volume of his own *Poems and Hymns*. He expressed the view that 'a good hymn is something like a good prayer – simple, real, earnest, and reverent'. His own hymns well fulfilled these requirements. Of the fifty-four he wrote a considerable number have survived. Most of the standard hymnals include between eight and a dozen of them. Among those which are well known (apart from 'For all the saints') are his children's hymn, 'It is a thing most wonderful'; his mission hymn, based on Holman Hunt's celebrated picture of the Light of the World, 'O Jesu, thou art standing'; his hymn for Rogationtide, 'To thee our God we fly'; and others like 'Summer suns are glowing', 'O Word of God Incarnate', 'Soldiers of the Cross, arise', and 'O my Saviour, lifted'.

We must agree with Dr Hugh Martin's judgment that How's contribution to English hymnody was a notable one and perhaps entitles him to rank as the finest hymn-writer of his century.

II

Few would dispute that 'For all the saints' is not only Bishop How's finest hymn but is one of the great hymns in the English language. While it comes into its own more especially at All Saints' tide, it is also frequently used at memorial services and on similar occasions. It consisted originally of eleven stanzas. Three of them are, quite properly, omitted from our hymnals. They were the third, fourth and fifth stanzas, dealing specifically in turn with the Apostles, the Evangelists, and the Martyrs. Apart from the fact that they are not up to the same high standard as the rest of the hymn, these verses do not fit happily into its general pattern; and in any case their inclusion would lengthen the hymn to an unreasonable degree.

Barnby's tune, familiar to the older generation and at one time immensely popular, is now entirely superseded by Vaughan Williams's splendid *Sine Nomine*, the tune he composed for the hymn for the *English Hymnal*. It perfectly matches the inspiration of the words.

The hymn begins on the note of thanksgiving:

> For all the saints who from their labours rest,
> Who thee by faith before the world confessed,
> Thy name, O Jesu, be for ever blest.
> > Alleluia.

The thanksgiving is expressed in the third line: *Thy name, O Jesu, be for ever blest*. It is important to note that the hymn, in so far as it comprises elements of praise and prayer, is addressed to Jesus. So it is him we bless *for all the saints* – or, as Bishop How originally wrote, 'all *thy* saints'. The saints are his. This is the thing that distinguishes them from the rest and best of mankind and unites them in one glorious company. They are Christ's, and now they are at rest with him; for the blessèd dead 'who die in the Lord . . . rest from their labours' (Revelation 14.13). For them the toil is past, the conflict finished. But while here on earth they bore a bold and faithful witness, and so the hymn describes them as those *who by faith before the world confessed* their Lord. They were not ashamed of him or his gospel (Mark 8.38; Romans 1.16). Their faith was such as to make them brave confessors of Christ; and, like the writer of this hymn, they confessed him not simply with their lips but in their lives. It is significant that the Prayer Book collect of All Saints' Day is a prayer that we may follow God's saints 'in all virtuous and godly living'. The witness of a genuinely holy life is likely to be a far more potent testimony before the world than any amount of holy talk.

The next stanza points to the secret of sainthood:

> Thou wast their rock, their fortress, and their might;
> Thou, Lord, their Captain in the well-fought fight;
> Thou in the darkness drear their one true Light.

The secret is revealed in the emphatic *Thou* repeated at the beginning of each line; in a word, the secret is Christ himself (see Colossians 2.2 NEB). Sanctity is not a product of the natural man. It is a gift of divine grace. This is the one clear message that sounds throughout the stanza. The saints would be the first to acknowledge that all that they became and all that they achieved was the Lord's doing, not theirs. They were human like the rest of us, and they shared our human weakness; but they had discovered and proved the sufficiency of Christ. In all their strivings and sufferings, in all their trials and temptations, he was *their rock, their fortress, and their might* (*cf.* Psalm 18.2 BCP). In every *well-fought fight* for the cause of truth and righteousness, he was *their Captain*, the one under whose banner they served and in whose name they conquered. And *in the darkness drear* (for the saints also have their hours of darkness) Christ was *their one true Light*.

This reflection on the saints and their spiritual resources leads to a prayer that we may be worthy to follow in their steps.

> O may thy soldiers, faithful, true, and bold,
> Fight as the saints who nobly fought of old,
> And win, with them, the victor's crown of gold.

It is not enough to admire the saints, to praise their virtues, or to applaud their achievements. We must seek to follow them, as they followed Christ. So we ask for his grace and pray that we his *servants*, like them, may be *faithful, true, and bold*: faithful to God, true to ourselves, bold in facing the foe. For again, like them, we must not shirk the battle but be prepared to *fight as the saints who nobly fought of old*. In every generation the holy war has to be carried on if the Church's witness is to be maintained and the kingdom of God advanced in the world. This is 'the good fight of the faith' (1 Timothy 6.12) in which we in our day are called upon to engage like those of old. If we accept the challenge which their lives present to us, and fight manfully under Christ's banner against sin, the world, and the devil, then – and only then – we may hope to *win, with them, the victor's crown of gold* (see 2 Timothy 4.8; Revelation 2.10).

III

O blest communion, fellowship divine!
We feebly struggle, they in glory shine;
Yet all are one in thee, for all are thine.

Here surely is the pivotal verse, the heart of the entire hymn. It is strange, then, that in the *English Hymnal*, followed by *Songs of Praise*, the stanza is marked with an asterisk to indicate that it may conveniently be omitted if it is desired to shorten the hymn. To omit this particular verse would, in our judgment, be a gross error. For at this point we affirm our belief in 'the communion of saints' – that is, the unbroken fellowship of all Christian believers in life and death, in time and eternity. In doing so we not only acknowledge the essential unity of the Church of God. We also express our conviction that the whole company of his people on earth and in heaven is 'knit together in one communion and fellowship in the mystical body of Christ our Lord', as the collect puts it. The living Christ, the conqueror of death, unites all who are united to him, in this world or the next.

It is this great Christian conviction which the hymn here asserts in such positive terms. *O blest communion, fellowship divine!* The communion of the saints is 'blest' because it is the company of those whom God has blessed. The fellowship is 'divine' because its members are the body of which Christ is the Head. Yet there is a difference to be recognized, the difference between the Church militant here in earth and the Church triumphant in heaven: *We feebly struggle, they in glory shine.* For us the struggle continues, and will continue until the end of life. For them the glory already shines. Nevertheless, *we* and *they*, though for a while divided by the incident of death, are still united in Christ: *all are one in thee, for all are thine.*

The doctrine of the communion of saints as thus expressed is the Christian answer to the claims of Spiritualism. As Hugh Burnaby wrote in his *Thinking through the Creed*:[1]

> The Spiritualist believes that he can communicate with the departed through a human medium. The Christian believes that his fellowship with the departed is mediated through Christ. If communion of the Christian with Christ is not broken by death, then neither can his communion with his fellow Christians be broken.

IV

The last four stanzas fall into two pairs. The first pair (vv. 5 and 6) presents a picture of the Church on earth as it bravely continues its work and warfare. The last pair (vv. 7 and 8) sets before us a vision of the Church in heaven, victorious and glorified.

> And when the strife is fierce, the warfare long,
> Steals on the ear the distant triumph-song,
> And hearts are brave again, and arms are strong.

> The golden evening brightens in the west;
> Soon, soon to faithful warriors cometh rest:
> Sweet is the calm of Paradise the blest.

In these two stanzas we see the Church in the world sustained in its struggles by the spirit of Christian hope. For us here on earth the battle is still on, and at times *the strife is fierce, the warfare long*. But as we recall the brave endeavours of those who fought and overcame in the past, we catch echoes of their *distant triumph-song* in heaven, and are given fresh courage and strength to continue the fight.

The sixth stanza portrays life's eventide. For God's *faithful warriors* it is a *golden evening*, brightened by the prospect of the rest that awaits them in *the calm of Paradise*, the abode of the blessèd who are with Christ (Luke 23.43).

In the closing stanzas the scene shifts from earth to heaven, and time is swallowed up in eternity.

> But lo, there breaks a yet more glorious day;
> The saints triumphant rise in bright array:
> The King of glory passes on his way.

> From earth's wide bounds, from ocean's farthest coast,
> Through gates of pearl streams in the countless host,
> Singing to Father, Son, and Holy Ghost.

In these exalted strains we catch our final glimpse of the saints, assembled in the presence of *the King of Glory*. Now, as *the saints triumphant*, clothed in *bright array*, they form part of the *countless host* of the redeemed, gathered into God's eternal kingdom from every part of the world – *from earth's wide bounds, from ocean's farthest coast* – who stream *through gates of pearl* singing their anthems of praise to the Triune God.

The symbolic language of these stanzas is derived largely from the last chapters of the book of Revelation. But in the end human language is inadequate to portray so magnificent a scene, and human imagination is incapable of grasping it. Nevertheless, he must be dull of mind and slow of heart who can sing these glowing lines without glimpsing something at least of the glory of the holy Catholic Church, the communion of saints, and the life everlasting.

NOTE
1 Hodder & Stoughton, 1961, p. 78.

II

GENERAL HYMNS

21

LIFE'S LITTLE DAY

Abide with me; fast falls the eventide

WHEN HENRY Francis Lyte wrote 'Abide with me' he was a dying man, and he knew it. For some twenty-four years he had been vicar of the Devonshire fishing village of Brixham, where he had exercised a devoted ministry among the simple fisher folk and won their confidence and affection. But the work made heavy demands upon him, and unfortunately his health was by no means robust. From time to time he was obliged to take long periods of rest abroad to recuperate his strength. From one such visit to the south of France he returned to Brixham in the spring of 1847, to spend a last few months among his beloved parishioners. By now he was a very sick man, fully aware that his life was nearing its end. It was during this valedictory period of his ministry that he wrote the last and greatest of his hymns.[1]

I

Lyte's final Sunday in Brixham was September 4, 1847. Though far from well, and despite the protests of his family, he determined to preach and celebrate Holy Communion at the morning service, and succeeded in carrying through this

his last duty. During the afternoon he rested, and in the evening after a short walk he withdrew to his study. When an hour or two later he rejoined the rest of the household he handed his sister-in-law the manuscript of 'Abide with me', together with a tune he had composed to suit the words. Within a few days he left home once again to return to the south of France. Less than three months later, on November 20th, he died of consumption and was buried in the grounds of the English Church at Nice, where his grave can still be seen.

The facts as stated are correct; but two things need to be added about the origin of the hymn. The impression given so far is that it was written by a sudden act of inspiration on the evening of Lyte's last Sunday in Brixham. That is not so. It is now known that a draft of it had been put together a week or two earlier. In a letter to a friend dated August 25th he refers to the hymn as 'my latest effusion' and quotes it at the end of the letter. It would seem that on the evening of September 4th he revised and rewrote it in its final form, so that he might share it with his family.

The other thing to be said is that the theory that the hymn had actually been written as far back as 1820 while Lyte was in Ireland (as propounded in *Songs of Praise Discussed* and other books) has no real authority and is to be dismissed as unauthentic. Apart from the fact that the words are in such complete harmony with the circumstances of Lyte's life as related above, it is difficult to believe that a hymn of this outstanding quality would have remained unknown, unpublished and unsung for twenty-seven years. There is also another consideration to which little attention appears to have been given. As far back as 1833 and 1834 Lyte had published two volumes of his hymns and poems. 'Abide with me' was not included in either of these. Why not? Why should this particular hymn be omitted from his collected works? There is only one logical answer to the question. The hymn was not included for the simple reason that it was not written until many years later.[2]

So much for the human background of 'Abide with me'. The biblical background is the story of the two disciples who on the first Easter Day walked to Emmaus in the company of the risen Lord, though they failed to recognize him.

> They drew nigh unto the village whither they went; and he made as though he would have gone further. But they constrained him, saying, Abide with us: for it is toward evening, and the day is far spent. And he went in to tarry with them. And it came to pass, as he sat at meat with them, he took bread, and blessed it, and brake it, and gave to them. And their eyes were opened, and they knew him; and he vanished out of their sight.
>
> (Luke 24.28–31 AV)

From this story Lyte drew the inspiration for his hymn, especially from the invitation the two disciples addressed to the Lord: 'Abide with us'. He uses the story as an allegory. The fading light of day, the gathering darkness, symbolize the eventide of life – and it was his own life of which he was thinking when he wrote the words. Though but fifty-four years of age he realized only too well that for him the day was far spent. The shadows were falling around him. Death could not be long delayed: how was he to meet it? The hymn supplies the answer by pointing to the risen, living, victorious, unchanging Christ.

As has so often been observed, this is not intended to be an evening hymn. The metaphor in the opening line does not allude to the close of the natural day. It refers to the close of life. The singer of the hymn, as one writer puts it, is not preparing for bed but for death. There is no reason why the words should not be sung in the morning as well as in the evening. The hymn is particularly suitable for funeral and memorial services. It is also a good hymn for Eastertide.

As already mentioned, Lyte wrote his own tune for the words. That tune has long since been discarded and superseded by Dr W. H. Monk's *Eventide*, written for the hymn in the first edition of *Hymns Ancient and Modern*, 1861. Three of Lyte's original eight verses have also disappeared. It is generally agreed that the hymn is better without them, for apart from making the hymn unduly long they tend to distract from the general theme. They constituted the third, fourth and fifth stanzas of the original:

Not a brief glance, I beg, a passing word;
But as thou dweltst with thy disciples, Lord,
Familiar, condescending, patient, free,
Come not to sojourn, but abide with me.

Come not in terrors, as the King of kings,
But kind and good, with healing in thy wings:
Tears for all woes, a heart for every plea –
Come, Friend of sinners, and thus 'bide with me.

Thou on my head in early youth didst smile;
And, though rebellious and perverse meanwhile,
Thou hast not left me, oft as I left thee;
On to the close, O Lord, abide with me.

II

The whole hymn is a prayer, an intensely personal prayer, the prayer of a man who is conscious of the swift passage of time, the brevity of life, the certainty of death. So in his desperate and urgent need he cries:

> Abide with me: fast falls the eventide;
> The darkness deepens; Lord, with me abide!
> When other helpers fail, and comforts flee,
> Help of the helpless, O abide with me.

When life reaches its *eventide* and *the darkness deepens*, there is only one prayer the Christian can offer: *Lord, with me abide!* Lyte felt the need of the Lord's abiding presence all the more keenly when he wrote the hymn because he had recently lost the support of some of his leading church workers. Several of the Sunday school teachers and most members of the choir had been caught up in the Plymouth Brethren movement which was then spreading in the West country; and as a result they had been persuaded to forsake the parish church and join the local Brethren assembly. This was a bitter blow to Lyte, especially in his weak state of health. At the very time he needed them most his friends had let him down; and it was with deep feeling that he wrote, *When other helpers fail* . . . In his grief he turned to the *Help of the helpless*, the Friend who would never forsake him but *abide with* him to the very end. And the end was not far off:

> Swift to its close ebbs out life's little day;
> Earth's joys grow dim, its glories pass away;
> Change and decay in all around I see;
> O thou who changest not, abide with me.

Not only the transitory character of *life's little day* but the changing nature of the world around are the dominant themes of this stanza. *Earth's joys grow dim, its glories pass away.* Nothing remains the same for ever. 'Fading is the worldling's pleasure, all his boasted pomp and show' – so wrote John Newton. Scripture says the same. The things that are seen are temporal. The fashion of this world is passing away. Here we have no continuing city. Lyte is simply reaffirming these undeniable truths. *Change and decay in all around I see*, for such in fact is the course of nature. To accept it is not to take a defeatist or pessimistic view of life. On the contrary, as Dr Routley points out in his study of this hymn, there is a note of healthy realism in recognizing the changeableness of things. But that is not the last word on the subject. The last word lies with Christ: *O thou who changest not, abide with me.* Things change: he does not. 'Jesus Christ is the same yesterday, and today, and for ever' (Hebrews 13.8); and with that glowing certainty in his heart the hymn-writer continues:

> I need thy presence every passing hour;
> What but thy grace can foil the tempter's power?
> Who like thyself my guide and stay can be?
> Through cloud and sunshine, O abide with me.

Well might Lyte say at the time he wrote this hymn, *I need thy presence every passing hour*; and we in our differing circumstances can echo his words. For most of us life is not a smooth, uneventful voyage, a simple, uncomplicated affair. There are trials and temptations to be faced: the devil sees to that; and *what but thy grace can foil the tempter's power?* Life makes other demands. There are tasks to be tackled, problems to be resolved, unexpected hardships and sufferings to be endured. At such times we may well ask, *Who like thyself my guide and stay can be?* The truth that shines out from all this is not only that Christ is unchanging but that his grace is all-sufficient in every circumstance and every need. Alike in *cloud and sunshine* he journeys with us along the road and abides with us as he promised 'all the days, until the end' – the end which in truth is simply a new beginning.

III

The hymn reaches its climax in the two final stanzas. Here the writer faces the grim fact of death – and faces it as only the Christian can, in a spirit of quiet trust and with a song of triumph.

> I fear no foe with thee at hand to bless;
> Ills have no weight, and tears no bitterness.
> Where is death's sting? Where, grave, thy victory?
> I triumph still if thou abide with me.

It will be noticed that each stanza ends with the same three words with which the hymn begins: *abide with me.* The simple phrase is the key to the whole work. From start to finish it revolves around the thought of Christ's abiding and unfailing presence. So this fourth stanza starts with the bold affirmation, *I fear no foe with thee at hand to bless.* And assuredly the Lord is at hand; 'for he has said, "I will never fail you nor forsake you." Hence we can confidently say, "The Lord is my helper, I will not be afraid; what can man do to me?"' (Hebrews 13.5,6). *Ills have no weight, and tears no bitterness.* The 'ills' of life happen to us all. As Christians we are not exempt from trouble and adversity, from illness and strain and the like. But in the apostle's words, these passing things are but a 'light affliction' compared with the 'eternal weight of glory' to come (2 Corinthians 4.17). Nor can we expect to escape 'tears' when bereavement comes to us, as it does to others. We should be less than human if we did not weep at such times. Jesus wept at the tomb of Lazarus. But our tears, though real, are without the bitterness of despair, for we do not grieve as those who have no hope (1 Thessalonians 4.13). We *have* hope, a hope that enables us to look beyond the grave and cry, *Where is death's sting? Where, grave, thy victory?* St Paul asked the same questions – and supplied the answer:

> O death, where is thy sting? O grave, where is thy victory? The sting of death is sin; and the strength of sin is the law. But thanks be to God, who giveth us the victory through our Lord Jesus Christ.
>
> (1 Corinthians 15.55–57)

The apostle's words are based on his faith in the risen Lord. Lyte's hymn is built on the same conviction. In considering the closing stanzas we do well to remember that the Christ of the Emmaus road to whom the disciples said 'Abide with us' was the Christ of Easter: the Christ who on the cross died for our sins and by his resurrection conquered death and is alive for evermore. It is those who share this faith that can say, *I triumph still, if thou abide with me.* And in that faith they can pray:

> Hold thou thy Cross before my closing eyes;
> Speak through the gloom, and point me to the skies;
> Heaven's morning breaks, and earth's vain shadows flee;
> In life, in death, O Lord, abide with me.

When Lyte – a convinced evangelical churchman – wrote *Hold thou thy Cross before my closing eyes*, he was not thinking of a crucifix being held before him on his deathbed. He was asking for a vision of the crucified Saviour whose blood had atoned for his sins. But he was asking for something more: *Speak through the gloom, and point me to the skies.* Our hymn books, following the amendment in *Hymns Ancient and Modern*, 1861, have changed the *Speak* to 'Shine'; but we have preserved the original reading. As Balleine remarks, Lyte asked for more than a gleam of light amid the darkness of death. He prayed that he might hear his Lord's voice speaking words of comfort to his soul and directing his thoughts above. *Heaven's morning breaks, and earth's vain shadows flee.* For the believer death, when it comes, is the dawning of eternal day, a passing from the shadowy things of earth to the glory of heaven. Yes, *when* it comes – and none of us knows when it will come. But come it will; so meanwhile we can only pray, *In life, in death, O Lord, abide with me.*

IV

In giving this hymn to the world Lyte fulfilled a deeply cherished wish: that of bequeathing to mankind some verse of enduring worth. In one of his poems entitled 'Declining Days' he wrote:

> If I might leave behind
> Some blessing for my fellows, some fair trust
> To guide, to cheer, to elevate my kind
> When I am in the dust,
> O thou, whose touch can lend
> Life to the dead, thy quickening grace supply,
> And grant me, swan-like, my last breath to spend
> In song that may not die.

Was ever a Christian man's prayer more gloriously answered? In 'Abide with me' – to say nothing of his other hymns – Henry Francis Lyte left behind undying verse, a legacy of song which has enriched the Church of God for well over a century and will continue to do so for generations to come.

NOTES
1 For further information about Lyte, and for another of his hymns, see chapter 32.
2 The facts relating to the origin of this hymn are taken from *Henry Francis Lyte* by B. G. Skinner (University of Exeter, 1974).

22

PURE IN HEART

Blest are the pure in heart

AT FIRST sight 'Blest are the pure in heart' might not appear to be the sort of hymn to single out for special consideration in a book of this kind. Not only is it very short, but it looks somewhat ordinary and to lack any particular distinction apart from having Keble's name attached to it. But that, we shall hope to show, is too hasty a judgment. There is quite a lot in this hymn which is of interest. It is certainly worth more than a passing glance. And the first thing to look into is the question of its authorship.

I

In the *English Hymnal* it is ascribed simply to John Keble. Most other hymnals give the authorship as 'J. Keble and others'. That at once suggests that there is some obscurity about the hymn's origin and that a number of people had a hand in its composition. Neither of these suggestions is true. There is in fact no mystery as to how the hymn came into being. We owe these verses partly to the saintly John Keble (1792–1866), one of the leaders of the Oxford Movement, and partly to another clergyman – admittedly a less distinguished personage but one who nevertheless deserves to be named, for without him the hymn would never have existed.

John Keble's contribution comes from his collection of religious verse called *The Christian Year*, 1827. The book won immense popularity and went through ninety-eight editions in Keble's own lifetime. Its design was to provide a poem for every Sunday and Holy Day of the Church's year, and also for certain other occasions. For example, the first poem in the book is entitled 'Morning', and from its sixteen stanzas is derived the hymn 'New every morning is the love'. From the next poem, 'Evening', come the six stanzas which make up 'Sun of my soul, thou Saviour dear'. When we turn to the end of the book we find the verses for Saints' Days, and among them a long poem appointed for the feast of the Purification, better known nowadays as the Presentation of Christ. This poem begins:

> Blest are the pure in heart,
> For they shall see our God;
> The secret of the Lord is theirs,
> Their soul is Christ's abode.

Now we have discovered the origin of the first verse of our hymn. But the fifteen stanzas which follow it in Keble's poem are entirely unfamiliar. They dwell in a devotional spirit on the people and events in the Gospel of the day (Luke 2.22–40). Not until the last verse of all do we find ourselves on familiar ground again with the words:

> Still to the lowly soul
> He doth himself impart,
> And for his cradle and his throne
> Chooseth the pure in heart.

Here then from *The Christian Year* we have the two stanzas which are Keble's contribution to the hymn, the first and third. What about the remaining stanzas, the second and fourth? These were composed by the Revd W. J. Hall, a minor canon of St Paul's Cathedral and later vicar of Tottenham, who in 1836 published a hymn book he had edited and which became known (on account of the design embossed on its cover) as the *Mitre Hymn Book*. It was this little known clergyman who took the two verses from Keble's poem and married them to two of his composition. This was done with Keble's full knowledge and consent. The result is a hymn which the Church has been singing for nearly a hundred and fifty years and is still today a hymn that lives.

It was a strange way for a hymn to be created. And in the circumstances it is remarkable that this composite effort should possess such a marked unity. Indeed, it is a tribute to Hall's editorial skill and poetical ability that the hymn gives no indication of its being the work of two authors. It could be claimed that 'Blest are the pure in heart' comes near to being a perfect hymn: short and simple, firmly based on the scriptures, devotional in spirit but with a doctrinal content – and not only thoroughly singable but suitable for use on any number of occasions.

II

What has the hymn to say? Quite a lot, brief though it is. Keble headed his poem in *The Christian Year* with the text 'Blessed are the pure in heart, for they shall see God' (Matthew 5.8). He takes up the theme of purity because he is writing for the feast of the Purification; but the Jewish ordinances described in the gospel of the day and duly observed by Mary in fulfilment of the law (Leviticus 12.2–8) were concerned simply with ritual purity. Not so the purity which is the theme of this hymn. What Jesus said was, 'Blessed are the pure in *heart*' – and the emphasis is on the last word. The *New English Bible* rendering helps to make this clear: 'How blest are those whose hearts are pure'. Jesus was not concerned with outward, ceremonial purity: the sort of purity emphasized by the Pharisees who made clean the outside of the cup while the inside was full of wickedness (Luke 7.39–41). He demanded the inward purity which David sought when he prayed, 'Create in me a clean heart, O God' (Psalm 51.10). This is the fundamental requirement. It is those whose hearts are pure who are blessed of God, who see the vision of God, who enter into intimate friendship with God, who experience the presence of God in their lives.

All this is what Keble expressed so clearly in the words which form the first stanza of the hymn, already quoted. Here is the ideal of Christian character, a sublime ideal indeed. But is it a possibility, or only an ideal? Can we achieve it? No – *we* cannot. Only God can. It is a work of grace, accomplished through his Son Jesus Christ. Therefore the next stanza, written by W. J. Hall, points us to him:

> The Lord who left the heavens
> Our life and peace to bring,
> To dwell in lowliness with men,
> Their Pattern and their King:

We have called this a simple hymn, and so it is in its wording. But now it introduces us to the most profound mystery of our Faith: the doctrine of the Incarnation, or the coming of *the Lord* from *the heavens* into the world, to visit us in great humility. The blessing of the pure heart can be ours only because of that fact, because of the coming of Christ *to dwell in lowliness with men*. The eternal Word was made flesh (John 1.14). He who was rich, rich with all the wealth of heaven, for our sake became poor (2 Corinthians 8.9). The King of glory emptied himself, stripped himself of the insignia of majesty, and took the form of a slave (Philippians 2.5–7). It was in this way he came. And why?

The hymn says he came *our life and peace to bring*. Perhaps we ought not to read too much into those little words 'life' and 'peace'; but in fact they answer to two of our deepest needs and longings. We are all searching for life, real life, life of a distinctive quality, life that is something more than a dreary and futile existence. It is the same with our quest for peace. We seek it, but we find little true peace in the warring world around us or in our own restless hearts. To a world such as ours, to people like ourselves, Jesus came as the author of both life and peace. They are his gifts to those who acknowledge his claims and who, as a result, follow and obey him, *their pattern and their King*.

174

What next? Something very wonderful; and to discover what it is we turn to the third stanza:

> Still to the lowly soul
> He doth himself impart,
> And for his dwelling and his throne
> Chooseth the pure in heart.

Here we are back to Keble, with the final verse of his poem. But there is one small change. In the third line Keble wrote 'And for his *cradle* and his throne'. His use of the word 'cradle' is understandable when we remember that the poem was written for a festival which commemorates events which happened on the fortieth day after the Nativity, when Jesus was a baby in a cradle. Hall did right to alter the word to 'dwelling', for the hymn he evolved from the poem had no particular connection with the Purification and was intended for general use.

Another point should be noted. In the hymn the second and third stanzas follow one another without a break; only a colon separates them. *The Lord who left the heavens* is the subject of them both. He who came to dwell among men in the miracle of his incarnate life now chooses to dwell by his Spirit in the hearts of his people. So while the second stanza is concerned with past history, the third has to do with present experience. The Lord who *came* is also the Lord who *comes*. But it is to the *lowly soul* that he comes; it is in the lives of *the pure in heart* that he not only makes *his dwelling* but establishes *his throne*.

As we thus return to the opening theme of the hymn we are confronted with a paradox. It is only the pure in heart who know the Lord's indwelling. Yet it is only by the Lord's indwelling that the heart can be pure. What then are we to do? We may well feel bound to say, like the centurion in the gospel story, 'Lord, I am not worthy that you should come under my roof' (Matthew 8.8). At the same time we must not say, with Simon Peter, 'Depart from me, for I am a sinful man, O Lord' (Luke 5.8). No. Unworthy and sinful as we are we will do better to pray:

> Lord, we thy presence seek;
> May ours this blessing be;

175

Give us a pure and lowly heart,
A temple meet for thee.

This is Hall's verse, and it makes a fitting end to the hymn. By the words *Lord, we thy presence seek*, he means we seek the Lord's presence in our lives. It is in effect an invitation to him to come and dwell in our hearts. *May ours this blessing be* is a glance back to the beatitude and a prayer that the blessing of *a pure heart* may be ours. And not only a pure heart: a *lowly heart* too – *a temple meet* for the Lord's presence.

In using the word 'temple' Mr Hall was perhaps recalling the original purpose of Keble's poem and its connection with the presentation of Christ in the temple at Jerusalem. To the Jews that majestic building was, in a special sense, God's dwelling-place, his shrine. The nearer they were to it the nearer they were to him. It is not so with us as Christians. The Lord does not dwell in temples made with hands. His dwelling is with the lowly in heart. We are his temple, 'a holy temple in the Lord, . . . a dwelling-place of God in the Spirit' (Ephesians 2.21,22). Long before the apostle's time the Hebrew prophet had said much the same thing: 'Thus says the high and lofty One who inhabits eternity, whose name is Holy: I dwell in the high and holy place, and also with him who is of a contrite and humble spirit' (Isaiah 57.15).

III

In dealing with this hymn and its origin we have assumed – rightly, we believe – that the second and fourth stanzas were written by W. J. Hall. It is only fair to admit that there is no absolute proof of this. What is certain is that the hymn, as we know it, first made its appearance in the *Mitre Hymn Book*, 1836, of which Hall was the editor. In that book he simply ascribed the hymn to Keble and gave no indication as to the authorship of the new stanzas. The obvious inference is that they were Hall's own work. The only other possibility, as Julian states, is that they were written by his co-editor,

Edward Osler; but in that case surely Hall would have acknowledged the fact and included Osler's name in the ascription.

It is pointless to pursue the matter further, and in any case it is not of any ultimate significance. What matters is the hymn itself, one of the minor treasures of English hymnody, which after the passage of nearly a century and a half still has something positive to say about the essence and secret of true religion. And a comment by Hugh Martin in *The Baptist Hymn Book Companion* is worth adding. 'Pure in heart' in the Beatitudes, he points out, does not refer only to chastity. 'A pure heart means here one that is sincere and single-minded in its desire to love and serve God, and free from any admixture of base matter, as we speak of pure food.'

23

GOD IN THE SILENCE

Dear Lord and Father of mankind

JOHN GREENLEAF Whittier, the author of this very popular
hymn, was a distinguished American poet whose life spanned
the greater part of the nineteenth century, for he was born in
1807 and died in 1892. The most important thing to
remember about him in connection with his religious verse is
that he was a Quaker. The Society of Friends, founded by
George Fox in the previous century, was largely a protest
against the formality of institutional religion, with its outward
forms, ceremonies and sacraments. Instead, it taught the
inwardness of true religion and made much of the 'Inner
Light', the direct illumination of the soul by God. Its worship
was marked by quietness, stillness, silence. It had no use for
organs and choirs, music and singing. The utmost simplicity
was demanded in all things, in life as well as in worship.

It is against this background that Whittier's verse in general, and 'Dear Lord and Father of mankind' in particular,
must be viewed.

I

The first thing to be said about the hymn is that it is not really
a hymn at all but a poem, or rather part of a poem. Quakers do

not sing hymns, and Whittier therefore was not concerned with hymnody. He himself declared, 'I am not really a hymn-writer, for the good reason that I know nothing of music. . . . A good hymn is the best use to which poetry can be devoted, but I do not claim that I have succeeded in composing one.'

Despite that modest disclaimer, it must be said that those parts of his poems which have been turned into hymns for use in Christian worship have achieved a large measure of success. Of none is this more true than of 'Dear Lord and Father of mankind'. The stanzas of which it is composed are the last part of a poem written in 1872 entitled 'The Brewing of Soma'. Soma was a potent drink made from a plant of that name, brewed by Hindu priests and declared to be the drink of the gods. When partaken of by their devotees it produced a state of frenzy, an outburst of drunken joy, as a result of which they indulged in wild and sensual orgies.

In the first part of his poem Whittier describes these pagan rites and then boldly asserts that they are finding fresh expression, though in a different form, in the traditional worship of the Christian Church. He castigates both Catholic ceremonialism, with its priests, vestments, sacraments and incense, and evangelical revivalism, with its noisy songs and emotional type of preaching. To Whittier the Quaker all this sort of thing was a sham religion, far removed from the spirit of Christ and more akin to the spirit of Soma. So he wrote:

> In sensual transports, wild as vain,
> We brew in many a Christian fane
> The heathen Soma still[1]

From the madness of these religious excesses, as he regarded them, the poet then turns away and with the twelfth stanza of his poem begins to describe what is for him the authentic spirit of Christ's religion· And it is at this point that our hymn begins.

II

In view of what has gone before the poet strikes a note of deep penitence:

> Dear Lord and Father of mankind,
>   Forgive our foolish ways!
> Re-clothe us in our rightful mind,
> In purer lives thy service find,
>   In deeper reverence praise.

Not *our foolish ways* but 'our feverish ways' was what Whittier wrote, with reference to religious emotionalism. And his prayer is not only that God will forgive us for our folly but *re-clothe us in our rightful mind*. It is a prayer for spiritual sanity instead of religious madness. Doubtless the poet had in mind here the story of the Gadarene demoniac, a wild and raving lunatic who, healed by Jesus, was found to be 'clothed and in his right mind' (Mark 5.15). It is in *purer lives* that his 'service' – that is, divine service, worship – is truly expressed, not in ceremonial acts; *in deeper reverence* for God and man and creation we offer our praise, not in words and songs. This is Whittier's meaning. All through the stanza he is stressing that real religion is inward and spiritual, concerned with the heart and life rather than with churchly activities.

He finds an illustration of this in the story of Jesus calling the Galilean fishermen to be his disciples:

> In simple trust like theirs who heard,
>   Beside the Syrian sea,
> The gracious calling of the Lord,
> Let us, like them, without a word,
>   Rise up and follow thee.

Simple trust! That was all Jesus demanded of those first disciples. Peter and Andrew and the others were not required to subscribe to a creed or perform a religious rite but simply to respond in faith to *the gracious calling of the Lord*. And this they did *without a word*. As far as we are told they said nothing, but simply, quietly and obediently left their nets and followed him.

The Quaker emphasis on silence is evident here, as it is also in the next stanza:

> O Sabbath rest by Galilee!
>   O calm of hills above,
> Where Jesus knelt to share with thee
> The silence of eternity,
>   Interpreted by love!

Having depicted the incident by the lakeside, the poet paints another Galilean scene. Drawing freely on his imagination he portrays Jesus at prayer in the course of the *Sabbath rest*, retreating from the noisy world and holding secret communion with God. The picture is beautifully drawn (perhaps based on Mark 1.35) and the words are pure poetry. The Son of God shares with the Father *the silence of eternity*; but it is not the silence of indifference or aloofness. The silence of God is *interpreted by love*, and in that silent love the soul communes with him in utter peace and quiet.

This is further expressed in the stanza that follows, which is omitted by many hymnals:

> With that deep hush subduing all
>   Our words and works that drown
> The tender whisper of thy call,
> As noiseless let thy blessing fall,
>   As fell thy manna down.

Our words and works – our forms of prayer, our songs of praise, our religious ceremonies: these can *drown the tender whisper* with which God speaks in the sacred hour of worship. We need to let the *deep hush* of heaven subdue our restless spirits. The illustration of the manna, which fell silently during the night, is striking (Exodus 16). This is the way God works still. His *blessing* falls *as noiseless as fell the manna down*. Perhaps we should remember here that in the fourth Gospel the manna is seen to be a picture of Christ, the living Bread from heaven (6.31–35).

With the next stanza we continue to pray in the same strain:

Drop thy still dews of quietness,
 Till all our strivings cease;
Take from our souls the strain and stress,
And let our ordered lives confess
 The beauty of thy peace.

The prayer sums up what the Quaker poet is saying to us about the inner stillness we need to cultivate at all times. Life is not meant to be an affair of *strain and stress*. God can take all that from *our souls* and constantly refresh us with his *still dews of quietness*. Then, and only then, will *our lives* be *ordered* aright and reflect *the beauty of* his *peace*. So we must pray that God will calm and heal our feverish, restless spirits:

Breathe through the heats of our desire
 Thy coolness and thy balm;
Let sense be dumb, let flesh retire,
Speak throught the earthquake, wind, and fire,
 O still small voice of calm!

Here is another scriptural illustration which, like the manna, is drawn from the Old Testament. It comes from the story of Elijah who after his contest with the priests of Baal on Mount Carmel withdrew to the quietness of Horeb, the mount of God. There God revealed himself to the prophet: not in the tempestuous wind or the shattering earthquake or the devouring fire, but in the accents of 'a still small voice' (1 Kings 19.9–17). In that way he spoke to the heart and conscience of his servant. In the same way he speaks to us today when we are quiet enough to hear his *still small voice of calm*.

III

So far we have looked at these verses in an uncritical manner and sought to interpret them from the Quaker poet's point of view. And let us readily admit that his point of view is deserving of attention. We must welcome what the hymn says on the positive side about the necessity of simple trust and obedience, about the importance of silent communion with God, about the value of a calm and restful spirit.

But that is only one side of the truth. Whittier's lines are right in what they affirm, wrong in what by implication they deny. For what they implicitly deny is that there is any need to worship God in words and music, or to make use of sacraments or ceremonial of any kind. As the poet says elsewhere,

> Our friend, our brother, and our Lord,
>   What may thy service be?
> Nor name, nor form, nor ritual word,
>   But simply following thee.

But is it really as *simple* as that? Do we need no form of prayer, no ritual word or act to assist us in our worship of God? If so, we might as well close our churches, throw away our prayer books and hymn-books, and abandon the ministry of music and song. But what then of the Lord's command at the Last Supper, 'Do this in remembrance of me'? What of St Paul's injunction to the early Christians to sing to God 'in psalms and hymns and spiritual songs'? Can we, any more than the apostolic Church, dispense with these means of grace?

Such questions cannot be evaded as we consider this hymn. Clearly it does not speak the whole truth about worship. Nevertheless, it has something important to teach us, and we should be grateful for its message as well as for its poetry. The worship in our churches would be the richer for more silence, greater simplicity, deeper spirituality. And we all need to cultivate in our own lives that spirit of true reverence, quiet trust, and inward peace which finds such sublime expression in Whittier's lines.

Whatever religious label we wear, we would surely agree with him in confessing,

> O Lord and Master of us all,
>   Whate'er our name or sign,
> We own thy sway, we hear thy call,
>   We test our lives by thine.[1]

NOTE

1 From the poem 'Our Master', as in *MHB* 102, v.8, and *CP* 102, v.8.

183

24

OUR SACRIFICE OF PRAISE

For the beauty of the earth

THERE IS a question to be faced at the outset in considering this hymn. What sort of a hymn is it? Into what category is it to be placed? Is it first and foremost a eucharistic hymn, designed to be sung at a celebration of the Holy Communion? Or is it simply a general hymn of praise, appropriate for use on many occasions and particularly suitable for harvest thanksgiving and flower services?

I

The answer to these inquiries is quite simple. It depends on the version of the hymn we follow. For it is to be found in virtually two distinct forms, what we might call the authorized version and the revised version. The authorized version appears in the *English Hymnal*, where we have the hymn in the original and complete form in which the author wrote it; and here it is rightly placed among the Communion hymns (*EH* 309). The revised version is an adaptation of the hymn by the editors of *Hymns Ancient & Modern*, and in that book it is placed among the general hymns (*AMR* 171).

A comparison of these versions reveals two main differences. The first has to do with the matter of length. The original hymn has eight stanzas. In its revised form it is reduced to five, verses 3, 7 and 8 being omitted. The other and more important difference concerns the refrain with which each stanza concludes. The author wrote

> Christ our God, to thee we raise
> This our sacrifice of praise.

The words are thus addressed specifically to our Lord as the Incarnate Son, and the 'sacrifice of praise' is quite clearly the eucharistic sacrifice. The language is that of the Prayer Book liturgy where we ask God 'mercifully to accept this our sacrifice of praise and thanksgiving'. In its amended form the refrain is deprived of its sacramental character and becomes

> Lord of all, to thee we raise
> This our grateful hymn of praise.

An examination of the hymnals in common use today reveals that it is in its revised and shortened form that the hymn has gained the most general acceptance and is therefore most widely known. There is certainly something to be said for the changes which have been made, and which were introduced it seems with the author's permission. They have the advantage of giving the hymn a broader appeal and a less limited use. At the same time it is well to bear in mind the purpose and pattern of the hymn as it was conceived in the mind of the man who wrote it. And before going further with our study we ought to inquire, Who was he?

Despite his somewhat high-sounding name, Folliett Sandford Pierpoint was very much one of the lesser Victorian hymn writers. He was a West countryman, born in Bath in 1835 and educated at the local grammar school and Cambridge University. A classical scholar and a devout Tractarian, he did a certain amount of teaching and tutoring in the course of a long and fairly leisurely life. But he also wrote a good deal of poetry, including a number of hymns; and it is by this one hymn that he is now remembered. It was published in an anthology called *Lyra Eucharistica*, second edition, 1864, when he was twenty-nine. He died in 1917.

We shall look at the hymn in its original form. It is essentially an act of praise to Christ with a strong eucharistic emphasis. Various subjects for praise are mentioned, beginning on the earthly and human level and rising at the end to sublime spiritual heights.

II

The first two stanzas are concerned with the world of nature. We offer praise for the wonder and loveliness of Creation.

> For the beauty of the earth,
>   For the beauty of the skies,
> For the love which from our birth
>   Over and around us lies.
>
> For the beauty of each hour
>   Of the day and of the night,
> Hill and vale, and tree and flower,
>   Sun and moon and stars of light.

What the hymn is saying in the first stanza is that the gifts of nature as revealed in *the beauty of the earth* and *the beauty of the skies* are not only tokens of God's creative power. They are also proofs and pledges of his love – the love which encircles our lives right *from our birth*, and is *over and around us* till the end of our days. The beauty of the world is a perpetual reminder of the Father's concern for his children's happiness. He has placed them in a world which is full of lovely things, things created not simply for their use but for their enjoyment.

There is *beauty* in *each hour*, as the second stanza says. Certainly *the night* has its beauty as well as *the day*, the sky as well as the earth. We look around in God's world and survey the glory of *hill and vale, and tree and flower* with their infinite variety of size and form and colour. We look up and discern the Creator's handiwork no less in *sun and moon and stars of light* and we gratefully acknowledge that 'The heavens

186

are telling the glory of God'. As the psalmist goes on to say:

> Day to day pours forth speech,
>   and night to night declares knowledge.
> There is no speech, nor are there words;
>   their voice is not heard;
> Yet their sound goes out through all the earth,
>   and their words to the end of the world.
>
> (Psalm 19.1–4)

These verses of the psalm are magnificently paraphrased in Addison's hymn 'The spacious firmament on high'. The eloquence of nature, 'the broad sweep of God's wordless revelation in the universe' (D. Kidner), should not only fill our hearts with joy and wonder but also enlarge our vision of God as the Lord and Maker of all things. Here assuredly is a fitting theme for our sacrifice of praise.

In the next stanza we give thanks for our physical faculties of hearing and sight, and the inner power to appreciate what we hear and see:

> For the joy of ear and eye,
>   For the heart and brain's delight,
> For the mystic harmony
>   Linking sense to sound and sight.

The stanza is omitted from some hymnals (e.g. *AMR*), presumably because the thought is regarded as obscure. But how fitting it is that we should praise God *for the joy of ear and eye*. So much of our deepest pleasure in life is dependent on what we hear and see. Too readily we take our hearing and sight for granted, whereas they are two of the greatest blessings of this life. Closely linked with them is their spiritual counterpart in *the heart and brain's delight*; for there is indeed a *mystic harmony* between our inward senses (what we feel and know) and the outward phenomena of *sound and sight*. Like so many of the mysteries of our human existence we may not be able to explain it; but that does not matter in the end. What matters is that we can experience and enjoy it – and this too calls for our sacrifice of praise.

187

The realm of personal relationships constitutes another source of joy:

> For the joy of human love,
>   Brother, sister, parent, child,
> Friends on earth, and friends above,
>   For all gentle thoughts and mild.

The words call for little comment and require no explanation, but they are assuredly deserving of thought and reflection. What would life be without *the joy of human love*? We would surely agree that the most enduring happiness of our days on earth is derived from the bonds of family life – *brother, sister, parent, child* – and from the gift of friendship. And the latter includes not only *friends on earth* but also *friends above*, such is our faith and hope in him who is the Resurrection and the Life. For this too we must offer our sacrifice of praise. And more still:

> For each perfect gift of thine,
>   To our race so freely given,
> Graces human and divine,
>   Flowers of earth and buds of heaven.

Here we are offering praise on a wider scale. We thank our Lord Christ *for each perfect gift* which he *so freely* and generously bestows upon *our race*. The gifts are described as *graces human and divine*, for these graces (*charismata*) are natural endowments strengthened by the Spirit (*cf.* 1 Corinthians 12.4–11). This much we can readily understand. But what are we to make of the final line which likens the graces to *flowers of earth and buds of heaven*? It is all too easy to sing words like these without grasping their meaning. And the meaning is not at first apparent. Probably what the writer is saying is that the gifts of God are, to some extent, already developed in this world and beautify our present life. These are the 'flowers of earth'. But at best they are only partially realized here on earth: they await their fulfilment in the life to come. These are the 'buds of heaven'. Also implicit in these words is the idea of continuity: the graces which are ours now will blossom in fuller flower in the heavenly life. Thoughts such as these are at least worth pondering as we offer our sacrifice of praise.

III

The last three stanzas lift our thoughts to a high spiritual plane and form a splendid climax to the hymn. First, we praise our Lord for the Church:

> For thy Bride, that evermore
> Lifteth holy hands above,
> Offering up on every shore
> This pure sacrifice of love.

The *Bride* of Christ is of course his Church. In *AMR* and other hymn-books which retain the stanza this is made explicit by changing the word. The analogy of the Church as the bride of Christ is developed by St Paul in Ephesians 5, where he likens the marriage bond which unites husband and wife to the spiritual relationship between the Lord and his people in what has been called the heavenly wedlock. Like the marriage bond, it is essentially a relationship of *love*:

> Husbands, love your wives, as Christ loved the Church and gave himself up for her, that he might sanctify her, having cleansed her by the washing of water with the word, that the church might be presented before him in splendour, without spot or wrinkle or any such thing, that she might be holy and without blemish.

> (Ephesians 5.25–27)

Christ's love for his Church is a sacrificial love. He gave himself up for her. The Church responds to that love in sacrificial terms, *offering up on every shore this pure sacrifice of love* – that is, the eucharistic sacrifice. Here is a further reminder of the original purpose and character of the hymn. The picture of the Church as a worldwide, worshipping community engaged in a ceaseless ministry of prayer and praise is an impressive one. The picture becomes more complete and even more attractive by the touches added in the final stanzas:

189

For thy Martyrs' crown of light,
For thy Prophets' eagle eye,
For thy bold Confessors' might,
For the lips of infancy.

For thy Virgins' robes of snow,
For thy Maiden-Mother mild,
For thyself, with hearts aglow,
Jesu, Victim undefiled.

The Church is not an institution. The Church is people; and now we catch a glimpse of some of its more illustrious company as a procession of saintly souls passes before our eyes. There is the noble army of *Martyrs*, crowned with the *light* of glory; the goodly fellowship of the *Prophets*, with their keen insight into the divine counsels; a band of *bold Confessors* strong in the Faith of Christ; a chorus of children singing their Saviour's praise; a band of white-robed *Virgins*, and foremost among them Blessed Mary, *Maiden-Mother mild*. For all these we offer our sacrifice of praise, rejoicing as we do so that as members of the Body of Christ we are one with them and belong to the same shining company.

Last of all, but most of all, we offer praise *with hearts aglow* for *Jesus* himself – *Victim undefiled*. The latter designation is given to him because of the eucharistic nature of the hymn. In the Lord's supper we celebrate his passion and 'remember' him in the mystery of his redeeming love: the one who, undefiled by sin, was nevertheless made sin for us; the Victim who is yet the Victor, the conqueror of death, the living Saviour and Lord. That being so,

Christ our God, to thee we raise
This our sacrifice of praise.

25

LIFE'S PILGRIMAGE

Guide me, O thou great Jehovah

THERE IS no foundation for the statement which is sometimes made that 'Guide me, O thou great Jehovah' was written at the request of the Countess of Huntingdon to mark the opening of Trevecca College, Talgarth, South Wales, in 1768. It is true that the author of the hymn was a close friend of the Countess, and that she both founded and financed the college, the purpose of which was to train 'godly and pious young men' to be preachers of the gospel. But the dates of the writing of the hymn and the opening of the college do not coincide. The actual connection between the hymn and the college will emerge in due course. First a word must be said about the man who wrote the hymn.

I

William Williams (1717–81) was one of the outstanding figures in the story of the Welsh evangelical revival in the eighteenth century. The leader of the movement was Howell Harris, who gathered round him a band of preachers, ordained and lay, to help him spread the gospel throughout Wales. By 1741 the revival was in full swing and great crowds of people were converted. Being Welsh, and having experienced the joy of Christ's salvation, they naturally wanted to sing. And here Howell Harris came up against a difficulty. There was a lack of good evangelical hymns in the Welsh language. Clearly new hymns had to be written – but by whom? He looked for the answer among his preachers and found it pre-eminently in William Williams.

As a young man of twenty Williams was preparing for the medical profession when he came under the spell of Howell Harris. He went to hear him preach with the intention of scoffing. He remained to pray. As a result he dedicated his life to the service of Christ and trained for the ministry. In due course he was ordained deacon in the Established Church and served a couple of curacies; but the Bishop of St David's took exception to his evangelical views and refused to ordain him priest. He thereupon threw in his lot with Harris and became a Dissenting preacher. For the next forty-eight years, as it has been said, 'he took all Wales for his parish' and travelled untiringly throughout the Principality as an itinerant evangelist.

By all accounts Williams was a great preacher. But he was an even greater poet and has deservedly been called the poet laureate of the Welsh revival. His hymns, of which he wrote some eight hundred, all in Welsh, had a profound influence on the spiritual life of the nation. Dr Elvert Lewis, in his *Sweet Singers of Wales*, wrote:

> What Paul Gerhardt has been to Germany, what Isaac Watts has been to England, that and more William Williams has been to the little Principality of Wales. His hymns have both stirred and soothed a whole nation for more than a hundred years; they have helped to fashion a nation's character and to deepen a nation's piety.

'Guide me, O thou great Jehovah' was published in Welsh in 1745. The great majority of Williams' hymns have not been translated into English. This is one of the few exceptions. The first English version was made by Peter Williams (no relation of the hymn's author) and published in 1771. It consisted of three of the original five stanzas. William Williams was satisfied with the rendering of the first of these stanzas and adopted it. But he considerably revised the second, entirely rewrote the third, and for good measure added a fourth. The resulting hymn was printed around 1772 in the form of a leaflet, headed:

A Favourite Hymn
sung by
Lady Huntingdon's Young Collegians.
Printed by the desire of many Christian friends.
Lord, give it thy blessing!

The young collegians were, in fact, the students of Trevecca College (later to become Cheshunt College, Cambridge). This explains how the hymn came to be associated with the college; and though it may well have been sung on the occasion when the college was opened in 1768, it had been composed many years earlier.

The hymn as we now have it comprises the first three verses printed in the leaflet. The fourth stanza, obviously an afterthought, has long been forgotten and the hymn is quite complete without it. It will be clear from what has been said that the English translation is the joint work of Peter and William Williams.

Cwm Rhondda, the tune we invariably associate with this hymn, is comparatively modern. It was composed by John Hughes (1873–1932) for a Welsh song festival in 1905 and rapidly gained popularity in Wales and far beyond. Hughes was an official of the old Great Western Railway, and like his father before him was a deacon and precentor of Salem Baptist Chapel, Pontypridd.

II

The imagery of the hymn is drawn from the record in the book of Exodus of the Israelites' journey through the wilderness to the promised land of Canaan. This is the key to the under-

193

standing of the hymn. It interprets the Christian life in terms of pilgrimage against the background of the biblical story. Only by keeping in mind some of the things that happened to the Israelites in the course of their long and weary journey is it possible to appreciate the vivid imagery employed. The whole hymn, in fact, is full of scriptural allusions and phrases of one sort or another. Another thing to note is that the hymn in its entirety is a prayer: a prayer for God's care and protection along the road of life, and for a safe arrival 'on Canaan's side' at the end of the pilgrimage.

> Guide me, O thou great Jehovah,
>   Pilgrim through this barren land;
> I am weak, but thou art mighty,
>   Hold me with thy powerful hand:
>   Bread of heaven,
> Feed me till I want no more.

Guide me, O thou great Jehovah – not 'O thou great Redeemer', as in *AMR* and *EH* and some other books. This is not only an unnecessary but an unfortunate alteration. The hymn is based, as we have observed, on a piece of Old Testament history, and *Jehovah* is the Old Testament name for God. Williams used it for this very reason. The hymn gains nothing but loses something of value at the outset when the word is changed. The prayer for guidance is a wise one, for the traveller is a *pilgrim through this barren land* – the barren land being 'the great and terrible wilderness' through which the Lord 'led forth his people like sheep' (Deuteronomy 8.15; Psalm 78.52). For the Christian believer the wilderness represents the world, as in the opening words of Bunyan's *Pilgrim's Progress*: 'As I walked through the wilderness of this world . . .' In that wilderness there are hazards and hardships to be met; so the pilgrim, recognizing that he is *weak* and God is *mighty*, prays, *Hold me by thy powerful hand*. The prayer recalls the psalmist's assurance, 'Thy right hand shall hold me' (Psalm 139.10; *cf.* also John 10.27–30).

But more. The pilgrim needs not only to be guided and guarded as he travels through the wilderness. He needs to be nourished and sustained as well; hence the prayer, *Bread of heaven, feed me till I want no more.* Now we are back in the Exodus story, chapter 16, verses 4–18. The Israelites 'murmured against Moses and Aaron' for bringing them into the wilderness 'to kill this whole assembly with hunger'. God's answer to Moses was, 'Behold, I will rain bread from heaven for you'; and so the 'manna' was given, to be gathered by the people each day. Moses told them, 'It is the bread which the Lord has given you to eat.' Jesus referred to this incident after he had fed the five thousand on the Galilean hillside and claimed:

> I am the bread of life. Your fathers ate the manna in the wilderness, and they died. This is the bread which comes down from heaven, that a man may eat of it and not die. I am the living bread which came down from heaven; if any man eats of this bread he will live for ever; and the bread which I shall give for the life of the world is my flesh.
>
> (John 6.48–51)

Christ is the 'Bread of heaven', and it is to him therefore we pray, 'Feed me till I want no more.' The word *want* is used here in the older sense of 'being in want', not in the modern sense of desiring or requiring. Hence what the prayer means is, 'Feed me till I am no more in need, till the hunger of my soul is satisfied.' The language is liable to be misunderstood, and for that reason some hymnals (e.g. *AMR* and *CP*) change the last line to 'Feed me now and evermore.' Our Lord's discourse in John 6, with its reference to the believer partaking of his flesh and blood (vv. 53–8), clearly has a sacramental meaning. In the Lord's supper we feed on Christ, the living Bread from heaven, and as we do so we find his promise true: 'He who comes to me shall never hunger' – or, in the language of the hymn, 'shall want no more'.

III

Open now the crystal fountain,
   Whence the healing stream doth flow;
Let the fire and cloudy pillar

Lead me all my journey through:
Strong Deliverer,
Be thou still my strength and shield.

Open now the crystal fountain, whence the healing stream doth flow. Here we are in Exodus chapter 17. Once again the Israelites are finding fault with Moses, this time because 'there was no water for the people to drink'.

> So Moses cried to the Lord, 'What shall I do with this people? They are almost ready to stone me.' And the Lord said to Moses, 'Pass on before the people, taking with you some of the elders of Israel; and take in your hand the rod with which you struck the Nile, and go. Behold, I will stand before you there on the rock at Horeb; and you shall strike the rock, and water shall come out of it, that the people may drink.'
>
> (vv. 4–6)

So a 'crystal fountain' was opened for the Israelites in the wilderness.

The meaning of this for the Christian is made clear in 1 Corinthians 10.4. St Paul sees in the story of the smitten rock a foreshadowing of the gospel and gives to the rock and the water a 'spiritual' or supernatural meaning, boldly declaring that 'the Rock was Christ'. It is from Christ that the 'healing stream' flows.

At the feast of Tabernacles in Jerusalem Jesus declared, 'If any one thirst, let him come to me and drink' (John 7.37). To the Samaritan woman at the well he promised 'living water' and said, 'Whoever drinks of the water I shall give him will never thirst' (John 4.14). Water in the Bible has many symbolical values. Here it is thought of as life-giving and thirst-quenching; and Christ is its source, its fountain-head.

The figure changes. *Let the fire and cloudy pillar lead me all my journey through.* This again takes us back to Exodus and the Israelites' pilgrimage. 'The Lord went before them by day in a pillar of cloud to lead them along the way, and by night a pillar of fire to give them light, that they might travel by day and by night' (Exodus 13.21). The pillar of cloud and fire was the sign of God's continual presence with his people. It was also the means by which he directed their path. They were not

196

to move a step forward unless he went with them (*cf.* Exodus 33.14–16). In our Christian pilgrimage we are assured of the daily companionship of the risen Lord by his word, 'Lo, I am with you always, to the close of the age' (Matthew 28.30). In his presence we find not only peace but protection, and therefore we pray that he will be our *strong Deliverer* – as he was to the people of Israel when he rescued them from the armies of the Egyptians (Exodus 14.26–31). Life's journey is beset by many perils and foes. As Christians we are not exempt from them, but we are promised grace to overcome, for the Lord is *still* our *strength and shield.*

The final stanza brings us to the end of the Israelites' journey through the wilderness and to the end of our own pilgrimage here on earth.

> When I tread the verge of Jordan,
>   Bid my anxious fears subside;
> Death of death, and hell's Destruction,
>   Land me safe on Canaan's side:
>   Songs of praises
>   I will ever give to thee.

When I tread the verge of Jordan. For the Israelites the long march from Egypt was now over. They had come to the Jordan, the last obstacle to be surmounted before they set foot in Canaan; but the river had to be crossed before they possessed the promised land. Such is the historical background of this stanza. In Christian symbolism Jordan is the river of death, and Canaan, the 'land flowing with milk and honey', is the heavenly country. Isaac Watts uses the same imagery in his hymn 'There is a land of pure delight'. At this point then the Christian pilgrim is looking ahead and praying that when the time comes for him to cross the river the Lord will *bid* his *anxious fears subside.* It is a prayer for a peaceful death.

That prayer is reinforced by another petition: *Death of death, and hell's Destruction, land me safe on Canaan's side.* Probably few people who sing this hymn realize that in these words Christ himself is being addressed. It is *he*, the living Lord, who is the 'Death of death', the one who by his cross and resurrection 'destroyed death' – that is, annihilated its power – 'and brought life and immortality to light' (2 Timothy 1.10). Likewise he is the 'Destruction' of hell, for hell means separation from God. Christ came to bridge the gulf between God and man and to reconcile them through the cross (2 Corinthians 5.19–21). This saving work of Christ is the ultimate ground of our faith and reason for our hope, and therefore we pray with confidence that he will bring us safely at last to our heavenly home.

With such a prospect before us we conclude the hymn on a note of joy and thanksgiving: *Songs of praises I will ever give to thee.* The hymn-writer had caught the spirit of the psalmist when he said, 'I will bless the Lord at all times; his praise shall continually be in my mouth' (Psalm 34.1). Praise is not intended to be an intermittent exercise, dependent on our changing moods and circumstances. It is for all times and seasons.

26

THE NAME OF JESUS

How sweet the name of Jesus sounds

IN THE Church of St Mary Woolnoth, adjoining the Mansion House in London, there may be seen on the north wall near the pulpit a memorial tablet with the inscription:

> JOHN NEWTON,
> Clerk,
> Once an infidel and libertine,
> A servant of slaves in Africa,
> was
> By the rich mercy of our Lord and Saviour
> Jesus Christ,
> Preserved, restored, pardoned,
> And appointed to preach the Faith
> He had long laboured to destroy.
> Near sixteen years at Olney in Bucks;
> And twenty-seven years in this Church.

Such is Newton's epitaph, written by himself, which tells in brief the record of his adventurous career. It gives some indication of the sort of man he had been in earlier life, as well as of the man he became 'by the rich mercy of our Lord and Saviour Jesus Christ'. It is to this man that we owe the hymn 'How sweet the name of Jesus sounds'.

I

John Newton was born in London in 1725. His mother, a godly woman, died when he was seven, and at the age of eleven he went to sea with his father who was a sailor. As a youth he served in turn with the Merchant and Royal Navy; but left to his own devices he drifted into the worst and lowest sort of company, discarded the faith his mother had taught him, and plunged headlong into a godless and profligate life. Worst of all, he got deeply involved with the iniquitous slave traffic off the coast of Africa and for some years he was himself commander of a slave ship. At this stage the one restraining and refining influence in his life was Mary Catlett, the girl at home with whom he fell violently in love when he was seventeen and whom he eventually married. She powerfully affected him for good and turned his thoughts back to God. Partly due to her, and partly through his reading of Thomas à Kempis and study of the scriptures, a change gradually took place in his life.

Matters came to a head when, at the age of twenty-three, he was caught in a sudden storm at sea and death stared him in the face. In desperation he cried to God for mercy – and was heard, delivered, and converted. Shortly after this he married, and four years later, abandoning the sea and all involvement in the slave trade, he took a shore job in the Port of Liverpool. In the years that followed he met up with Whitefield and Wesley, who turned his thoughts towards the ministry. After much hard study he was eventually ordained at the age of thirty-nine to serve as curate-in-charge of Olney in Buckinghamshire. During his sixteen years of ministry there he collaborated with his friend and neighbour, the poet William Cowper, in producing the *Olney Hymns*. The hymns were written to be sung at the weekly prayer meetings, not for use in the church services. Due to his mental illness Cowper's share in the making of this book was much smaller than had been intended (sixty-eight hymns). It was left to Newton to contribute the larger number of hymns (280) and complete the collection, which was published in 1799. Later that same year, at the age of fifty-six, he left Olney to become rector of St Mary Woolnoth, where he remained for the rest of his days.

Such in bare outline is the record of his life. It is with his hymns that we are concerned here, and with one hymn in particular; but in studying his writings it is impossible to forget the unusual circumstances of his life and the manner of man he was. Newton was no ordinary clergyman, and his was no ordinary ministry. It is not surprising therefore that his hymns have a distinctive flavour – and a strongly evangelical flavour. For the most part they are homely and personal in character. Many of them are simply the expression of his own first-hand experience of the 'amazing grace' of God. He did not aspire to the same poetical heights as Cowper, for he knew that this was beyond him. Nevertheless the best of his hymns will bear comparison with those of his friend. If he did not write great poetry, he composed good hymns. Of those which still survive, the two finest and best known are 'How sweet the name' and 'Glorious things of thee are spoken'. These may be regarded as complementary: between them they glorify Christ and his Church. Among his other hymns are: 'Great Shepherd of thy people, hear'; 'Come, my soul, thy suit prepare'; 'Amazing grace! how sweet the sound'; and 'May the grace of Christ our Saviour'.

II

'How sweet the name of Jesus sounds' comes from Part One of the *Olney Hymns* entitled 'On Select Passages of Scripture'. The scripture reference given for this one is Song of Solomon 1.3, 'Thy name is as ointment poured forth, therefore do the virgins love thee.' The hymn consisted originally of seven stanzas. The central one (Newton's fourth) is omitted from all hymnals, and wisely so; for it does not really match up with the rest of the hymn and it interrupts the natural sequence between the third and fourth verses of the hymn as we now have it. It runs:

> By thee my prayers acceptance gain,
>   Although with sin defiled;
> Satan accuses me in vain,
>   And I am owned a child.

The six stanzas we have in our hymn books fall into three pairs. The first pair deals particularly with the healing power of the name of Jesus.

> How sweet the name of Jesus sounds
>   In a believer's ear!
> It soothes his sorrows, heals his wounds,
>   And drives away his fear.

> It makes the wounded spirit whole,
>   And calms the troubled breast;
> 'Tis manna to the hungry soul,
>   And to the weary rest.

The whole hymn is a jubilant and grateful celebration of the Saviour's name, setting forth the glory of his person: his titles, attributes and offices. In these first two stanzas Newton clearly has in mind the words of his text, 'Thy name is as ointment poured forth.' One of the properties of ointment is that of sweet fragrance, and this accounts for the opening line, *How sweet the name of Jesus sounds*. But there is a proviso: his name sounds sweetly only *in a believer's ear*. Newton would doubtless have emphasized the word 'believer'. He could never forget that at one time he himself, far from being a believer, had been an infidel and blasphemer who took delight in profaning the sacred name. Now, by the grace of God, all that was changed, for he himself was changed, and he lived only to magnify and adore the name he once had scorned.

In the lines that follow he recalls that ointment, in addition to its fragrant odour, also possesses healing properties. Similarly with the name of Jesus and the believer: *it soothes his sorrows, heals his wounds, and drives away his fear.* The same thought is repeated in the next stanza: *It makes the wounded*

spirit whole, and calms the troubled breast. No one is wholly
free from affliction. Sorrow and suffering leave their scars on
every life. At this point the hymn comes very close to our
human condition. The great Joseph Parker of the City Temple
used to say, 'Preach to broken hearts, and you will never
lack an audience.' One can go a step further. Tell of Jesus, the
Great Physician, and the broken-hearted will find healing,
consolation and peace in his name.

New metaphors are introduced in the last two lines of the
second stanza. The name of Jesus is now likened to food and
rest, two of the basic necessities of life. First, *'Tis manna to the
hungry soul* – manna being the 'bread from heaven' with
which God sustained the Israelites in the wilderness (Exodus
16.4f.). In referring to that story after the feeding of the five
thousand, Jesus claimed that he himself was the true bread
from heaven and promised, 'He who comes to me shall never
be hungry' (John 6.32–35). Next, he offers *to the weary rest* –
that is, 'relief', as in the invitation of Matthew 11.28,29 (see
NEB). 'Jesus does not promise his disciples a life of inactivity
or repose, nor freedom from sorrow and struggle, but he does
assure them that, if they keep close to him, they will find relief
from such crushing burdens as crippling anxiety, the sense of
frustration and futility, and the misery of a sin-laden conscience' (R. V. G. Tasker).[1]

III

In the single name 'Jesus' is hidden a variety of other names
and titles. A dozen or more of these are set before us in the
next pair of stanzas, which form the heart of the hymn.

> Dear name! the rock on which I build,
>   My shield and hiding-place;
> My never-failing treasury, filled
>   With boundless stores of grace.
>
> Jesus! my Shepherd, Husband, Friend,
>   My Prophet, Priest, and King;

My Lord, my Life, my Way, my End,
Accept the praise I bring.

Dear name! The words have a spontaneous ring about
them. They seem to have come instinctively into Newton's
mind as he reflected on the name which had become so
inexpressibly dear to him – and remained so to the end of his
long life. When in his last years someone asked him about his
health, he confessed that his powers were failing. 'My memory is almost gone,' he said; 'but I still remember two things:
that I am a great sinner, and that Jesus is a great Saviour.'
Dear name indeed! *The rock on which I build*, for Jesus is the
firm foundation of the believer's life, and no other foundation
can anyone lay (1 Corinthians 3.11). *My shield and hiding-
place*, two metaphors which are taken from the Psalms. They
are found separately in many passages, and together in Psalm
119.114: 'Thou art my hiding-place and my shield; I hope in
thy word.' Another Old Testament verse which comes to
mind in this connection is Proverbs 18.10: 'The name of the
Lord is a strong tower; the righteous man runs into it and is
safe.'

But more. The Lord is not only our protection and defence
in time of adversity; he is also our *never-failing treasury, filled
with boundless stores of grace*. Christ vastly enriches life. In
him the believer has an inexhaustible treasury of grace, for as
the prologue to the fourth Gospel puts it, 'Out of his full store
we have all received grace upon grace' (John 1.16 NEB).
William Temple comments: 'In our own experience we have
drawn upon that treasure store, and have found that the more
we drew the more remained that we might also draw from
that; for every grace received there was more grace offered.'[2]

Jesus! my Shepherd, Husband, Friend. The first and third of
these titles raise no problems. 'Shepherd' is derived directly
from the New Testament (e.g. John 10.1–18). 'Friend'
belongs rather to the language of Christian devotion. Its
significance is expressed in another of Newton's hymns,
beginning 'One there is above all others, well deserves the
name of Friend' (*MHB* 100; *BHB* 214), based on Proverbs
18.24. But what about the title 'Husband'? Newton's reason

for using it is clear. He is interpreting his text from the Song of Solomon in allegorical fashion. The bridegroom in the ancient love-song is Christ, his bride is the Church. St Paul uses the same metaphor in Ephesians 5.21f.; so does the writer of the Apocalypse (Revelation 21.9). But Christ is not the 'husband' of the individual soul and cannot therefore be addressed by the believer as 'my Husband'. The bride of Christ is the Church in its corporate and collective sense. Moreover, as Julian's *Dictionary* points out, 'the expression *Husband* is unsuited to congregational use, as in no sense can it be said that Jesus is the Husband of *men*.' Some hymnals still retain the word (as *EH*); most books change it to something more suitable, such as 'Brother' (*AMR* and *MHB*) or 'Guardian' (*CP*).

My Prophet, Priest, and King. These three titles are part of the biblical terminology in which the coming of the Messiah is both foretold (in the OT) and fulfilled (in the NT). Thus Prophet (Deuteronomy 18.15,18; Acts 3.22; 7.37); Priest (Psalm 110.4; Hebrews 5.6,10, etc.); King (Zechariah 9.9; Matthew 21.5). It may be said that as Prophet Jesus reveals God to men; as Priest he reconciles men to God; and as King he rules over men for God.

The stanza concludes with a further catena of titles: *My Lord, my Life, my Way, my End.* The first three of these are purely biblical in character. Thomas addressed the risen Jesus as 'My Lord and my God' (John 20.28). The Church's earliest confession of faith was 'Jesus is Lord' (1 Corinthians 12.3; *cf.* Romans 10.9). He himself claimed to be the source of Life as well as the Way to the Father (John 14.6). Elsewhere in the New Testament he is spoken of as 'Christ our life' (Colossians 3.4) and as the 'new and living way' by which we draw near to God's holy presence (Hebrews 10.19,20). The phrase 'my End' represents Jesus as the ultimate goal of the believer's life, the prize to be grasped when the race is finished (Philippians 1.21; 3.14).

IV

The fourth stanza finishes with the words *Accept the praise I bring*. The two concluding verses take up this theme and develop it further.

> Weak is the effort of my heart,
>   And cold my warmest thought;
> But when I see thee as thou art,
>   I'll praise thee as I ought.

> Till then I would thy love proclaim
>   With every fleeting breath;
> And may the music of thy name
>   Refresh my soul in death.

Only too often we are aware of the feebleness and unworthiness of the praise we offer to our Lord. We can therefore share Newton's feeling when he says, *Weak is the effort of my heart, and cold my warmest thought.* This is something we are all obliged to confess. Yet in that very confession there is a reminder that true worship does demand an effort of the heart and should be marked by warmth of spirit. All too easily our acts of praise become a formality, nothing more than a matter of words. The words are on our lips, but our hearts are not in the words. Yet the apostle exhorts us to sing and make melody to the Lord with all our hearts (Ephesians 5.19). If Jesus is to us all that this hymn asserts, we shall not be content with anything less than heartfelt praise. Hereafter, like Newton, we shall hope to do better: *when I see thee as thou art, I'll praise thee as I ought.* Heaven is perfect vision and unending praise in the presence of the Lord. There 'we shall see him as he is' (1 John 3.2), for faith will give place to sight, and with the whole company of the redeemed we shall indeed praise him as we ought.

What in the meantime? *Till then I would thy love proclaim with every fleeting breath.* While life remains it must be used in the service of Christ. Such was Newton's firm conviction, and he carried it into good effect by continuing to preach the gospel from his London pulpit till he was over eighty. When, a year or two before his death, he was urged to give up preaching because of his failing sight, he repudiated the suggestion. 'What!' he replied, 'shall the old African blasphemer stop while he can speak?' Because he found difficulty in reading his sermon manuscript, he would take a servant with him into the pulpit who stood behind him and with a pointer traced out the lines. One Sunday morning Newton came to the words, 'Jesus Christ is precious,' which he repeated for the sake of emphasis. His servant, thinking he was getting confused, whispered, 'Go on, go on, you said that before.' Newton looking round replied, 'John, I said that twice, and I am going to say it again.' Then with redoubled force he sounded out the words, 'Jesus Christ is precious.'

He died in 1807 at the age of eighty-two. Who can doubt that *the music of* his Saviour's *name refreshed* his *soul in death*?

NOTES
1 Tyndale New Testament Commentaries: *St Matthew* (Tyndale Press, 1961), p.122.
2 *Readings in St John's Gospel* (Macmillan, 1945), p.16.

27

THE SOUL'S REFUGE

Jesu, Lover of my soul

WHAT IS the correct assessment of 'Jesu, Lover of my soul'? Is it true, as has often been asserted, that it is the greatest and best loved of all Charles Wesley's thousands of hymns? Or ought we to recognize that, despite all that has been claimed for it, the hymn has some serious defects and does not come out too well when placed under close scrutiny?

Two observations may be made at the outset as we look into these questions. The first is that the hymn is not as popular or as widely used now as it was a generation or two ago: a fact which may or may not be significant. The second is that from the very beginning the hymn has been subject to criticism of one sort or another: not everyone has praised it. So clearly there are two sides to the question, and both require careful examination.

I

The first critic of the hymn was John Wesley himself. So far did he disapprove of what his brother had written that he excluded it from his collection of hymns for the Methodist people. The reason for this, it has been assumed, is that he objected to the title given to Jesus in the opening line: *Lover of my soul*. He had a strong dislike of anything savouring of the sentimental in hymns, his brother's or anyone else's, and no doubt he regarded 'Lover' as too familiar and amatory a word to ascribe to the Lord.

But Charles was not coining a phrase when he used the expression 'Lover of my soul'. It was suggested to him by a passage in the Wisdom of Solomon which concludes, 'Thou sparest all: for they are thine, O Lord, thou lover of souls' (Wisdom 11.26). That God loves all his creatures there can be no doubt. He can therefore truthfully be called the lover of souls; and in that case why should not the title be applied to Jesus Christ?

So much for John Wesley's rejection of the hymn, at least as far as the opening line is concerned. But possibly he had other objections as well. He may have felt that the hymn was unsatisfactory from a literary point of view: that it was something of a hotchpotch and contained too many mixed metaphors.

Strong criticism on grounds like these was levelled against the hymn by the illustrious Victorian statesman, W. E. Gladstone. In a letter to a friend written in 1894 he stated his opinion in the following terms:

> I cannot assign a high rank to this extremely popular hymn. It has no unity, no cohesion, no procession, and no special force. A number of ideas are jumbled together rather than interwoven. The paths of the metaphors cross one another, not always on the same level. . . . This is not a whole, for the parts seem to have no relation to one another.

He proceeded to give examples to justify his view. He thought it incongruous that in the first verse the 'bosom' should be regarded as a refuge from a storm at sea, and that at the end of the verse the figure of 'flying to the bosom' should be displaced by the different idea of being guided safe into the haven. Again, in the next stanza he failed to see any connection between the first two lines, the one conveying the idea of shelter ('Other refuge have I none'), the other the thought of dependence ('Hangs my helpless soul on thee'), while in the

209

final lines yet another metaphor is introduced in the words 'Cover my defenceless head'. Once more, in the last stanza he found further ground for complaint in that water, 'the element which at the opening of the hymn was the great enemy and the great danger, is now presented as the source of hope and life. "Healing streams" are to abound.'

What are we to make of this criticism? Is the hymn really just a jumble of ideas and metaphors haphazardly strung together, so that it lacks any clear shape or unity? Or what is it all about?

II

By way of answer let us begin by noting that Wesley wrote the hymn soon after his evangelical conversion, when his heart was still aglow with the glory of God's grace revealed to him in Christ. He had exchanged a dutiful religion for a living Saviour and Lord. Christ had become his all in all; and in trying to give expression to his new-found faith a host of ideas flooded his mind and spilt over into words – perhaps not in calm, clear, connected fashion but vivid and arresting for all that. Wesley here is writing out of his own experience, and he is writing not a poem but a hymn. A good hymn may not necessarily be a good poem. It may fail as a poem but succeed as a hymn. Whatever may be said about 'Jesu, Lover of my soul', it is not a failure. History is agreed about that. It is full of memorable pictures and phrases and has a way of speaking to the heart that is equalled by few other hymns.

Another point to bear in mind in interpreting the hymn is that when it was published in 1740 Wesley gave it the title 'In Temptation'. This at least suggests that in writing these verses he was following a theme, not 'zigzagging' about, as Gladstone suggested. The theme of temptation imparts to the hymn a large measure of unity. 'This,' remarks Timothy Dudley-Smith, 'is a key which helps to explain and justify the changing metaphors, the progression of verses, and the element of pleading – the arrow prayer in the moment of testing.'[1]

Another key is provided by what we may call the missing stanza. Wesley wrote five stanzas in all. In some hymnals (e.g. *AMR* 193) only three are printed (vv. 1, 2, 5). Most books do better and include the fourth – 'Thou, O Christ, art all I want'. That still leaves Wesley's third, the central stanza, which runs:

> Wilt thou not regard my call?
> > Wilt thou not accept my prayer?
> Lo! I sink, I faint, I fall!
> > Lo, on thee I cast my care!
> Reach me out thy gracious hand!
> > While I of thy strength receive,
> Hoping against hope I stand,
> > Dying, and behold I live.

From this it is clear that Wesley had vividly in mind the story of Peter's attempt to walk to Jesus on the storm-tossed sea when 'beginning to sink he cried out, "Lord, save me." Jesus immediately reached out his hand and caught him, saying to him, "O man of little faith, why did you doubt?" ' (Matthew 14.30, 31). Against this background, as Balleine remarks, Wesley's 'maze of metaphors coalesces into a moving picture of a storm-tossed soul flying to Christ for safety.'[2]

III

We are now in a better position to understand and interpret the opening stanza:

> Jesu, Lover of my soul,
> > Let me to thy bosom fly,
> While the nearer waters roll,
> > While the tempest still is high;
> Hide me, O my Saviour, hide,
> > Till the storm of life is past;
> Safe into the haven guide,
> > O receive my soul at last.

211

The metaphors employed in these lines – *the nearer waters* swirling around, *the tempest* raging high, *the storm of life* and the eventual shelter of *the haven* – are not really so mixed as Gladstone made out. Here is Peter as he gets out of the boat to walk to Jesus crying out, 'Lord, let me come safely to the embrace of your arms while the tempest rages and the waves surge so close at hand! Guard me from danger till the storm has passed, and then bring me safely to land.'

The first two lines of the second stanza, which Gladstone also criticized,

> Other refuge have I none,
> Hangs my helpless soul on thee,

are simply asserting that in the storm of life Christ is the only secure *refuge*, the all-sufficient object of faith for the *helpless soul*. The last four lines of the stanza repeat this in even more explicit terms:

> All my trust on thee is stayed,
> All my help from thee I bring;
> Cover my defenceless head
> With the shadow of thy wing.

In the final stanzas there is a change of emphasis, and this is marked by a change of imagery. In the previous part of the hymn the picture is that of the believer looking to Christ for aid and protection amid the temptations and perils of the world. Now he is aware of a yet more deadly danger to be faced. His own nature is corrupt; his heart is sinful and treacherous; so his prayer now takes on another note, the note of penitence and contrition. In the presence of Christ he sees himself as he really is:

> Just and holy is thy name;
> I am all unrighteousness;
> False and full of sin I am,
> Thou art full of truth and grace.

When placed in a similar situation the apostle Peter prayed, 'Depart from me, for I am a sinful man, O Lord.' That may sound the logical thing to do, but it is not the logic of the gospel; for he who is *just and holy* is also *full of grace and truth*.

Therein lies our salvation: 'Grace and truth came through Jesus Christ' (John 1.17). Hence we can go on to say,

> Plenteous grace with thee is found,
> Grace to cover all my sin.

Grace is the love of God in action, love lavished on the unworthy and undeserving, love doing for the sinner what he could never do for himself. And God's grace is *plenteous*, grace abounding to the chief of sinners, as Bunyan, like St Paul before him, discovered (Romans 5.20; 1 Timothy 1.14,15). It is from that inexhaustible spring that *the healing streams* flow forth, not only to pardon but to sanctify, not only to quicken but to renew; and on that high note the hymn reaches its sublime conclusion:

> Thou of life the fountain art,
> Freely let me take of thee;
> Spring thou up within my heart,
> Rise to all eternity.

IV

Nothing more need be added as to the message and meaning of the hymn.[3] But it is interesting to see in these last four lines an illustration of Wesley's skilful use of biblical phraseology, which is so striking a feature of his hymns in general. Dr Henry Brett, the Methodist scholar, has pointed out that in the lines quoted there are allusions to the following passages of scripture.

> 'With thee is the fountain of life' (Psalm 36.9).
> 'Let him take the water of life freely' (Revelation 22.17).
> 'Spring up, O well; sing ye unto it' (Numbers 21.17).
> 'The water that I shall give him shall be in him a well of water springing up into everlasting life' (John 4.14).

The quotations are from the Authorized Version, which was the Bible of Wesley's day. They are sufficient to show how deeply his mind was steeped in the scriptures. The language of scripture was instinctively called to mind as he composed his hymns, which in many cases, as Dr Brett remarks, 'are a mere mosaic of biblical allusions'.[4]

Without pursuing the matter further, we may justly claim that this is one reason among others why the hymns of Charles Wesley have stood the test of time. They owe their literary inspiration to the scriptures; and impregnated as they are with the Word of God, they share in some measure the same enduring quality.

NOTES

1 *Bulletin* of The Hymn Society, October 1976.
2 *Sing with the Understanding*, p. 108.
3 For two other of Wesley's hymns, see chapters 2 and 31.
4 *The Hymns of Methodism* (Epworth Press, 1945), pp. 71–2.

28

THE PRAYING CHURCH

Jesus, where'er thy people meet

It is not often that a prayer meeting has to be moved to a larger building on account of the overflowing congregation. All too often numbers tend to dwindle rather than increase in such cases – at any rate in these days. But in the parish of Olney in Buckinghamshire, where John Newton was the minister-in-charge in the latter part of the eighteenth century, the weekly prayer meeting grew to such an extent that a change of venue had to be sought. And in this unusual circumstance lies the origin of our hymn.

I

In a letter written in April 1769 John Newton told a friend about the new arrangements.

> We are going to remove our prayer meeting to the great room in the Great House [a mansion in Olney belonging to Lord Dartmouth, the patron of the living]. It is a noble place, with a parlour behind it, and holds 130 people conveniently. Pray for us, that the Lord may be in our midst there, and may be pleased to add to our numbers.

It was for these parish prayer meetings that Newton and his

poet-friend William Cowper wrote the celebrated *Olney Hymns*. The book was published in 1779 with a view, so Newton said in his preface, to 'promoting the faith and comfort of sincere Christians'.

To mark the removal to the Great House both men wrote a special hymn. Newton's was the one beginning:

> Dear Shepherd of thy people, hear;
> Thy presence now display;
> As thou hast given a place for prayer,
> So give us hearts to pray.

Cowper's contribution was the hymn we are to consider in this chapter. To appreciate it fully it is important to bear in mind the occasion which called it forth; it then becomes all the more meaningful. But it need hardly be said that the hymn is suited to any occasion when the people of God meet together to pray. It is a hymn that combines devotional feeling and spiritual depth with sound biblical teaching. And, as we should expect from a man of Cowper's gifts, it is also marked by a touch of poetic beauty.

The hymn as he wrote it consisted of six stanzas. One of these is missing from all our hymnals, as it is too closely associated with the hymn's origin. Reference will be made to it in due course. Apart from this omission, the hymn as we now have it is exactly as Cowper wrote it, mercifully free from any editorial emendations or 'improvements'. 'On Opening a Place for Social Prayer' is the title given in the *Olney Hymns* to this and the hymn which Newton wrote for the same occasion. The first two stanzas have a direct bearing on the occasion. It is more than likely that some of the Olney folk were apprehensive about the change of meeting place. Some, remembering the good times they had enjoyed before, may even have resented it. Wouldn't everything be different in the larger and grander building? No! is the reassuring answer given by Cowper in his hymn. One thing, at any rate – and that the all-important thing – would be the same. They could be sure that the Lord would be present in their midst.

> Jesus, where'er thy people meet,
> There they behold thy mercy-seat;

216

Where'er they seek thee, thou art found,
And every place is hallowed ground.

The *mercy-seat* formed part of the furnishing of the Jewish tabernacle, and later of the temple. It was situated in the Holy of Holies, the innermost sanctuary which only the high priest was permitted to enter, and that but once a year on the solemn Day of Atonement. He entered it with the blood of sacrifice and sprinkled it on the mercy-seat, which thus symbolized the meeting place – the place of at-one-ment – between God and man.

What for the Jews was the prerogative of one man on one day of the year is now the privilege of all Christian people, at all times and in all places. The veil of the temple, shrouding the mercy-seat, has been torn in two (Mark 15.38). The way into the Holiest – the holy presence of God – is open to everyone by the blood of Jesus (Hebrews 10.19). This is the essential meaning of the phrase 'the priesthood of all believers'. All now have access by faith to the mercy-seat; and in the New Testament (Romans 3.25, *Gk.*) Jesus himself through his passion is the *hilasterion*, the mercy-seat, 'the place where God's forgiveness meets man's sin' (William Temple).

We must beware of attaching too much importance to sacred sites, consecrated buildings, and the like. The presence of God is not located in any one spot. Christianity has no holy places as such. The Lord is with his people *where'er* they *meet* and *where'er they seek* him, and as a result *every place is hallowed ground.*

II

The next stanza develops and explains this theme:

For thou, within no walls confined,
Inhabitest the humble mind;
Such ever bring thee where they come,
And going, take thee to their home.

217

Not holy places but holy people: that is the Christian concept when it comes to prayer and worship. Jesus made this plain when he spoke to the Samaritan woman at the well. She had raised with him the question of the correct place to worship God. The Samaritans had their temple on Mount Gerizim; the Jews had theirs in Jerusalem. Which was right?

Jesus answered by declaring the question to be totally irrelevant. He said:

> Believe me, the hour is coming when neither on this mountain nor in Jerusalem will you worship the Father. . . . The hour is coming, and now is, when the true worshippers will worship the Father in spirit and truth, for such the Father seeks to worship him. God is spirit, and those who worship him must worship in spirit and truth.

(John 4.21–4)

Jesus swept aside the rival claims of Gerizim and Jerusalem for the simple reason that, as a spiritual being, God does not dwell in temples made with hands. And that is what Cowper is saying in this hymn. God is *within no walls confined*, whether they be 'consecrated' walls or any other. He inhabits *the humble mind*, the hearts of his holy people. Such are the 'true worshippers' who bring the Lord's presence with them *where they come.* So where they worship matters little. How they worship matters everything: it must be spiritual and real. And what is true of worship in general is equally true of prayer as one of its basic elements.

In the third stanza the poet glances back again and remembers – perhaps a bit nostalgically – the old meeting place with all its precious memories, and prays,

> Dear Shepherd of thy chosen few,
> Thy former mercies here renew;
> Here to our waiting hearts proclaim
> The sweetness of thy saving name.

The title *Dear Shepherd* is found also in the companion hymn by John Newton, already quoted: 'Dear Shepherd of thy people, hear'. But in many hymnals the 'dear Shepherd' in this case is changed to 'great Shepherd', though it remains unaltered in Cowper's hymn. The ways of hymn-book editors are mysterious indeed. Is 'dear Shepherd' too familiar a title to apply to Jesus? Not everyone would agree. On the other hand biblical authority can be claimed for 'great Shepherd' (Hebrews 13.20).

The prayer is that the Lord's *chosen few* – a phrase which perhaps reflects Cowper's Calvinistic views – may experience his *former mercies* as they meet to pray. The recollection of past blessings was an encouragement to them to expect fresh ones in the future. So they come together with *waiting hearts*, ready to listen to what the Lord has to say to them as well as to make their petitions known to him.

III

This expectant spirit is reflected in the next stanza:

> Here may we prove the power of prayer
> To strengthen faith and sweeten care;
> To teach our faint desires to rise,
> And bring all heaven before our eyes.

The power of prayer! Here is a theme on which both Cowper and Newton delight to dwell in their hymns. They had proved the power of prayer in their own lives as well as in the work of the parish. In another of his hymns Cowper wrote the well-known lines:

> Restraining prayer, we cease to fight;
> Prayer makes the Christian's armour bright;
> And Satan trembles when he sees
> The weakest saint upon his knees.

In the stanza before us he gives an indication of what believing prayer can accomplish. It has power *to strengthen faith*, for prayer not only demands faith: it deepens faith. Prayer also has power to *sweeten care*, to relieve our anxiety as we cast our burdens on the Lord; power to lift up *our faint desires* to the giver of all grace; and power to enlarge our spiritual vision and *bring all heaven before our eyes*.

Next we come to the stanza omitted from the hymnals, with its reference to the immediate occasion of the hymn's composition, the removal of the prayer meeting to the Great House.

> Behold, at thy commanding word,
> We stretch the curtain and the cord;
> Come thou, and fill this wider space,
> And bless us with a large increase.

The second line, *We stretch the curtain and the cord*, is a reference to Isaiah 54.2: 'Enlarge the place of your tent, and let the curtains of your habitation be stretched out; hold not back, lengthen the cords'. Cowper was convinced that the move was being made at God's *commanding word*, and therefore he confidently asks the Lord to *fill this wider space* (the 'great room') with *a large increase* of numbers. That hope was shared by Newton, as stated in his letter quoted at the beginning of the chapter.

But it was not only for bigger numbers at the prayer meeting that these two men were praying. They had a deeper concern. They were looking to God for a spiritual revival throughout the parish:

> Lord, we are few, but thou art near,
> Nor short thine arm, nor deaf thine ear;
> O rend the heavens, come quickly down,
> And make a thousand hearts thine own!

The Church should always be outward looking, giving thought and prayer to those outside its fellowship as well as to those within. This final stanza reflects that attitude. Here petition gives place to intercession. The poet does not dwell on the fact that *we are few* or let it depress him. His faith is in God, whose presence is *near* and whose power is boundless. He recalls the words of scripture: 'Behold, the Lord's arm is not shortened, that it cannot save, or his ear dull, that it cannot hear' (Isaiah 59.1). He is assured that when the Church meets to pray the Lord is not far away but close at hand; not impotent but mighty to save; not deaf to his people's cry but ready to hear. So he is led to pray for a new and greater work of grace which will result in a multitude of people being won for Christ.

The praying church is the church that may expect such things to happen. Whether they who pray be many or few is not the main consideration. Let them but be of one heart and mind in their faith, and let them meet in the name of their Lord, and they will prove the truth of his promise:

> If two of you agree on earth about anything they ask, it will be done for them by my Father in heaven. For where two or three are gathered in my name, there am I in the midst of them.
>
> (Matthew 18.19,20)

29

COMING TO CHRIST

Just as I am, without one plea

CHARLOTTE ELLIOTT (1789–1871) is a good example of the devout and cultured Christian women who contributed to the vast output of Victorian hymnody. A member of a well-known evangelical and clerical family, she lived a long but comparatively uneventful life. This was due in large measure to the fact that at the age of thirty-two she suffered a serious illness, which left her an invalid for her last fifty years. It was a year or so after that illness that she passed through the spiritual crisis which resulted eventually in the writing of 'Just as I am'.

I

In 1822, when her father was vicar of Clapham, there came to stay at the house the Genevan evangelist, Dr César Malan. He closely observed the young woman who, despite her strong Christian background, appeared to him to be restless and unhappy. Had she found God's peace? Was she really a Christian? He decided he must ask her, and did so. She much resented his question, and more or less told him to mind his own business – which in fact was what he was doing, since he was an evangelist. However, he did not press her further but promised to pray for her.

The question stuck in Charlotte's mind. She could not evade the issue; and some days later she sought out Dr Malan, apologised for her rudeness, and admitted, 'I do want to come to Christ, but I don't know how to come.' 'Come to him just as you are,' was his answer. The simple words were enough. She came, just as she was, and found peace of heart. At once her life took on a new meaning. She dedicated herself to God's service and asked him to use her as he would, despite her weak state of health. Her sphere of service proved to be the writing of poetry, including hymns (she wrote about a hundred and fifty), and her various collections of verse had a wide circulation.

It was twelve years after her encounter with Dr Malan that she wrote the hymn for which she is now chiefly remembered. At this time she was living with her brother, the Revd Henry Venn Elliott, vicar of St Mary's, Brighton. He had launched an ambitious scheme to found a school for clergy daughters, and in order to raise money for this project a great bazaar was organized in the parish. Preparations were made on a wide scale; but when the actual day came Charlotte was too unwell to take any part, and she was left at home on her own while the rest of the household set off for the hall. A mood of deep depression overwhelmed her as she reflected on her helplessness and apparent uselessness. Had God cast her off? Was she no longer of any service to him?

As she struggled with her doubts and fears her mind went back over the past. She recalled the crisis of twelve years earlier when she had anxiously asked Dr Malan how to come to Christ. 'Come to him just as you are,' he had assured her, and her heart had found rest. That afternoon, as she lay weak and despondent on the drawing room sofa, the words took hold of her afresh. She reached for paper and pencil as, with no apparent effort, the words of the hymn 'Just as I am' flowed into her mind. She wrote them then and there for her own comfort. They have brought consolation and help to untold thousands down the years. Her clergyman brother stated near the end of his life, 'In the course of a long ministry

I hope I have been permitted to see some fruit of my labour, but I feel that far more has been done by a single hymn of my sister's.'

Like many another favourite, this is a hymn of an intensely personal and subjective character. It came from the heart and speaks to the heart. Because of its frequent use in evangelistic services we might be tempted to think of it as essentially a 'conversion' hymn, designed to express the penitent's initial response to the love of Christ. But that would be wrong. Charlotte Elliott wrote it, as we have seen, many years after her conversion. There is no such thing as a once-for-all coming to Jesus. We must come again and again, day after day, to renew our fellowship with him. It is noteworthy that the *English Hymnal* includes the hymn in its Holy Communion section. At every celebration of the sacrament not only does our Lord come to us: he also invites us to come once again to him.

II

Each stanza of the hymn begins and ends with the same pattern of words. The closing phrase is *O Lamb of God, I come*. It was John the Baptist who, pointing his disciples to Jesus, gave him this title: 'Behold, the Lamb of God, who takes away the sin of the world!' In the Bible the lamb is the symbol of sacrifice. Jesus is God's Lamb, the Lamb of infinite worth, who voluntarily gave himself for us to bear away our sin. It is to him, the Sin-bearer, we must come, each one of us, *just as I am*. This, the opening phrase of every stanza, is the dominant note of the entire hymn. From beginning to end it is designed to make clear how we are to come to Christ.

The first verse tells us, in effect, to come in simple faith:

> Just as I am, without one plea
> But that thy blood was shed for me,
> And that thou bidd'st me come to thee,
> O Lamb of God, I come.

We come to Jesus 'not trusting in our own righteousness' – and therefore *without one plea* connected with our own works or worthiness. We come relying wholly on what he has done for us and acknowledging, with penitence and gratitude, *thy blood was shed for me*. And we come in response to his own gracious invitation: *thou bidd'st me come to thee*. It is of the essence of faith that it looks away from self to Christ, rests on his saving work, and takes him at his word. In that spirit of simple trust we come to him, whether it be for the first or the hundredth time.

The next stanza urges us to come without delay:

> Just as I am, and waiting not
> To rid my soul of one dark blot,
> To thee, whose blood can cleanse each spot,
>   O Lamb of God, I come.

Some hymnals (for example, *AMR* 349 and *EH* 316) omit this second stanza. It ought not in our judgment to be left out, for it is very much part of the hymn and has two values. For one thing, it directs me to come to Jesus without delay, *and waiting not*; for however long I wait I cannot make myself more presentable to him or *rid my soul of one dark blot*. Secondly, it is here, in this stanza alone, that we face the fact of sin and our need of forgiveness. At the same time, of necessity, we face the fact of the cross as the remedy for sin, for we come to him *whose blood can cleanse each spot*. In writing like this Charlotte Elliott is not simply expressing (as one writer suggests) the old-fashioned and out-dated evangelical belief of her day. She is affirming the timeless and unchanging truth which lies at the very heart of the apostolic gospel.

Again, we must come to Jesus despite our feelings:

> Just as I am, though tossed about
> With many a conflict, many a doubt,
> Fightings within, and fears without,
>   O Lamb of God, I come.

These words reflect more clearly than any others the author's state of mind when she wrote the hymn. She was feeling weak and helpless, despondent and cast down in spirit, beset with

225

many a conflict, many a doubt. There were *fightings* going on *within* her soul and *fears* pressing upon her from *without.* She was experiencing in that dark hour something of what Bunyan in his immortal allegory represented as the Valley of Humiliation. What was she to do in such a situation? Recalling the wise words of her Evangelist she looked away from herself and, with all her conflicting emotions, came again to Jesus – just as she was. In him, and in his love, she found once more acceptance, assurance, and peace.

III

We look again at the hymn and learn to come to Jesus expectantly:

> Just as I am, poor, wretched, blind;
> Sight, riches, healing of the mind,
> Yea, all I need, in thee to find,
>   O Lamb of God, I come.

When we come to Jesus just as we are, we come *poor, wretched, blind* – like Bartimaeus in the Gospel story (Mark 10.46–52). And like Bartimaeus we find every need supplied. Such is the sufficiency of Christ that we can always come to him with an expectant faith. He gives us *sight*, enlightening the eyes of our hearts (Ephesians 1.18) and granting us spiritual understanding. *Riches* too are ours, riches beyond our reckoning, the unfathomable riches of Christ (Ephesians 3.8). And *healing of the mind*: freedom from the bondage of the past, release from present depression and fear, a calm and restful spirit as we face the unknown future.

We can also come to Jesus confidently:

> Just as I am, thou wilt receive,
> Wilt welcome, pardon, cleanse, relieve:
> Because thy promise I believe,
>   O Lamb of God, I come.

We need have no doubt as to how Jesus will *receive* us. He

will *welcome* us to himself and to his company, he will *pardon* our sins and failures, he will *cleanse* our hearts and imaginations from evil thoughts, he will *relieve* our every anxiety and care. Why? The writer of this hymn replies, *Because thy promise I believe.* And there is no doubt as to the promise Charlotte Elliott had in mind. At the head of the hymn when it was published she put the text, 'Him that cometh to me I will in no wise cast out' (John 6.37). Here is the reason why we may come to our Lord with confidence.

And when we come, we should come in full surrender:

> Just as I am (thy love unknown
> Has broken every barrier down),
> Now to be thine, yea, thine alone,
> O Lamb of God, I come.

The words in parenthesis are fundamental to the sense of this verse. It is the all-conquering love of Christ which captures our hearts and claims our lives. His is *love unknown* in the sense that it is love that surpasses human thought and knowledge (Ephesians 3.19). But it is that love which, however imperfectly grasped, *breaks every barrier down*: the barriers of pride, self-sufficiency, the fear of man, the love of the world – the things which all too often keep us from yielding ourselves wholly to Christ. It is only when the last of them has been demolished that we can make the act of total committal and say, *Now to be thine, yea, thine alone.* And we can add, in the words of the final and supplementary stanza, written and published some four years later than the rest of the hymn:

> Just as I am, of that free love
> The breadth, length, depth, and height to prove,
> Here for a season, then above,
> O Lamb of God, I come.

227

30

GENERAL THANKSGIVING

Now thank we all our God

MORE HYMNS have been written in German than in any other language. A good many years ago it was stated that the number cannot fall short of a hundred thousand. Yet this is not altogether surprising when it is remembered that hymn singing as we now know it had its beginning in Germany. To quote Julian: 'The church hymn, in the strict sense of the term, as *a popular lyric in praise of God to be sung by the congregation in public worship*, was born with the German Reformation, and most extensively cultivated ever since by the evangelical church in Germany.'

The vast wealth of German hymnody is, of course, largely unknown to us, and would be totally unknown were it not for the fact that many of the finest German hymns have been translated into English. For this we are primarily indebted to Catherine Winkworth (1829–78), who earned for herself the title 'the Queen of translators'. In all she wrote and published translations of nearly four hundred German hymns.

What sort of person was she?

I

Somebody once described her as a quiet middle-aged English lady who to her family was a lovable maiden aunt with an inexhaustible genius for inventing stories for children. But there was more to Catherine Winkworth than that. She was a highly cultured woman, a devout Christian, an expert linguist. Intellectually she was probably the most gifted and brilliant of our women hymn-writers.

Born in London, she spent most of her life in Manchester; but in her later years she moved to Bristol where she took a prominent part in pioneering and promoting the higher education of women. In her day the universities were not open to women. With others she helped in founding University College, Bristol – now the University of Bristol. She died suddenly of heart disease at the age of forty-eight. The memorial to her in Bristol Cathedral states that through her translations she 'opened a new source of light, consolation and strength in many thousand homes'.

Among her translations in common use today are 'Praise to the Lord, the Almighty', 'Christ the Lord is risen again', 'O Love, who formedst me to wear', 'Deck thyself, my soul, with gladness', and of course the hymn which now concerns us in this chapter, 'Now thank we all our God'.

This, the best known of all her hymns, is the English rendering of Martin Rinkart's *Nun danket alle Gott*. Rinkart (1586–1649) was a pastor in his native town of Eilenberg, Saxony, during the grim days of the Thirty Years War. The walled town became a refuge for homeless and hungry people from far and wide. The war inevitably brought famine and pestilence in its train, and when things were at their worst Rinkart – at the time the only clergyman in the place – sometimes conducted forty to fifty funerals a day. It is extraordinary that under such conditions he not only maintained his strong faith in God but also succeeded in writing a hymn which is dominated by the note of thanksgiving.

II

To begin with, it may help to take an overall look at the hymn and observe its general features. Four things may be noted.

First, while the hymn consists of three stanzas, the first two constitute the body of the work and were written independently of the third. The latter, a Trinitarian doxology, was added later to complete the hymn and give it a distinctive Christian character.

Next, it is worth mentioning that the first two stanzas were originally intended not for church use but as a grace to be sung after a meal by Rinkart's household. From such a simple domestic beginning has emerged a hymn which nowadays graces big national and state occasions.

The third thing to note, and the most important, is that these first two stanzas are a free paraphrase of Ecclesiasticus 50.22–4:

> Now bless the God of all,
>   who in every way does great things;
> who exalts our days from birth,
>   and deals with us according to his mercy.
> May he give us gladness of heart,
>   and grant that peace may be in our days in Israel,
>   as in the days of old.
> May he entrust to us his mercy!
>   And let him deliver us in our days!

It was in these words that Rinkart found his inspiration. He put the prose into verse, and more than two hundred years later Catherine Winkworth beautifully turned the German verse into English poetry.

The last point to observe is that the two opening stanzas form a complementary pair. The first is an act of praise and looks back to the past in grateful recognition of the goodness and providence of God. The second is an act of prayer and looks to the future, seeking grace and guidance for the days to come.

III

Now to examine the hymn in a little more detail. The first two lines set the keynote.

> Now thank we all our God,
> With heart and hands and voices,

The call is to *thank God* – *our* God – and it is addressed to us *all*, whoever we are, wherever we may be, whatever our circumstances. Such a call may not be easy to obey; but it is in line with St Paul's exhortation to give thanks 'always and for everything . . . in the name of our Lord Jesus Christ to God the Father' (Ephesians 5.20). Next, we are told how to give thanks: *with heart*, from the depth of our being; with *hands*, in our everyday deeds and activities; and with *voices*, in word and song, especially in our worship.

Why are we to give thanks? The answer is found in the remaining lines of this stanza. It is given first in general terms.

> Who wondrous things hath done,
> In whom his world rejoices;

Our thanksgiving here embraces all God's marvellous acts and is as wide as the world itself – *his world*, be it noted. But next it is expressed in more personal terms:

> Who from our mother's arms
> Hath blessed us on our way
> With countless gifts of love,
> And still is ours to-day.

God 'exalts our days from birth', as the Ecclesiasticus passage puts it (*cf.* Psalm 71.6). Whatever our age, however long or short a time we have lived, we can gratefully acknowledge that *from our mother's arms*, from life's very beginning, God has *blessed us on our way with countless gifts of love*. To 'count' our blessings, as we are often urged to do, is really an impossible task; it is like trying to count the stars. But the greatest blessing of all consists not in what God gives us but in what he is to us. He *still is ours today*. Yes, today! That brings the record up to date. However we are placed, whatever we have or lack, nothing can rob us of God or separate us from his love. And as he is ours, so we are his, now and for ever (Romans 8.38–9).

In the second stanza thanksgiving gives place to prayer.

The prayer echoes the request in Ecclesiasticus for gladness of heart and peaceful days, for God's mercy and deliverance.

O may this bounteous God
Through all our life be near us,
With ever joyful hearts
And blessed peace to cheer us;
And keep us in his grace,
And guide us when perplexed,
And free us from all ills
In this world and the next.

The prayer begins by asking that God, *this bounteous God*, for whose goodness and generosity we have given thanks in the previous stanza, may be with us *through all our life* – that is, through all our remaining days. For if he is *near us*, and we have the assurance of his presence, we can face whatever comes without anxiety or fear. Hence the prayer continues with the petition that he will *cheer us* with *ever joyful hearts* and *blessèd peace*. Here are two of God's richest gifts, worth more than anything that money can buy: hearts that are constantly filled with his joy and blessed with his peace.

In the second half of the stanza we ask God to do three other things for us. First, to *keep us in his grace*; for it is tragically possible to fall from grace, to be ensnared by evil and lose touch with God. Second, we ask him to *guide us when perplexed.* And who is not perplexed at times amid the conflicting voices of the world and the problems of life? To pray for God's guidance is as necessary as to pray for his grace.

The third and final petition is all-embracing and covers every contingency here and hereafter, for we ask God to *free us from all ills, in this world and the next.* There are plenty of ills from which we may well pray to be released, such as sickness, pain, sorrow, and loneliness. We may not be wholly spared such things in this world, nor should we expect to; but it is a comfort to know that we shall be free from them in the world to come, for we are assured that 'God will wipe away every tear, and death shall be no more, neither shall there be mourning nor crying nor pain any more' (Revelation 21.4, 5).

IV

The third stanza, as we have noted, takes the form of a Trinitarian doxology. Here we are singing, 'Glory be to the Father, and to the Son, and to the Holy Spirit; as it was in the beginning, is now, and ever shall be, world without end.'

> All praise and thanks to God
> The father now be given,
> The Son, and him who reigns
> With them in highest heaven,
> The one eternal God,
> Whom earth and heaven adore,
> For thus it was, is now,
> And shall be evermore.

The *him who reigns* with *the Father* and *the Son* is of course the Holy Spirit. To make this quite plain, the third and fourth lines sometimes have been re-phrased (as in *With One Voice* 14) to read

> The Son and Holy Ghost,
> One Lord in highest heaven.

This is a justifiable amendment, though it is unfortunate that 'Holy Ghost' has to be used instead of 'Holy Spirit' to suit the metre. Ghost and spirit are no longer interchangeable words in the English language, as they once were, and we ought to give up speaking of the third person of the Trinity as the Holy Ghost.

This apart, the words of the stanza call for no particular comment. But how splendid and majestic is this final outburst of adoring worship, giving *all praise and thanks to God* the Holy Trinity, *the one eternal God.* And how fittingly it rounds off this great hymn of general thanksgiving which, with its splendid tune by Rinkart's contemporary, Johann Crüger

(1598–1662), has been well described as one of the universal hymns: a hymn which transcends all national and denominational boundaries and is known and sung the whole world over.

31

CELEBRATING A CONVERSION

O for a thousand tongues to sing

EVER SINCE John Wesley's Collection of *Hymns for the Use of the People called Methodists*, published in 1780, 'O for a thousand tongues' has been the opening hymn in each edition of the *Methodist Hymn Book*. It well deserves that place of honour, not only because it is indisputably one of Charles Wesley's finest hymns but also because it is representative of his hymnody at its best. It rings with the notes of Christian praise, joy, and assurance. It magnifies the name of Jesus and the power of his atoning sacrifice. It affirms that the gospel of salvation is for all mankind. And it abounds in scriptural phrases and allusions. These are the things that characterize so many of the six thousand and more hymns that Wesley wrote. Perhaps it is not surprising that there is something special about this particular one, for it was written just a year after his evangelical conversion and published in 1740 under the title 'For the Anniversary Day of One's Conversion'.

I

We know from his journal that Charles Wesley dated his conversion from May 21, 1738. At the time he was just over thirty years of age, an ordained priest of the Church of England, an earnest, devout, scholarly man yet full of religious unrest. He was no sceptic or unbeliever. He accepted every word of the Bible, every article of the Church's creed. But while he was fully convinced of the truth of the gospel, he was conscious that its saving message had not become real in his own experience. He longed for the joyous assurance and radiant faith exhibited by his German Moravian friends. He knew that some vital element was missing in his spiritual life. And then quite suddenly he found it; or, as no doubt he himself would have wished to express it, the light of God broke upon him, and he became a new man in Christ.

It was on Whit Sunday when the transforming event took place, just three days before his brother John's conversion. Encouraged by the Moravians he had been studying Luther's commentary on the Epistle to the Galatians and had been deeply impressed by the text, 'The Son of God loved me, and gave himself for me' (Galatians 2.20). 'Dwell long,' Luther counselled, 'on this little word *me*.' Wesley did so, and on that memorable Whit Sunday received a truly pentecostal blessing. He laid hold of the promises of the gospel. He discovered what it meant to trust in Jesus personally for salvation. He entered into the full assurance of faith. In his own words, 'I now found myself at peace with God, and rejoiced in hope of loving Christ.'

A year passed, a year of energetic service in company with his brother as they engaged in the work of evangelism up and down the land; and then in May 1739, to celebrate the anniversary of his conversion, he wrote the hymn we know as 'O for a thousand tongues to sing'. But when Wesley wrote it, it did not begin like that. It was a long hymn of eighteen stanzas, beginning:

> Glory to God, and praise and love
>   Be ever, ever given,
> By saints below and saints above,
>   The Church in earth and heaven.

> On this glad day the glorious Sun
>   Of Righteousness arose;

On my benighted soul he shone,
And filled it with repose.

Here we catch the spirit of praise and thanksgiving which
filled the heart of this man as he looked back to the day when
for him all things became new. Two other early verses in the
hymn explain exactly what his conversion meant for him (the
italics are his own).

Then with my *heart* I first believed,
Believed with faith divine;
Power with the Holy Ghost received
To call the Saviour *mine*.

I felt my Lord's atoning blood
Close to my soul applied;
Me, me he loved – the Son of God:
For *me*, for *me* he died.

From this we can see that a number of elements entered into
Wesley's new-found experience. For one thing, it was a matter of the heart, not simply of the intellect. For another, the
faith he exercised was itself a divine gift, not a human acquisi-
tion. Yet again, it was faith that rested wholly on the Son of
God and his sacrificial death. And it was faith of a deeply
personal character: 'for *me*, for *me*, he died.'

The hymn as we now have it in our books comes from the
version reproduced by John Wesley in his *Collection* referred
to at the outset. He omitted Charles's first six stanzas and
started with the seventh ('O for a thousand tongues'), adding
nine others to make a hymn of ten stanzas in all. Modern
hymnals reduce it still further and print no more than five or
six. What appears to be the most generally accepted form of
the hymn, in six stanzas, is that given in *EH*, *CP* and *AHB*. In
this form the final stanza is 'My gracious Master and my God',
which actually came second in John Wesley's version; but
since it is a prayer, it provides a suitable and satisfactory
ending. An alternative (adopted by *CH*) is to finish with
Charles's original opening stanza, 'Glory to God, and praise
and love', as quoted above.

II

In looking at the stanzas we shall note their relation to Wesley's conversion experience, and also see in them an epitome of the gospel which lay at the heart of the Methodist revival.

> O for a thousand tongues to sing
> My great Redeemer's praise!
> The glories of my God and King,
> The triumphs of his grace!

The stanza makes a splendid opening to the hymn in its abbreviated form. Wesley longed for *a thousand tongues to sing* his *Redeemer's praise*, such was the debt of gratitude he felt he owed him. The phrase is said to have been suggested by a remark made by his Moravian friend and spiritual counsellor, Peter Böhler: 'If I had a thousand tongues, I would praise Christ with them all.' The words exactly matched Wesley's mood at the time he wrote this hymn and celebrated the anniversary of his conversion. He had originally written 'my *dear* Redeemer's praise', the 'dear' being a spontaneous expression of his love for his Lord. His brother John changed the word to 'great': he disapproved of anything of a sentimental nature in hymns.

The poet's heart continues to overflow with praise as he extols *the glories of* his *God and King* and celebrates *the triumphs of his grace.* In these latter words he was doubtless recalling how the grace of the Lord Jesus Christ had triumphed in his own life a year before, and in the lives of hundreds more in the intervening period. Hence the note of exultation is sustained in the next stanza:

> Jesus! the name that charms our fears,
> That bids our sorrows cease;
> 'Tis music in the sinner's ears,
> 'Tis life, and health, and peace.

The name of Jesus is a favourite theme with the hymn-writers. Here Wesley joins their company, as he does indeed in many of his hymns, and rejoices that *Jesus* is *the name that charms our fears* and *bids our sorrows cease.* He means, to put it plainly and positively, that the name of Jesus is the source of peace and joy to the believer. But take note of the word *charms*, an unusual word to use in this context. We associate a charm with the world of magic rather than with religious faith. We say that a thing works like a charm. Yes, says Wesley, and so it is with the name of Jesus. It has a magical, a supernatural effect in the lives of those who love him, banishing their fears and dispelling their sorrows. There is *music* in that name, the music of the gospel which sounds sweetly *in the sinner's ears* and echoes with the notes of *life, and health, and peace.*

But that is not all. In Christ there is more than joy and peace, life and health. Charles Wesley could testify from his own experience:

> He breaks the power of cancelled sin,
> He sets the prisoner free;
> His blood can make the foulest clean,
> His blood availed for me.

This stanza is unhappily – and surely mistakenly – omitted from *AMR*, for it strikes one of the characteristic notes of the Wesleys' preaching – the note of freedom. They were insistent that God in Christ not only forgives and justifies the sinner by faith, but that *he breaks the power of cancelled sin, he sets the prisoner free.* Yes, *free!* That is the keyword here. And the freedom is twofold. To use the imagery of the hymn, the 'prisoner' is both pronounced not guilty *and* released from his captivity. In Christian terms, and in relation to ourselves, it means, first, that the guilt of sin is 'cancelled' and we are free from the condemnation of the law through the cross of Christ (see Colossians 2.13,14). Secondly, it means that the power of sin is broken and we are free from the bondage of the 'flesh' through the liberating, life-giving Spirit of Christ at work within us. The best commentary on what Wesley is saying here is Romans 8.1–17, with its wealth of teaching on the Holy Spirit and the life of sanctification.

There is a third freedom which Christ offers: freedom from the filth or defilement of sin. *His blood can wash the foulest clean.* Wesley knew this to be true from his work as an evangelist. He had not confined his preaching to the churchy, respectable people of his day. He had gone with the gospel of redeeming love among the outcasts of society, the profligates, the drunkards, the fallen, the inmates of Newgate gaol; and in the lives of such people he had witnessed amazing triumphs of grace, just as St Paul did at Corinth centuries earlier (see 1 Corinthians 6.9–11). Wesley knew well the power of the blood of Jesus to cleanse from sin and all unrighteousness (1 John 1.7–10): knew it not only because of what he had seen happen to other people but because of what he had experienced in his own life: *his blood availed for me.*

III

In the next two stanzas the poet illustrates the transforming power of the gospel by reference to the reply Jesus gave to the inquiry of John the Baptist: 'Are you he that should come, or are we to look for another?' John was seeking some convincing evidence that Jesus really was the promised Messiah. The Lord readily supplied that evidence. He pointed out to John's messengers that his miraculous works vindicated his claims; he was doing precisely what Isaiah foretold the 'Coming One' would accomplish (see, e.g., Isaiah 35.4,5; 61.1):

> Go and tell John what you hear and see: the blind receive their sight and the lame walk, lepers are cleansed and the deaf hear, and the dead are raised up, and the poor have good news preached to them.
>
> (Matthew 11.4,5)

Wesley paraphrases the Lord's words and at the same time gives them a spiritual interpretation:

> He speaks – and listening to his voice
>   New life the dead receive;
> The mournful, broken hearts rejoice,
>   The humble poor believe.

240

> Hear him, ye deaf; his praise, ye dumb,
> Your loosened tongues employ;
> Ye blind, behold your Saviour come,
> And leap, ye lame, for joy.

Most of the language of these stanzas has its counterpart in the message of Jesus to John and the Isaiah quotations. The first two lines of the fourth stanza about the *new life* which *the dead receive* come from another source: the words of Jesus in John 5.25, 'The hour is coming, and now is, when the dead will hear the voice of the Son of God, and those who hear will live.' The next two lines, about *the broken, mournful hearts* and *the humble poor*, are based on Isaiah 61.1: 'The Lord has anointed me to preach good tidings to the poor, he has sent me to heal the broken hearted.' Wesley's metrical rendering of these two passages is skilfully made and requires no comment.

The other stanza is derived entirely from Isaiah 35.5,6, with its references to *the deaf* whose ears shall be unstopped, *the dumb* whose tongues shall sing for joy, *the blind* whose eyes shall be opened, and the *lame* man who shall *leap* like a hart. These works of healing were performed literally by Jesus in the course of his messianic ministry. They are repeated and reproduced after a spiritual fashion in the lives of those who now commit themselves to him in faith. Their ears are opened to his word, their lips show forth his praise, their eyes behold his glory, and their feet walk rejoicingly in his way.

The final stanza, as we have it in most of our hymnals, is a prayer that we who have received the good news of Christ may share it far and wide:

> My gracious Master, and my God,
> Assist me to proclaim,
> To spread through all the earth abroad
> The honours of thy name.

We note that our Lord is addressed not only as *my gracious Master* but as *my God*, for Wesley had no doubts about the deity of Jesus; and the petition is for divine assistance to *proclaim* the gospel of Christ, and so *to spread the honours of*

241

his name. Where? How far? *Through all the earth abroad*, says the hymn, and the answer is significant. One of the dogmatic notes in the theology of the Wesleys was that of 'universal redemption'. They firmly rejected the Calvinistic idea of a limited atonement, as though the cross availed only for the 'elect'. They were emphatic that Christ died for the sins of the whole world: that he was, as a line from another hymn puts it, 'the general Saviour of mankind'. The stanza with which the hymn ends in the *Methodist Hymn Book* reinforces this teaching:

> See all your sins on Jesus laid:
> The Lamb of God was slain,
> His soul was once an offering made
> For every soul of man.

If that is true, it follows that the good news must be made known throughout the world, that all may know Christ died for all, and thousands more tongues may sing their great Redeemer's praise.

32

A SYMPHONY OF PRAISE

Praise, my soul, the King of heaven

HENRY FRANCIS Lyte is not usually ranked among the more distinguished hymn-writers. In many books on hymnody he receives but scant attention, and in all likelihood his name is not familiar to the ordinary churchgoer. Nevertheless the fact remains that this humble and little known evangelical clergyman was the author of two of the most popular hymns in the English language: 'Praise, my soul, the King of heaven' and 'Abide with me'.[1]

I

The son of English parents, Lyte was born in Scotland in 1793 but spent his early life in Ireland. He graduated at Trinity College, Dublin, where for three successive years he won the prize for an English poem. A year or two after his ordination he moved to England and became assistant curate in the parish of Marazion, Cornwall. Here, as a result of attending the death-bed of a neighbouring clergyman, he experienced a deep evangelical conversion which gave a new direction to his ministry and preaching. After serving a number of short curacies in the West country he was appointed in 1823 to the living of Lower Brixham, then a small Devonshire fishing village, where he remained for the last twenty-four years of his life.

During that time he wrote a considerable number of hymns. Some of these were collected in a book called *The Spirit of the Psalms*, published in 1834. The title of the book is significant. The hymns it contained were not simply paraphrases, like the metrical psalms of earlier times. Lyte was concerned with the spirit rather than the letter of the psalms he selected: to convey their essential message and to express it in a poetical form suitable for congregational singing.

Among the hymns he produced in this way were 'God of mercy, God of grace', his version of Psalm 67, and 'Pleasant are thy courts above', a rendering of Psalm 84. But his masterpiece undoubtedly was his treatment of Psalm 103 in 'Praise, my soul, the King of heaven'.

In its original form the hymn comprised five stanzas, not just the four with which many of us are familiar. Some Free Church hymnals (e.g. *CP* 18; *BHB* 23) reproduce all five. Another point to be noted is that in the fifth line of each stanza Lyte wrote 'Praise him! Praise him!', as in the two books just mentioned and also in *EH* 470. The editors of *Hymns Ancient and Modern* changed the twofold 'Praise him!' to 'Alleluia!' and this use has been adopted by some other hymnals. The meaning in either case is the same, *Alleluia* representing the Hebrew form of 'Praise the Lord'.

The hymn magnificently expresses the spirit of the psalm on which it is based. The one hundred and third psalm as a whole may be regarded as a symphony of praise – and a symphony in three movements. The praise begins on the personal level; then it takes on a corporate or churchly character; and finally it expands to cosmic dimensions.

II

The first stanza covers the first five verses of the psalm, which

will be quoted throughout in the Prayer Book version as being
that with which Lyte was probably most familiar.

> Praise the Lord, O my soul: and all that is within me praise
> his holy Name.
> Praise the Lord, O my soul: and forget not all his benefits;
> Who forgiveth all thy sin: and healeth all thine infirmities;
> Who saveth thy life from destruction: and crowneth thee
> with mercy and loving-kindness;
> Who satisfieth thy mouth with good things: making thee
> young and lusty as an eagle.

The praise here is personal, and the hymn accordingly begins
on this note:

> Praise, my soul, the King of heaven,
>   To his feet thy tribute bring;
> Ransomed, healed, restored, forgiven,
>   Who like me his praise should sing?

My soul must praise the Lord, my soul being 'all that is
within me', heart and mind and will. I myself as an individual
matter to God and must bring my own grateful *tribute* to *the
King of heaven*. And there is a reason why I am compelled to
do this. My soul must praise the Lord because of all that he
has done for me, because of 'all his benefits'.

Ransomed, healed, restored, forgiven – these are the
benefits referred to, and they are epitomized in a memorable
line. How much four words can say! In picture language they
succinctly express the Christian experience of salvation on the
personal level.

What has the Lord done for my soul?

He has *ransomed* me: that is, rescued and liberated me at
great cost, saved me from the power of sin and death.

He has *healed* me: made me whole, sanctified me, cured my
soul's ills and infirmities.

He has *restored* me: renewed my spiritual vigour and vital-
ity, made me 'young and lusty as an eagle'.

He has *forgiven* me: pardoned, accepted, acquitted me, so
that I am justified freely by his grace through the redemption
which is in Christ Jesus.

If this is true in my own experience, how can I forget all

God's benefits? And if I recall but a fraction of them – then, *who like me his praise should sing?*

> Praise him! Praise him!
> Praise the everlasting King.

The next stanza begins:

> Praise him for his grace and favour
> To our fathers in distress.

Who were they – *our fathers in distress*? The psalm supplies the answer. At verse 6 the writer turns his thoughts from what the Lord has done for him personally to what he has done for Israel, his own nation. And in that connection he calls to mind that critical turning-point in Jewish history, the exodus, and the deliverance God wrought for his afflicted people.

> The Lord executeth righteousness and judgement: for all them that are oppressed with wrong.
> He shewed his ways unto Moses: his works unto the children of Israel.
>
> (vv. 6, 7)

The mention of *Moses* identifies the situation. In Egypt the Israelites are 'oppressed with wrong'. God raises up his servant and sends him to be their saviour. The people witness his mighty works, both in judgment and grace, and they are emancipated. This is the picture the psalmist has in mind as he recalls God's redeeming mercy to Israel. To look back in history and remember what the Lord has done for his Church in times of oppression and persecution is always a salutary exercise, for he is unchanging in *his grace and favour*. That being so,

> Praise him, still the same for ever,
> Slow to chide and swift to bless.

The expression *slow to chide* is an echo of the next part of the psalm:

> The Lord is full of compassion and mercy: long-suffering, and of great goodness.
> He will not alway be chiding: neither keepeth he his anger for ever.
>
> (vv. 8, 9)

To 'chide' has the meaning here of to contend, to accuse, to keep up a quarrel. But that is not God's way with his people. He does not deal with them after their sins, or reward them according to their wickedness (v. 10). And just as he is slow to chide, so is he *swift to bless*, because he is 'full of compassion and mercy'. His steadfast love is higher than the heavens towards those who fear him, and he removes our transgressions from us as far as the east is from the west (vv.11, 12). This also calls for praise:

> Praise him! Praise him!
> Glorious in his faithfulness.

III

The psalm continues:

> Yea, like as a father pitieth his own children: even so is the Lord merciful unto them that fear him.
> For he knoweth whereof we are made: he remembereth that we are but dust.
>
> (vv.13,14)

This surely is one of the tenderest passages in the psalms, if not in the whole of the Old Testament. And Lyte beautifully matches its language and spirit in his third stanza:

> Father-like he tends and spares us,
> Well our feeble frame he knows;
> In his hands he gently bears us,
> Rescues us from all our foes.

Father-like he tends and spares us. The thought of the Fatherhood of God is not often found in the Old Testament. God is conceived rather as Creator, King and Judge – and so of course he is. But he is something more, as Jesus made clear. It was he who unveiled the ultimate truth about God and taught us to think of him as Father, and as such to trust in him and pray to him. We now accept the Fatherhood of God as a commonplace; but we should never cease to regard it as a marvellous revelation, an amazing mercy, that the Maker of heaven and earth, transcendent in his glory, majesty, holiness and power, is also our loving Father who *tends and spares us* and *knows well our feeble frame*. So again we must sing:

> Praise him! Praise him!
> Widely as his mercy flows.

The psalm goes on to reflect upon the twin truths of man's mortality and God's eternity:

> The days of man are but as grass; for he flourisheth as a flower of the field.
> For as soon as the wind goeth over it, it is gone: and the place thereof shall know it no more.
> But the merciful goodness of the Lord endureth for ever and ever upon them that fear him: and his righteousness upon children's children.
>
> (vv. 15–17)

It is at this point that the stanza which is missing from some of our hymnals fits in:

> Frail as summer's flower we flourish,
> Blows the wind, and it is gone;
> But while mortals rise and perish
> God endures unchanging on:
> Praise him! Praise him!
> Praise the high Eternal One.

'Fading life, eternal love' is how Derek Kidner in his commentary[2] sums up the thought expressed in this part of the psalm. The fading life is ours: *frail as summer's flower we flourish*. The eternal love is God's, who *endures unchanging on*. Our life ends; his love never does. And because that is true, because God's love for us never ends, we may be sure that our life fades and dies only as far as this world is concerned. In the world beyond we shall continue to live in the unending and unchanging love of the Father; or, to keep to the metaphor of the psalm, the flower that fades on earth blooms again in the Paradise of God.

IV

In the final section of the psalm the horizon widens still farther:

> The Lord hath prepared his seat in heaven: and his kingdom ruleth over all.
>
> O praise the Lord, ye angels of his, ye that excel in strength: ye that fulfil his commandments, and hearken unto the voice of his words.
>
> O praise the Lord, all ye his hosts: ye servants of his that do his pleasure.
>
> O speak good of the Lord, all ye works of his, in all places of his dominion: praise thou the Lord, O my soul.
>
> (vv. 19–22)

The Lord is King! His throne is established in the heavens and his sovereignty embraces the entire universe. On this triumphant note the psalm reaches its conclusion. Hence the praise now is on a cosmic scale. Everything in creation is called upon to swell the chorus, including the angelic hosts that serve God's will; 'and I too,' says the psalmist, as he ends his song in the same way that he began it: 'praise thou the Lord, O my soul!'

Lyte superbly catches the spirit of all this in his final stanza:

> Angels, help us to adore him,
> Ye behold him face to face;
> Sun and moon, bow down before him;
> Dwellers all in time and space:
> Praise him! Praise him!
> Praise with us the God of grace.

Like the end of the psalm, this verse has an all-embracing character. It broadens our vision of God's creation. It lifts us out of our narrow selves. It helps us to see that our own praise is only a tiny part of the whole. Everybody and everything must pay homage to the Lord: the *angels* who *behold* his *face* in heaven; the created order above and around us, including *sun and moon*; and the whole of humanity, *all* who dwell *in time and space*.

That last includes every one of us. Our own praise must not be missing, poor and unworthy though it may be. We all have our own individual part to play, a part which each alone *can* play and without which the symphony would be incomplete. So in the end we too must say,

> My soul, bear thou thy part,
> Triumph in God above,
> And with a well-tuned heart
> Sing thou the songs of love!
> Let all thy days
> Till life shall end,
> Whate'er he send,
> Be filled with praise.[3]

NOTES
1 For this hymn see chapter 21.
2 Tyndale Old Testament Commentaries: *Psalms 73–150* (IVP, 1975), p. 366.
3 The final stanza, by J. H. Gurney (1802–62), of 'Ye holy angels bright'.

33

THE SINGING CHURCH

Songs of praise the angels sang

A NAME TO be honoured in the story of English hymnody is that of James Montgomery. Hymn lovers are indebted to him for two reasons. First and foremost he was a distinguished and gifted hymn-writer. His work at best bears comparison with that of Watts and Wesley, and indeed he stands next in succession to them in the line of English hymn writing. Most modern hymnals contain upwards of a dozen of his compositions (*Congregational Praise* has twenty-two) and they include such favourites as 'Angels from the realms of glory', 'Hail to the Lord's Anointed', 'Lord, teach us how to pray aright', 'For ever with the Lord', and 'Stand up and bless the Lord' – apart from the hymn we are to deal with in this chapter. Erik Routley has described him as 'without question ... the greatest of Christian lay hymn-writers.'[1]

But Montgomery was not only a writer of hymns. He was also a hymnologist. Canon John Ellerton (himself a noted hymn-writer) described him as 'our first hymnologist; the first Englishman who collected and criticized hymns, and who made people ... understand something of what a hymn meant, and what it ought to be.' By his painstaking work of selecting, editing and revising hymns for publication – and discarding those which were unworthy or unsuitable – Montgomery did much to raise the standard of hymnody in his day and to influence its future development.

I

We shall return to his hymns in a moment, but at this point it would be good to find out something about their author. Born in Scotland in 1771, James Montgomery was the son of a Scottish minister of Irish extraction. While his parents were serving as missionaries to the West Indies he was educated at a Moravian settlement in Yorkshire with a view to entering the ministry of the Moravian Church. This however did not prove to be his vocation, and after trying his hand at various jobs he settled down at length as assistant to a Sheffield bookseller and publisher. He quickly developed his literary gifts and at the age of twenty-three became editor of the *Sheffield Iris*, a journal with a strongly radical flavour. He was twice imprisoned for expressing his political views too freely.

An ardent evangelical – and an enthusiast for overseas missions and the work of the Bible Society – he was nevertheless a man of broad sympathies and ecumenical spirit. This is reflected in his church connections. He was in turn Presbyterian, Moravian and Methodist, while in his later years he became an Anglican, drawn to St George's church, Sheffield, by his close friendship with its vicar, William Mercer. Like Montgomery, Dr Mercer was also a writer of hymns, and with the help of his friend he did much to encourage the introduction of hymn singing into the Church of England.

Montgomery lived to the age of eighty-two and was a voluminous writer; but his literary works in general, including his large number of poems, have been forgotten. His hymns live on. He wrote about three hundred and fifty in all, and they are notable for their consistency of quality, their unity of theme, and their suitability of form for their subject. Their over-all excellence is due not only to their author's very considerable poetical powers but to the care he gave to their composition and the skilful use he made of the scriptures.

The hymn we have chosen to look at, 'Songs of praise the angels sang', is characteristic of Montgomery's work and illustrates the features to which we have drawn attention. It makes plentiful use of the Bible; it keeps to a definite theme; it has a clear shape and design; and it is good poetry. Its theme is epitomized in the phrase 'songs of praise' which runs all through the hymn. It occurs at least once in every stanza, ten times in all, and its repetition gives strength and unity to the hymn. It is a simple but expressive phrase, recalling St Augustine's definition of a hymn:

> It is a song with praise of God. If you praise God and sing not, you utter no hymn. If you sing and praise not God, you utter no hymn. A hymn then contains these three things: song, and praise, and that of God.

Regarding the shape of the hymn, the first three stanzas show how the great crises of biblical history – creation, redemption, judgment – are celebrated by songs of praise, while the last three apply the principle of praise to the life and worship of the Church both on earth and in heaven. From this it will be clear that the hymn consists of six stanzas; but in some hymnals (e.g. *AMR* 369, *EH* 481) Montgomery's final stanza is omitted and replaced by a trinitarian doxology:

> Hymns of glory, songs of praise,
> Father, unto thee we raise;
> Jesu, glory unto thee,
> With the Spirit, ever be.

This was apparently the work of Sir Henry Baker when he included the hymn in the first edition of *Hymns Ancient and Modern*, 1861. In our study we shall keep to Montgomery.

II

> Songs of praise the angels sang,
> Heaven with alleluias rang,
> When creation was begun,
> When God spake and it was done.

253

This first stanza is not exactly as Montgomery wrote it. In his own version the last two lines ran:

> When Jehovah's work begun,
> When he spake and it was done.

The alteration, probably also made by the editors of *Hymns Ancient and Modern*, must be regarded as an improvement. It not only makes the meaning more explicit; it also removes a grammatical infelicity. When did Jehovah's work begin? The answer is in the opening words of the Bible: 'In the beginning God created the heavens and the earth'. So the reference is to the work of creation, *when God spake and it was done.* His word has creative energy. Montgomery presumably had in mind Psalm 33.6,9: 'By the word of the Lord the heavens were created, and all their host by the breath of his mouth. . . . For he spoke, and it came to be; he commanded, and it stood fast.'

When this happened, *Songs of praise the angels sang.* The allusion here is clearly to the magnificent Old Testament passage where Job is dramatically confronted with the marvels of God's work in creation 'when the morning stars sang together, and all the sons of God shouted for joy' (Job 38.7). The sons of God here are commonly taken to be the angelic hosts.

The poet passes from the crisis of creation to the crisis of redemption:

> Songs of praise awoke the morn
> When the Prince of Peace was born;
> Songs of praise arose when he
> Captive led captivity.

When Montgomery published the hymn in his *Christian Psalmist and Original Hymns*, 1825, he gave it the title of 'Glory to God in the Highest'. Here then is the multitude of the heavenly host glorifying God with their *songs of praise* on the first Christmas Day *when the Prince of Peace was born.* The coming of Christ is welcomed by the choir of angels because it is 'good tidings of great joy' to the Church and to all mankind. Christianity began in an outburst of song, and

Gloria in excelsis Deo is ever the keynote of the Church's worship.

The Incarnation, however, is not the whole gospel. The purpose of Christ's coming was to save men from their sins, to break the power of evil, to overcome death – and this redeeming work he accomplished by his cross and resurrection, crowned by his exaltation 'when he ascended on high' and 'led a host of captives' (Ephesians 4.8, quoting Psalm 68.18). Here is another theme for *songs of praise* on the part of both men and angels, *when he captive led captivity*. The apostle takes the words of the ancient psalm, with their picture of the victorious king returning from battle with his captives in his train, and applies them to the conquering Christ, now exalted to the throne of heaven, his work completed, his conflict won. This indeed calls for songs of praise. 'Lift up your heads, O ye gates! and be lifted up, ye everlasting doors, that the King of Glory may come in!' (Psalm 24.8).

Third, there is the crisis of Judgment.

> Heaven and earth must pass away,
> Songs of praise shall crown that day;
> God will make new heavens and earth,
> Songs of praise shall hail their birth.

Heaven and earth must pass away. Jesus himself said something very like that (Mark 13.31). In fact, references to the dissolution of heaven and earth and to the 'winding up' of the present created order are scattered throughout the Bible (e.g. Psalm 102.25–7; Isaiah 51.6; 2 Peter 3.10). But the most impressive language is found in the book of Revelation, with its solemn and majestic imagery of the Last Judgment. 'Then I saw a great white throne and the One who sat upon it; from his presence earth and heaven vanished away, and no place was left for them' (Revelation 20.11 NEB). Mention of the 'throne' is a reminder of the sovereignty of God – one of the dominant notes of the Apocalypse, and certainly a theme for *songs of praise*. 'Hallelujah! For the Lord our God the Almighty reigns. Let us rejoice and exult and give him the glory' (Revelation 19.7).

God will make new heavens and earth, for his new creation

takes the place of the old. 'Then I saw a new heaven and a new earth, for the first heaven and the first earth had passed away. . . . And I saw the holy city, new Jerusalem, coming down out of heaven from God. . . . And he who sat on the throne said, Behold, I make all things new" ' (Revelation 21.1,2,5). *Songs of praise shall hail their birth* – the birth of God's new order in which 'there shall be an end to death and mourning and crying and pain; for the old order has passed away' (v.4).

III

The last three stanzas continue the theme of 'songs of praise', but they do so on a different level, relating it to the life of mankind and the worship of the Church.

> And shall man alone be dumb
> Till that glorious kingdom come?
> No! the Church delights to raise
> Psalms and hymns and songs of praise.

The example of the heavenly hosts as they pour out their ceaseless praise to God presents a challenge to humanity. *Will man alone be dumb?* Can he keep silent while he awaits the coming of God's glorious kingdom of righteousness and peace and joy? The question is answered by a decisive *No!* – and for a very good reason: *the Church delights* to emulate the angels and give glory to God in the highest, and it does so in *psalms and hymns and songs of praise.*

From the beginning this has been characteristic of the Church. It has always been a singing Church. St Paul's repeated exhortation to the early Christians to join in singing 'psalms and hymns and spiritual songs' (Ephesians 5.19; Colossians 3.16) throws an interesting light on the worship of the primitive church. The 'psalms' doubtless represent the heritage of the past: the Hebrew psalmody which was taken over by the Christian church from the Jewish church and which formed a bond of unity between the people of the new covenant and those of the old. 'Hymns' we may take to represent the fresh element in Christian worship: hymns newly written to show forth the praises of Christ and celebrate the mysteries of the gospel. Here we glimpse the beginnings of the great treasury of hymnody which has so abundantly enriched the Church's praise down the centuries. 'Spiritual songs' is a more general expression and would include any canticles of a spiritual nature, such as the songs found in the beginning of St Luke's Gospel, in the Epistles (e.g. Ephesians 5.14; Philippians 2.6–11; 1 Timothy 3.16), and in the Apocalypse (e.g. Revelation 5.9–10; 11.17–18; 15.3–4).

Such was the place of 'songs of praise' in church life in the apostolic age. The position has not altered today:

> Saints below, with heart and voice,
> Still in songs of praise rejoice,
> Learning here, by faith and love,
> Songs of praise to sing above.

God's *saints* – by which is meant here, as in the New Testament, all believers who live up to their profession – *still in songs of praise rejoice.* Seldom do they meet together in worship without raising their voices in song, whether it be in the splendour of an ancient cathedral or a great parish church, or in the plainer setting of a village chapel, a Salvation Army citadel, or a Brethren assembly. All such singing is equally acceptable to God provided it be *with heart and voice* – and not with the voice alone. The heart of praise is the praise of the heart. So St Paul wrote to the Ephesians: 'Sing and make music in your hearts to the Lord' (5.19), and to the Colossians, 'Sing thankfully in your hearts to God' (3.16).

Montgomery suggests that the singing of Christians on earth is a fit prelude to, and preparation for, the worship of heaven: they are *learning here, by faith and love, songs of praise to sing above.* One thing the scriptures seem to make clear about heaven is that it is a place of song. If that is so, we would surely be well advised to get into practice here and now.

One thing further is noted about the singing of the saints:

> Borne upon their latest breath,
> Songs of praise shall conquer death;
> Then, amidst eternal joy,
> Songs of praise their powers employ.

Here is the final stanza with which Montgomery completed his hymn. The doxology substituted for it in some hymnals is by no means inappropriate or unsuitable. On the other hand the author's own verse finishes the hymn according to the pattern he had planned. It is clear that he wished to round off his hymn by affirming that the ministry of song never ceases for the people of God. They sing to God's glory all through their earthly days. They meet their end and *conquer death* with *songs of praise* on their lips. And finally, in the world to come, *amidst eternal joy*, they continue to sing, blending their voices with angels and archangels and all the company of heaven, crying,

> Holy, holy, holy, is the Lord God Almighty,
> who was, and is, and is to come!

NOTE
1 *Hymns and Human Life*, p.124.

258

34

A CALL TO ARMS

Stand up, stand up for Jesus

OF THE many hymns that came to Britain from America in the latter half of the last century, few made a bigger impact than 'Stand up, stand up for Jesus'. Almost at once it became immensely popular. Perhaps this was due to its robust and stirring character, so different from many of the subjective and sentimental Victorian hymns then in vogue. It has retained its popularity for well over a century, and with its vigorous call to arms it still has a message for the Church today.

Behind the hymn there lies a story, or more truly a tragedy; yet if it had not been for the tragedy the hymn would never have been written.

I

The story takes us back to the city of Philadelphia in the great revival of 1858. One of the most influential forces in the city at that time was the Revd Dudley A. Tyng, a young Episcopalian minister who was rector of the Church of the Epiphany. A powerful preacher, he courageously opposed the iniquitous slave trade which was still tolerated then in the

USA, even by many of the churches. His outspoken sermons on the subject gave offence to some of the wealthy members of the congregation, themselves slave owners, with the result that he was compelled to resign. But his friends in the city who shared his convictions determined that his voice should not be silenced. They hired for him the largest hall in the city, and there, in those stirring days of spiritual awakening, he held regular services and preached to large congregations.

During this time he conducted a mission for young men under the auspices of the YMCA. On a certain Sunday evening he preached to a crowd of five thousand from the text, 'Come now, ye that are men, and serve the Lord' (Exodus 10.11). Hundreds responded to his call and signified their decision to enlist in the service of Christ.

It proved to be Dudley Tyng's last sermon. A few days later he met with a terrible and fatal accident. Watching a mule at work on a winnower, he approached too near the animal to pat its neck, so that his sleeve got caught in the machinery. At once his arm was wrenched from its socket. He died shortly afterwards from the injury and shock. On his deathbed he asked his friend George Duffield, a Presbyterian minister in the city, to preach to the young men at the YMCA service the following Sunday. Dr Duffield agreed and asked, 'What message shall I send them from you?'

'Tell them to stand up for Jesus,' was the reply.

Duffield preached the funeral sermon from Ephesians 6.14 ('Stand, therefore, having your loins girt about with truth'), and after referring to his friend's dying message he concluded by reading some verses he had written, inspired by that message. Those verses were the hymn 'Stand up, stand up for Jesus'.

As far as George Duffield was concerned, that was the end of the matter. He never dreamt that his verses would be heard of again. But his Sunday school superintendent asked for a copy of the words and had them printed on a leaflet, for the children to sing. A stray copy found its way into a church newspaper, where it caught the eye of the editor of a new American hymn-book. Set to the music of a popular song called *Morning Light*, the verses were soon being sung in churches all over America, and not long afterwards they met with an enthusiastic welcome in this country.

When Duffield's poem was adopted as a hymn one of the original verses was rightly omitted. It contained a reference to the tragic circumstances in which the words had been written and the death of Dudley Tyng:

> Stand up, stand up for Jesus!
>   Each soldier to his post;
> Close up the broken column,
>   And shout through all the host!
> Make good the loss so heavy
>   In those that still remain,
> And prove to all around you
>   That death itself is gain.

II

The theme of the hymn is, clearly enough, the holy war: the battle in which all Christians are called to engage as soldiers of the cross. The theme is a familiar one on the part of hymn-writers. Charles Wesley's 'Soldiers of Christ, arise' is the finest example and like the present hymn is based to a large extent on the picture of the Christian soldier in Ephesians 6.10–20. Reference will be made to this in the course of our study.

The first stanza is introductory. In striking and powerful words the call to arms sounds out and epitomizes the message of the entire hymn.

> Stand up, stand up for Jesus,
>   Ye soldiers of the Cross!
> Lift high his royal banner,
>   It must not suffer loss.
> From victory unto victory
>   His army he shall lead,
> Till every foe is vanquished,
>   And Christ is Lord indeed.

There is both challenge and comfort in these lines. The challenge, addressed to all who have enlisted as *soldiers of the Cross*, is boldly to maintain the cause of Christ and *lift high his royal banner* before the world. This is what it means to *stand up for Jesus*, in accordance with Dudley Tyng's dying message; and the exhortation is repeated at the beginning of each stanza. The comfort to be found here, expressed in the latter half of the verse, is the assurance that the final issue of the war is not in doubt. Christ is leading *his army* to ultimate triumph, *from victory unto victory*; and the conflict will not end till *every foe is vanquished* and every tongue confesses that *Christ is Lord indeed* (Philippians 2.11).

Meanwhile, we must be on the alert and recognize the strenuous character of the fight in which our Lord calls us to take up arms:

> Stand up, stand up for Jesus!
>   The solemn watchword hear;
> If while ye sleep he suffers,
>   Away with shame and fear.
> Where'er ye meet with evil,
>   Within you or without,
> Charge for the God of battles,
>   And put the foe to rout.

This is not a phoney war. We are not like children playing at soldiers, fighting make-believe battles. The struggle is utterly real, and we must therefore heed the *solemn watchword* to be wakeful and watchful and do *away with shame and fear.* For what is it we are fighting? In a word we are doing battle with *evil.* This is the special point St Paul makes in the Ephesian passage. We are not contending against merely human foes – 'flesh and blood' – but 'against the spiritual hosts of wickedness in the heavenly realms'. We *meet with evil* in two directions: first *within* us, for our own hearts are not free from the taint of sin; and secondly *without* in the form of social wrong and injustice.

When George Duffield wrote this hymn it was social evil that was very much in his mind, and particularly the evil of slavery. He, like Dudley Tyng, was convinced that to stand up for Jesus was to stand against the traffic in human flesh and blood. Such evil could not be condoned or ignored. It must be attacked. Hence the call to *charge for the God of battles, and put the foe to rout.* In our own day the foe may not be the same; but the Christian duty to fight such evils as racism, terrorism, world poverty, and religious persecution, remains the same.

The call to arms is reinforced in the next stanza:

> Stand up, stand up for Jesus!
>   The trumpet call obey;
> Forth to the mighty conflict
>   In this his glorious day.
> Ye that are men now serve him
>   Against unnumbered foes;
> Let courage rise with danger,
>   And strength to strength oppose.

The first part of this verse does not call for comment; but note the words, *Ye that are men now serve him.* At this point of the hymn the writer recalls the text from which Dudley Tyng preached his last sermon: 'Go now, ye that are men, and serve the Lord.' The service of the Lord, as the hymn makes abundantly clear, is military service. Christ has no place for spiritual pacifists. There is a *mighty conflict* to be fought and won. We are up against *unnumbered foes.* In such a situation *courage* and *strength* are called for: courage to match every danger as it arises, and strength to *oppose* the strength of the enemy.

III

Where are we to find such strength? The answer is given in the apostle's words at the beginning of the Ephesian passage: 'Be strong in the Lord and in the power of his might. Put on the whole armour of God . . .' This is the answer repeated by the hymn in the stanza that follows.

> Stand up, stand up for Jesus!
>   Stand in his strength alone;

263

The arm of flesh will fail you,
  Ye dare not trust your own.
Put on the gospel armour,
  Each piece put on with prayer;
Where duty calls or danger,
  Be never wanting there.

One thing we discover only too quickly when we engage in this sort of warfare. We cannot overcome the enemy in our own strength. *The arm of flesh* – that is, self-effort, self-reliance – is doomed to failure. The foe is too powerful and we are too feeble. But the Captain under whom we serve has provided us with armour, *the gospel armour*, to equip us for the fight. We have but to take it up and make use of it, to *put on* what is already at our disposal:

> Stand firm then, with the belt of truth buckled around your waist, with the breastplate of righteousness in place, and with your feet fitted with the gospel of peace as a firm footing. In addition to all this, take up the shield of faith, with which you can extinguish all the flaming arrows of the evil one. Take the helmet of salvation and the sword of the Spirit, which is the word of God.

(Ephesians 6.14–17 NIV)

This is 'the whole armour of God'. *Each piece* is essential and must be *put on with prayer*; for the list of spiritual equipment ends with the words, 'Pray at all times in the Spirit, with all prayer and supplication'. Bunyan in *Pilgrim's Progress* spoke of a time when Christian in the midst of fierce conflict 'was forced to put up his sword, and betake himself to another weapon, called All-prayer'. That weapon is an indispensable part of the Christian warrior's armoury, for it enables him in every situation to keep in touch with his Commander-in-Chief.

In this way, strong in the Lord though weak in ourselves, we go forth at the call of duty to serve and to fight, encouraged by the prospect set before us in the final stanza.

Stand up, stand up for Jesus!
  The strife will not be long;
This day the noise of battle,

> The next the victor's song.
> To him that overcometh
> A crown of life shall be;
> He with the King of Glory
> Shall reign eternally.

The battle we are fighting as soldiers of the Cross is a tough one, but it is not an interminable one. *The strife will not be long.* At any rate it will not last for ever. *The noise of battle* will at length give place to *the victor's song.* The overcomers will receive the *crown of life* and *reign eternally* with Christ *the King of Glory.*

The imagery and language here, as in so many hymns, is derived from the Revelation of St John. To the church at Smyrna the risen Lord says:

> Be faithful, even to the point of death, and I will give you the crown of life;

and to the lukewarm church at Laodicea he gives the promise:

> To him who overcomes, I will give the right to sit with me on my throne, just as I overcame and sat down with my Father on his throne.

> (Revelation 2.10; 3.21 NIV)

35

THE CONSECRATED LIFE

Take my life, and let it be

PROBABLY A GOOD many people who are familiar with the
hymns of Frances Ridley Havergal but know little or nothing
about the author envisage her as a typically pious old Victorian lady who, after the fashion of her day, wrote a lot of
religious verse but otherwise was in no way out of the ordinary. To think of her like that is to be hopelessly mistaken.
True, she was a Victorian, and equally true, she was a woman
of deep and genuine piety. But she was certainly not old, for
she died at the age of forty-two, and by no manner of means
could she be described as 'ordinary'.

I

Born in 1836, she was the youngest daughter of the Revd
W. H. Havergal, one of the most eminent church musicians
and composers of his day. Early in life she revealed outstanding gifts, especially literary gifts. She began composing verse
at the age of seven, and in the course of her life she wrote an
enormous amount of prose and poetry, apart from her sixty or
so hymns. From her father she inherited a quite remarkable
musical talent, not only as a singer and pianist but also as a

composer. In her mid-twenties she considered taking up music as a profession, after obtaining a favourable opinion from the German musician Hiller. Languages were another of her accomplishments. She had a good working knowledge of Latin, Hebrew and Greek, and could speak French, German and Italian. She had a prodigious memory. She knew whole books of the Bible by heart, and according to her sister 'would play through Handel, and much of Beethoven and Mendelssohn, without notes'. Added to all this she possessed a bright and charming personality which drew people naturally to her side.

But with FRH, as we may call her, everything was subordinated to her Christian faith. At about the age of fourteen, through the witness of a school fellow, the Lord Jesus became 'a living bright reality' to her, and thenceforth he took first place in her life. Her religion was one of uncomplicated, unquestioning faith as she dedicated herself, with all her varied gifts, to the service of her Lord. She devoted a great deal of her time to writing books, poems and music. She was constantly in demand for her singing and piano playing. She engaged in a voluminous correspondence with people all over the world who sought her help; and she was highly skilled as a personal evangelist and spiritual counsellor. She was a diligent Bible student, a keen temperance worker, an enthusiast for overseas missions.

Although never enjoying robust health, she pursued a very active life until the age of thirty-seven, when a severe attack of typhoid fever laid her low for the best part of a year. Other illnesses followed, and in her later years she was obliged to restrict some of her activities; but she was ceaselessly busy with her pen almost to the day of her death, on June 3rd, 1879.

As a hymn-writer she is recognized as being, in a special sense, the singer of consecration. Her hymns belong to what has been called 'the hymnody of Christian experience'. She was not a great poet, but her verse glows with spiritual warmth and speaks to the heart. She testified, 'I can never set myself to write verse. I believe my King suggests a thought and whispers me a musical line or two, and then I look up and thank him delightedly, and go on with it. That is how the hymns and poems come.'

A good many of her hymns are still in use, especially in evangelical circles. Among the best known are 'Who is on the Lord's side?'; 'Lord, speak to me, that I may speak'; 'I gave my life for thee'; and the Keswick Convention favourite, 'Like a river glorious'. Her own personal favourite was 'I am trusting thee, Lord Jesus'. By many she is remembered only for 'Take my life'.

II

It is impossible to divorce FRH's hymns from herself. They are the expression of her own radiant faith and deep devotion to Christ. As Julian's *Dictionary* remarks, 'She lives and speaks in every line of her poetry.' Of no hymn is this more true than 'Take my life' – her consecration hymn, as she herself called it. Only a person as totally dedicated to God as she was had the right to pen such lines or invite others to sing them. We know from one of her letters just when and how the hymn was written. The date was February 4th, 1874; the occasion was the end of a five days' visit to the house of some friends. She had prayed that God would so use her visit that all ten members of the household might become genuine, rejoicing Christians; and he answered her prayer.

> Before I left the house every one had got a blessing. The last night of my visit, after I had retired, the governess asked me to go to the two daughters. They were crying, etc.; then and there both of them trusted and rejoiced; it was nearly midnight. I was too happy to sleep, and spent most of the night in praise and renewal of my own consecration; and these little couplets formed themselves, and chimed in my heart one after another, till they finished with *Ever*, ONLY, ALL for thee![1]

From this it will be clear that FRH wrote the hymn in couplets, and in this form it was printed in her *Loyal Responses*, 1878. There are twelve couplets in all, not eleven as stated by Julian and copied by others. In most hymn books the couplets are paired, to form six four-line stanzas.

We shall consider the hymn as she wrote it, couplet by couplet. The first of them is general and introduces the theme of the consecrated life. The ten that follow are specific and deal in turn with those elements of the personality that are involved in true consecration. The final couplet integrates these into one, namely, the consecrated self. Each couplet begins with the word *Take*, and this is a key to the interpretation of the hymn. When we use it as a prayer we are offering ourselves, all we are and all we have, to the Lord for his acceptance and use. It is for *him* to decide what that use shall be. Our part is to place ourselves unreservedly at his disposal: to make our various powers of body, mind, and spirit available for his service. This is the meaning of consecration, as FRH knew so well; and much of the hymn can be illustrated, as we shall see, from the record of her own life and experience.

III

In *Loyal Responses* the hymn is prefaced with the words from the Communion service in the Book of Common Prayer: 'Here we offer and present unto thee, O Lord, ourselves, our souls and bodies, to be a reasonable, holy, and lively sacrifice unto thee.' The first couplet epitomises this:

> Take my life, and let it be
> Consecrated, Lord, to thee.

Take my life: here is the substance of the whole prayer. Life is the most precious thing we possess, for as Jesus said, 'What does a man gain if he wins the whole world and loses his life? Or what can a man offer in exchange for his life?' (Mark 8.36,37). We each have only one life to live, and we are free to choose what we do with it. We can squander it on selfish pursuits and worldly ambitions, or dedicate it to the service of Christ. FRH had made her own choice long before she wrote this hymn; but it was only a few months earlier that she had experienced something of a spiritual crisis and entered into a new and deeper relationship with her Lord. She told her sister:

> It was on Advent Sunday, December 2nd, 1873, I first saw clearly the blessedness of true consecration. . . . There must be full surrender before there can be full blessedness. God admits you by the one into the other. He himself showed me all this most clearly. First, I was shown that 'the blood of Jesus Christ his Son cleanseth us from all sin,' and then it was made plain to me that he who had thus cleansed me had power to keep me clean. So I just yielded myself to him, and utterly trusted him to keep me.

The second couplet is about the consecration of our time:

> Take my moments and my days;
> Let them flow in ceaseless praise.

My moments are the fragments of *my days.* All time, however we measure it, belongs to God and we are responsible to him for the use we make of it. In a letter to a friend in February 1875, FRH wrote: '*I realize,* "Lord, I have given my life to thee, and every day and hour is thine." For, literally, every hour seems in his hand and filled with his work in some form or another, either preparation, actual service, or, as now, weakness and pain.'

Next, our actions:

> Take my hands, and let them move
> At the impulse of thy love.

My hands represent my work. Our hands are most marvellous instruments, instruments which fit us for an infinite variety of tasks; and when they *move at the impulse of* God's *love* both they and the tasks accomplished are sanctified. FRH's hands were constantly employed in a ministry of writing – letters, poems, articles, books, music – as well as in playing the piano and organ. But she had other manual skills as well. She was an expert needlewoman; she could use the sign language in speaking to the deaf and dumb; and her sister recalled her as 'the merry carpenter, deftly dovetailing and contriving'.

Take my feet, and let them be
Swift and 'beautiful' for thee.

Just as our hands represent our work, so our *feet* symbolize our journeys – more especially in this instance the errands we carry out in the Lord's service. FRH put the word *beautiful* in inverted commas to indicate that she was quoting what the apostle said about the heralds of the gospel: 'How beautiful are the feet of those who preach good news!' (Romans 15.15; *cf.* Isaiah 52.7). Commenting on these words Bishop Handley Moule remarked, 'From the viewpoint of heaven there is nothing on the earth more lovely than the bearing of the name of Jesus Christ into the needing world.' This undoubtedly is what FRH had in mind: going out to witness for her Master wherever she went.

That witness, in song and speech, is the theme of the next two couplets.

Take my voice, and let me sing
Always, only, for my King.

In earlier years music had threatened to take first place in FRH's life, so greatly was she in demand for her singing and playing. But she resisted the temptation and resolved that in all things Christ should have the pre-eminence. She was able to testify, 'Singing for Jesus is to me the most personal and direct commission I hold from my beloved Master.' On one occasion she was asked to sing the part of Jezebel in Mendelssohn's *Elijah* at a Kidderminster concert. She mentioned this to a friend, who asked her, 'How can a Christian girl personate Jezebel?' She thought about it, saw the inconsistency, and declined the part. This happened a few months before she wrote the consecration hymn and vowed to *sing always, only, for my King.*

Take my lips, and let them be
Filled with messages from thee.

FRH did not engage in much public speaking (it was not normal in those days for a woman to do so), but she was constantly busy in spiritual counselling, conducting Bible classes, addressing small groups. She wrote to a friend, 'I want

271

Jesus to speak to me, that I may speak for him to others with real power. It is not knowing doctrine, but *being with* him, which will give this.' Hence her prayer that her *lips* might *be filled with messages from* him, as a result of her being much with him. Her hymn 'Lord, speak to me' amplifies this thought.

IV

Many find it difficult to sing with honest hearts the seventh couplet:

> Take my silver and my gold;
> Not a mite would I withhold.

FRH was aware that *Take my silver and my gold* was open to question and raised problems, for in a letter to a friend in 1877 she wrote:

> I do think that couplet, 'Take my silver and my gold, Not a mite would I withhold', is peculiarly liable to be objected to by those who do not really understand the *spirit* of it. So I am not a bit surprised! Yes, 'not a mite would I withhold'; but that does not mean that, because we have ten shillings in our purse, we are pledged to put it *all* into the next collecting plate, else we should have none for the next call. But it does mean that every shilling is to be, and I think I may say *is*, held at my Lord's disposal, and is distinctly not my own; but, as he has entrusted to me a body for my special charge, I am bound to clothe that body with his silver and gold, so that it shall neither suffer from cold, nor bring discredit upon his cause!

Those words explain the sensible and responsible attitude she adopted towards money and possessions. The year before she died she sorted out her jewel cabinet and 'with extreme delight' sent off nearly fifty articles of value to be disposed of for the work of the Church Missionary Society.

Next comes the consecration of the mind:

> Take my intellect, and use
> Every power as thou shalt choose.

FRH's *intellect* was developed to a quite exceptional degree in an age when higher education for women was unknown. She made her own Canon Hay Aitken's prayer, 'Lord, take my mind and think through it' and sought to dedicate *every power* she possessed – poetical, linguistic, scholastic, musical – to his service.

The secret of it all was the consecration of her will:

> Take my will, and make it thine;
> It shall be no longer mine.

Take my will, and make it thine is the prayer of one who is fully surrendered to God and accepts his will as good and perfect (Romans 12.1,2). FRH suffered a keen disappointment when arrangements for the publication of her poetical works in America fell through; but so sure was she that God's purpose was being worked out in every detail of her life that she found 'an actual accession of joy' in accepting the situation and declared, 'Now "Thy will be done" is not a sigh but only a *song*!' *Master* was her favourite title for Jesus, 'because it implies submission; and this is what love craves. Men may feel differently; but a true woman's submission is inseparable from deep love.'

> Take my heart, it is thine own;
> It shall be thy royal throne.

The verbs in these two lines distinguish between the present and the future. *My heart*, the seat of my affections, *is thine own* – now, already. But that is not enough. Consecrated to the Lord, henceforth *it shall be thy royal throne.* The throne is the symbol of kingship. This is why FRH so often spoke of Jesus as 'my King'. It was the recognition of his sovereignty in her heart and life.

The next couplet is closely allied to this:

> Take my love; my Lord, I pour
> At thy feet its treasure-store.

This prayer *Take my love* caused FRH some concern when she renewed her consecration on December 2nd, 1878, the fifth anniversary of that memorable Advent Sunday, 1873.

She examined her life in the light of the hymn, going through it verse by verse, and remarked, '. . . the eleventh couplet, "love" – that has been unconsciously *not filled up*. Somehow I felt mystified and out of my depth here . . .' It was lack of feeling, it seems, that troubled her. She sensibly told the Lord about it and decided to 'hand over the whole concern to him, and implore him to make it clear and definite.' Her deep devotion to Christ was indeed a *treasure-store* which her life proved beyond all shadow of doubt.

The final couplet reaffirms the total consecration expressed in the preceding words:

> Take myself, and I will be
> Ever, only, all for thee.

There are no half measures here. FRH wished her dedication to the Master to be unending, single-hearted, complete. So should we. *Take myself*! I cannot give God more than myself. I ought not to give him less.

NOTE
1 Quotations in this chapter are derived mainly from *Memorials of Frances Ridley Havergal* by her sister Marion Havergal (Nisbet, 1880).

36

GOD IN THE EVERYDAY

Teach me, my God and King

ONE OF the most attractive figures in the story of English hymnody is that of George Herbert, the seventeenth-century country parson and poet. Born in 1593, a member of a noble English family, he was educated at Westminster School and Cambridge University. As a young man, pleasure-loving and ambitious, fortune smiled upon him. At Cambridge he distinguished himself as a Latin and Greek scholar, and in due course he became a Fellow of Trinity College and Public Orator of the University. Following a family tradition, he also spent time at the court of James I and won the favour of the King. He seemed destined for a brilliant career in the service of the State. But something happened, something which changed the whole current of his life.

I

King James died, and deprived of the royal patronage Herbert decided to abandon the glittering life of the court. Perhaps he had already become disenchanted with its false glamour and empty pleasures. At any rate, at this point in his life he passed through a deep spiritual crisis. The conviction grew within him that God was calling him to something higher. So he withdrew from the life of London society and for the next four or five years devoted himself to the study of divinity. Eventually, at the age of thirty-two, he took holy orders. Four years later he became rector of Bemerton, a small village in Wiltshire, near Salisbury, where he spent the last three years of his life. He died in 1633 at the age of thirty-nine.

Short as was his incumbency of Bemerton, he made a profound and enduring impression on the parish by his saintly character, his exemplary home life, his deeds of charity, his pastoral devotion, and above all by his ordering of public worship. Morning and evening prayer were said daily in the village church. The word of God was preached and the gospel sacraments administered in accordance with the Church's rules. As a result, George Herbert has become a legendary figure in the story of the English Church, a model of what a parish priest should be. During his incumbency he wrote a book called *The Priest to the Temple.* This work not only set forth the ideals of the pastoral ministry but also mirrored the soul of the man behind the book: a man wholly consecrated to the service of Christ.

In addition to his scholarly gifts Herbert had considerable musical talent; and he was a poet. It is for his poetry that he is now chiefly remembered. His poetical style is quaint, epigrammatic, witty, sometimes elusive and obscure, but it has great charm. He is recognized as being among the foremost devotional poets of the Church of England. His poems, it has been rightly said, 'breathe a gentle piety and a sincere love of Christian virtue'.

Though not written as hymns or intended for use in church, several of his poems have found their way into our hymn-books and become deservedly popular. Among them are 'King of glory, King of Peace'; 'Let all the world in every corner sing' (headed 'Antiphon'); 'The God of love my Shepherd is' (a paraphrase of the 23rd psalm); and of course 'Teach me, my God and King'.

II

This hymn is an excellent example of the enigmatic quality of Herbert's religious verse. It does not yield its meaning at first glance. Doubtless many sing the hymn in church – carried along by its attractive carol melody *Sandys* – without really grasping what the words are all about. It is worth trying to find out, for behind the various figures and illustrations employed there is a message which closely touches our daily life. In fact it is about God in the everyday.

Herbert headed his poem *The Elixir*. The term refers to the hope cherished by the medieval philosphers – or alchemists as they were called – of discovering a touchstone which had the property of changing base metals into gold, or a tincture which could infuse spiritual qualities into material things. In his poem Herbert asserts that there is indeed an elixir which possesses these supernatural powers and can marvellously transform and enrich the whole of life. It is found in the simple phrase 'for his sake'. Life's most ordinary activities take on an entirely new meaning when they are performed not merely from a sense of duty or for the sake of money but out of a sincere love for God and a single eye to his glory. In a word, the thing that matters most in life is not *what* we do but *why* we do it. The deed may be all right; the motive may be all wrong. But if the motive *is* right, then the deed itself assumes a new value.

This is the theme of Herbert's *Elixir*. John Wesley in the next century was particularly attracted to the poem – as he was to many other of Herbert's works – and he included it in his earliest collection of hymns. But recognizing that the language was puzzling in places, he rewrote much of it with a view to removing the obscurities and making the meaning plain to his simple Methodist folk. The result, alas, was not very happy. While Herbert's message was correctly and clearly interpreted, in the process the magic of his poetry was lost, and the hymn as Wesley printed it was flat and uninspiring. The only stanza of the poem which he did genuinely improve was one dropped from the hymn-books, no doubt on account of its awkward rhythm as well as its abstruse meaning. Herbert wrote as his second verse:

> Not rudely, as a beast,
> To run into an action;
> But still to make thee prepossest,
> And give it his perfection.

Wesley entirely rewrote this, skilfully interpreting its meaning:

> To scorn the sense's sway,
> While still to thee I stand,
> In all I do be thou the Way;
> In all be thou the End.

Such a verse is not unworthy to join company with Herbert's own poetry.

III

The first stanza sets the keynote of the work:

> Teach me, my God and King,
> In all things thee to see,
> And what I do in anything,
> To do it as for thee.

The hymn thus begins with a prayer, and out of this prayer the other stanzas develop. It is a prayer that God will enable us to *see* him *in all things*: that he will give us such spiritual sensitivity and insight that we may be aware of his presence in all our affairs and do our work as in his sight and for his approval. With this we may compare the words of Bishop Ken's morning hymn:

> Direct, control, suggest, this day
> All I design, or do, or say;
> That all my powers, with all their might,
> In thy sole glory may unite.

The next stanza illustrates the peril of spiritual short-sightedness: the peril of failing to see God in daily life because our gaze is directed towards lesser objects:

> A man that looks on glass
> On it may stay his eye;
> Or if he pleaseth, through it pass
> And then the heaven espy.

The words conjure up a picture. You are sitting in a room looking at the window. What do you see? Your eyes may penetrate no farther than the window-pane itself, arrested possibly by some defect in the glass or some mark on the pane. And perhaps that is all you see. Or you may of course ignore the window-pane entirely and look right through it – and catch sight of the beauty of the sky above, the wonder of creation.

So with ourselves and the everyday things of life. We may be so absorbed in our tasks and duties that we lose all sight of God. We are then like the *man that looks on glass* – looks on it but does not see through it. The glass itself holds all his attention. When that happens to us, life becomes a mundane and monotonous affair. On the other hand we may make our work, however humdrum, an act of Christian service, an offering to God for his glory. It all depends on how we look at life.

The next stanza carries on this thought:

> All may of thee partake:
> Nothing can be so mean,
> Which with this tincture, 'for thy sake',
> Will not grow bright and clean.

By *all may of thee partake* the poet means that all may share in God's service. It is not something reserved for the clergy or the ultra-pious. And the meanest task shines with a new lustre and grows *bright and clean* when it is motivated by love and obedience. '*For thy sake*' – this is the heavenly elixir which transfigures the value of the most ordinary deed.

To make this meaning clear, a simple, homely illustration is provided:

A servant with this clause
Makes drudgery divine;
Who sweeps a room, as for thy laws,
Makes that and the action fine.

A servant who sweeps a room. What could be more ordinary than that? But the tincture 'for thy sake' *makes* the *drudgery divine.* The humble task is performed *as for thy laws* – as though in obedience to God's own command – and the result is twofold. Not only is the job well done, but *the action* itself has a *fine* quality, an enhanced worth.

In his *Priest to the Temple* George Herbert wrote: 'Nothing is little in God's service. If it once have the honour of that Name, it grows great instantly.' Little is much when God is in it. The woman who had a card over her kitchen sink inscribed 'Divine service performed here thrice daily' had got hold of the right idea.

In the final stanza the elixir is identified with the philosopher's touchstone:

This is the famous stone
That turneth all to gold:
For that which God doth touch and own
Cannot for less be told.

In his valuable commentary in *The Works of George Herbert*[1] Canon T. E. Hutchinson remarks:

The word *touch* was used of testing the fineness of gold by rubbing it with the touchstone; also of officially marking metal as of standard quality after it had been touched. What God has 'touched' and approved as gold, no one may rightly reckon *for less.*

God tests and approves (or disapproves) our actions by the spirit in which they are done. It is this that decides their value and determines whether they are base metal or true gold.

Three sentences from St Paul sum up everything that Herbert says to us in *The Elixir*:

'Whatever you do, do all to the glory of God' (1 Corinthians 10.31).

GOD IN THE EVERYDAY

'Whatever you do, in word or deed, do all in the name of the Lord Jesus' (Colossians 3.17).

'Whatever you do, do it heartily, as serving the Lord and not men' (Colossians 3.23).

NOTE
1 Oxford University Press, 1941, p. 541.

37

THE CHURCH OF CHRIST

The Church's one foundation

QUITE A NUMBER of hymns had their origin in the religious controversies of their day. For example, the hymns of Martin Luther were to some extent battle songs of the Reformation, affirming the great liberating truths rediscovered in the holy scriptures. Some of Charles Wesley's fine hymns two centuries later were the direct product of the Calvinistic controversy and were designed to proclaim God's everlasting love for all mankind in face of the 'horrible decree' that multitudes of souls were divinely predestined to eternal damnation, because Christ died only for the 'elect'. And in the next century it was another fierce theological conflict, known as the Colenso affair, which inspired the writing of the hymn we are going to consider in this chapter.

I

John Colenso was Bishop of Natal in South Africa. In 1861 he published a commentary on Romans and in the following year began to issue a series of papers on the Pentateuch. These writings, adopting as they did a 'critical' attitude towards the Bible and questioning certain articles of the Christian faith,

282

aroused a storm of protest. His Metropolitan, Bishop Robert Gray of Cape Town, denounced his opinions and deposed him from office. The details of the case need not concern us here, but the whole affair caused a big religious upheaval at the time. This was the case not only in South Africa but equally in Britain, where Colenso was considered by many to be a 'heretic' whose teaching undermined the very foundations of the Christian Church.

It is here that a certain young clergyman, Samuel John Stone, a member of the High Church party, comes into the picture. Like those who shared his outlook, he supported Gray and opposed Colenso; and as his contribution to the controversy he wrote this hymn, 'The Church's one foundation', in defence of the Church and the historic Christian faith. At the time, 1866, he was curate of Windsor and twenty-seven years of age.

As regards Stone himself, perhaps the most important thing to be said is that he was a strong man. He was strong and muscular physically, strong and resolute in character, and above all strong in the faith of Christ and in his devotion to the Church. This is clearly reflected in the hymn. It is emphatically a strong hymn: dogmatic, positive, decisive. There was nothing soft or flabby about the Revd S. J. Stone or his Christianity. He was a fearless defender of the faith. He was prepared to fight for it, and fight for it he did.

As we look at the hymn and what it has to say to us we shall do well to bear in mind the kind of man who wrote it and the circumstances that gave it birth. Clearly enough it is a hymn about the Church of Christ, and in effect it offers us three pictures of the Church: the Church as it should be, the Church as it is, and the Church as it will be.

II

The first picture is that of the Church in God's design, the Church as he intends it to be, according to the scriptures. Such is the picture provided by the first two stanzas. They have accordingly a firm biblical basis, as is apparent in the very opening lines:

> The Church's one foundation
> Is Jesus Christ, her Lord.

This bold affirmation has as its authority the words of St Paul: 'Other foundation can no man lay than that which is laid, even Jesus Christ' (1 Corinthians 3.11). The point the apostle is making in the passage from which the words are taken is that while men have their part in the building up of the Church – as Paul and Apollos had done at Corinth – its *foundation* is not human but divine: *Jesus Christ, our Lord*. This at once gives us a high view of the Church and assures us that because it is built on rock the forces of death shall never overpower it (Matthew 16.18 NEB).

> She is his new creation
> By water and the Word.

Under this figure the Church takes on a more personal aspect. It is a regenerate society, Christ's *new creation*, a company of people born again 'of water and the Spirit' (John 3.5), or as the hymn puts it, echoing Ephesians 5.26, *by water and the Word*. The water is the water of baptism, the regenerating sign; the Word is the word of the gospel, the regenerating agency.

The passage in Ephesians 5 just alluded to has as its theme the marriage relationship. The apostle says, 'Husbands, love your wives, as Christ loved the church and gave himself up for her, that he might sanctify her' (verse 25). So the hymn continues:

> From heaven he came and sought her
> To be his holy Bride;
> With his own blood he bought her,
> And for her life he died.

This opening stanza of the hymn is stressing throughout that the Church is wholly Christ's. Our English word 'church' is derived from the Greek *kyriakos*, meaning that which belongs to the Lord. The most important thing about the

Church is that it belongs to the Lord Christ. And the hymn makes clear why it belongs to him: he founded it; he created it; he purchased it *with his own blood*; and he espoused it to himself as *his holy Bride*. This is the measure of Christ's love for the Church.

The second stanza asserts two further truths about the Church: its catholicity and its unity.

> Elect from every nation,
>   Yet one o'er all the earth,
> Her charter of salvation
>   One Lord, one faith, one birth;
> One holy name she blesses,
>   Partakes one holy food,
> And to one hope she presses
>   With every grace endued.

The Church's catholicity is stated in the opening words, *Elect from every nation*, and implied in the reference to *all the earth* in the second line. However, it is the Church's unity that is enlarged upon in the remainder of the verse, in words derived largely from Ephesians 4.4, 5:

> There is one body and one Spirit, just as you were called to the one hope that belongs to your call, one Lord, one faith, one baptism, one God and Father of us all, who is above all and through all and in all.

The Church's *one Lord* is, of course, the Lord Jesus; and this, significantly, is the central fact in the sevenfold unity stated by the apostle. By the *one faith* Stone was doubtless referring to the Church's historic faith as confessed in her creeds, though Paul was probably thinking of faith in the subjective sense, the believer's response of trust to the Lord. The *one birth* – the new birth of the Spirit – in the hymn corresponds to the 'one baptism', as being the sacrament of regeneration. The *one holy name* which the Church *blesses* is the strong name of the Trinity; the *one holy food* of which she *partakes* is the body and blood of Christ in the eucharist; and the *one hope* to which *she presses*, assisted by *every* means of *grace*, is the hope of glory.

III

From the biblical ideal of the Church presented in the first two stanzas the hymn-writer turns to the reality of the Church as it is, the Church as it appears only too often in the pages of history and in the eyes of the world. Accordingly in the third stanza he faces facts and portrays the Church afflicted by many a foe, divided in the Lord's service and threatened by false teaching.

> Though with a scornful wonder
>   Men see her sore opprest,
> By schisms rent asunder,
>   By heresies distrest,
> Yet saints their watch are keeping,
>   Their cry goes up, 'How long?'
> And soon the night of weeping
>   Shall be the morn of song.

We have called this the third stanza, and so it is as far as our hymn-books are concerned. But when Stone wrote the hymn he inserted a verse before the present one. This is now always and rightly omitted; but it is worth quoting, for it recalls very clearly the spirit of the times and the deep feelings of the author when the hymn was composed.

> The Church shall never perish!
>   Her dear Lord to defend,
> To guide, sustain, and cherish,
>   Is with her to the end;
> Though there be those who hate her,
>   And false sons in her pale,
> Against or foe or traitor
>   She ever shall prevail.

Stone was very conscious of the presence of the *foe* and *traitor* in the Church of his day; and so he went on, in the verse which followed the above, to lament the fact that the Church was *by schisms rent asunder, by heresies distrest.* We ought to note the difference between 'schism' and 'heresy'. To put it simply, schism is separation from the Church's fellowship; heresy is denial of the Church's faith. In practice the two are, inevitably, closely related. Normally it is heresy which occasions schism. In fact the very word 'heresy' (Greek *hairesis*) originally meant separation or faction and is used in this sense in 1 Corinthians 11.19. The early heretics were those who abandoned the apostolic church because they had abandoned the apostolic faith.

To come back to the hymn: its author was genuinely disturbed by the elements of schism and heresy in the Church of his day, which is why he expressed himself as he did. Perhaps we in our own time take too complacent a view of the ecclesiastical scene and are not as ready to face facts as he was. But however we look at things, we can scarcely deny that the Church is still in schism, broken up into different parts. The situation is sad when those parts are content to remain in a state of separation. It is sadder still, tragic indeed, when the parts are not even prepared to be in communion with one another at the Lord's table. It is ludicrous in the extreme when one part virtually claims to be the whole. But such situations do in fact exist.

The hymn is right in recognizing the Church's imperfections and inconsistencies. But it also recognizes something else: that within the mixed body of those who profess and call themselves Christians there are always God's faithful ones: the *saints* who hold fast to their faith and *watch* for their Lord's appearing when the world's dark *night of weeping* will end and the Day of God will break in *the morn of song*.

This is the Church's glorious hope; and it is this hope that dominates the final stanzas and evokes the third picture of the Church in this hymn. Here we see the Church as at last it will be – triumphant, glorified, and at rest.

> 'Mid toil and tribulation,
>   And tumult of her war,
> She waits the consummation
>   Of peace for evermore;
> Till with the vision glorious
>   Her longing eyes are blest,

And the great Church victorious
Shall be the Church at rest.

For the time being *toil, tribulation, and tumult* are the Church's lot. But only for the time being, for *she waits the consummation of peace for evermore.* And then – *the vision glorious*! What is that? Nothing less than the vision of God; for while now we walk by faith, not by sight, at the last 'his servants shall see his face' (Revelation 22.4). 'Now we see in a mirror dimly; but then face to face' (1 Corinthians 13.12). Such is the dazzling prospect in view for the Church militant here in earth: no longer engaged in *her war* but *at rest* with Christ.

Yet she on earth hath union
With God the Three in One,
And mystic sweet communion
With those whose rest is won.

Union and *communion*. The Church's union is with the Triune God through faith and baptism, prayer and worship. Her communion is with the faithful departed through Jesus Christ, the risen and living Lord; and as we think of them with joy and thanksgiving, we lift up our hearts in prayer:

O happy ones and holy!
Lord, give us grace that we
Like them, the meek and lowly,
On high may dwell with thee.

IV

To that prayer we can say nothing but Amen. But a final reflection suggests itself. It is strange that out of the heat and bitterness of religious controversy there should have emerged a hymn of such fine spiritual quality as this: certainly one of the greatest hymns about the Church ever to have been written. It has survived for well over a hundred years and is likely to survive much longer.

But stranger still, in a sense, is the fact that though the young curate of Windsor in later years composed a considerable amount of religious verse, little of it, if any, is on the same level as this hymn or has been deemed worthy to find a place in our hymnals. To all intents and purposes the name of the Revd S. J. Stone is perpetuated by one hymn.

The hymn is invariably associated with the tune *Aurelia*, by S. S. Wesley (1810–76). He composed it originally for 'Jerusalem the golden'; hence the title of the tune, derived from the Latin *aureolus*, golden.

38

THE GOOD SHEPHERD

The King of love my Shepherd is

THE BEST known hymn-book in the world, certainly as far as this country is concerned, is *Hymns Ancient and Modern*, first published in 1861. That book owed its birth and growth and outstanding success to the genius of one man, the Revd Sir Henry Williams Baker, who not only inspired and promoted the book but was from the first chairman and acknowledged leader of the committee responsible for its production. The task he undertook was an arduous one and made enormous demands upon him. The publication of an Anglican hymnal was very much a pioneer effort at that time. No one previously had attempted such a thing, especially on so ambitious a scale. The question then may well be asked, How was a busy clergyman, with a parish to look after, able to accomplish so big an undertaking?

I

The answer is that Sir Henry Baker, though a beneficed clergyman, was a country vicar whose small rural parish of Monkland in Herefordshire required of him only very light duty. It left him with sufficient freedom to devote to the writing and editing of hymns, engaging in a vast amount of correspondence with hymn-writers and musicians, attending frequent committees in London, and coping with printers and proofs. For the latter part of his life *Hymns Ancient and Modern* absorbed most of his time and energy. He remained at Monkland until his death in 1877 at the age of fifty-six. In a comparatively short life he did more than any other man for the promotion of hymnody in the English Church.

Sir Henry wrote a large number of hymns, and also made translations of a good many Latin hymns. A lot of these naturally found their way into the early editions of the hymnal. Not all have retained their appeal through the years; nevertheless the latest revision (*AMR*, 1950) contains sixteen of his hymns and translations. Among those in common use are 'Lord, thy word abideth', 'We love the place, O God', 'Praise, O praise, our God and King', and 'O praise ye the Lord'. But assuredly the hymn by which he is best remembered is 'The King of love my Shepherd is' – a hymn which is never likely to lose its place in the Church's worship.

The hymn is sometimes described as a paraphrase of the 23rd Psalm. So it is in a sense; but it is more than that. It is not simply another metrical version of the psalm, like the Scottish 'The Lord's my Shepherd, I'll not want', or George Herbert's 'The God of love my Shepherd is'. These are paraphrases pure and simple and keep as close as possible to the biblical text. Sir Henry's aim was different. While basing his hymn on the psalm he treated it with a large degree of freedom, and moreover gave it a definitely *Christian* interpretation. This is the distinctive feature of the hymn. In it we have an ancient Hebrew song – itself a marvellous devotional treasure – transformed into a fully Christian act of praise.

Our purpose in examining the hymn is to see how this is done. It could be said that Sir Henry was following in the tradition of Isaac Watts, who in paraphrasing the psalms made it his business to spiritualize and Christianize them. But his style of composition is markedly different from that of Watts. It bears all the marks of the nineteenth-century Anglican hymn-writer and is typical of the best of its kind.

II

The King of love my Shepherd is,
Whose goodness faileth never;
I nothing lack if I am his
And he is mine for ever.

This first stanza covers the opening words of the psalm and is based on the Prayer Book version: 'The Lord is my Shepherd: therefore can I lack nothing.' The Lord, of course, is Jehovah, the God of Israel, God in his holiness, majesty, and power. Baker invests the sacred name with a new tenderness, more in harmony with the Christian revelation: *The King of love.* Perhaps the title owes something to George Herbert's 'The God of love'; but 'King of love' is better and more effective. It recognizes not only God's sovereignty but also his sovereign grace. He exercises his reign in love. His throne is the throne of grace. In keeping with this thought are the words that follow: *whose goodness faileth never.* The goodness of God is an aspect of his love: love in its generosity.

The psalm continues: 'therefore can I lack nothing.' The hymn echoes the words but at the same time expands and explains them. *I nothing lack*, it says, *if I am his and he is mine for ever.* The *if* governs both phrases and is all-important. It defines the relationship between the Shepherd and the sheep. In his parabolic discourse in John 10 Jesus speaks of us as 'my sheep'; we are his. We on our part can speak of him as 'my Shepherd': he is ours. He makes us *his* own, and as a result he becomes our own. And the relationship is an abiding one: it is 'for ever'. Of his sheep Jesus declared, 'I give them eternal life, and no one shall snatch them out of my hand' (v.28).

'He maketh me to lie down in green pastures; he leadeth me beside the still waters.' The psalm puts the green pastures first, the still waters second. The hymn, for purely poetical reasons, reverses this.

> Where streams of living water flow
> My ransomed soul he leadeth,
> And where the verdant pastures grow
> With food celestial feedeth.

Apart from the difference of order, the hymn introduces a subtle change of language. The psalmist's 'still waters' (or 'waters of quietness', as the marginal reading has it) suggests a placid pool. In the hymn, however, the pool becomes *streams of living water*, and the picture is quite different. The phrase recalls the words of Jesus to the woman at Sychar's well (see John 4.10–14), as also the invitation he issued in Jerusalem at the feast of Tabernacles:

> On the last and greatest day of the festival Jesus stood and cried aloud, 'If anyone is thirsty let him come to me; whoever believes in me, let him drink. As Scripture says, 'Streams of living water shall flow out from within him.' He was speaking of the Spirit which believers in him would receive later; for the Spirit had not yet been given, because Jesus had not yet been glorified.
>
> (John 7.37–39 NEB)

The Evangelist thus makes it clear that the living water which Jesus promised is the Holy Spirit; and this second stanza portrays the *ransomed soul* of the believer as renewed by the Spirit of God and nourished with the Word of God. That Word is the *food celestial* on which he feeds and which he finds *where the verdant pastures grow* – in the pages of holy scripture.

The third stanza is particularly beautiful and had a special value for its author:

> Perverse and foolish oft I strayed,
> But yet in love he sought me,
> And on his shoulder gently laid,
> And home rejoicing brought me.

The verse takes up and makes explicit the psalmist's words, 'He restoreth my soul'. We may well have wondered at times just what that means. The hymn tells us. It means the Lord restores us to himself when 'we have erred and strayed from his ways like lost sheep'. Sir Henry puts it in pictorial form, derived from the parable Jesus told:

> What man of you, having a hundred sheep, if he has lost one of them, does not leave the ninety-nine in the wilderness, and go after the one which is lost, until he finds it? And when he has found it, he lays it on his shoulders, rejoicing. And when he comes home, he calls together his friends and his neighbours, saying to them, 'Rejoice with me, for I have found my sheep which was lost.'
>
> (Luke 15.4–6)

The hymn turns the prose into poetry. The sheep, *perverse and foolish*, has strayed from the flock and is lost. It is only one out of a hundred in the flock; but the shepherd cares for each of his sheep, and in his love he goes after the one that is lost and searches for it till he finds it. Then *on his shoulder gently laid* it is brought *home* with *rejoicing*. The story is our Lord's own portrayal of *grace* – the love of God in action for the salvation of the lost – and the assurance that every individual soul is of worth to him.

The words of this stanza, we have said, had a special value for their author. When Sir Henry Baker was on his deathbed, those around him heard him quietly repeating to himself, 'Perverse and foolish oft I strayed . . .' The words which have brought comfort to so many in the varying phases of life were his own consolation in the hour of death.

This brings us appropriately to the fourth stanza and the part of the psalm which says, 'Yea, though I walk through the valley of the shadow of death, I will fear no evil: for thou art with me; thy rod and thy staff they comfort me.'

> In death's dark vale I fear no ill
> With thee, dear Lord, beside me;
> Thy rod and staff my comfort still,
> Thy Cross before to guide me.

On the whole the hymn here keeps close to the psalm, with its reference to *death's dark vale* where *I fear no ill with thee, dear Lord, beside me*, and the *comfort* of the Shepherd's *rod and staff*. But we cannot fail to note the addition which has no equivalent in the psalm: *thy Cross before to guide me*. Why

294

does the author introduce the cross at this point? Is it just a devotional touch, or a poetic device to produce a rhyme? No. Sir Henry remembered that Jesus said, 'I am the good shepherd. The good shepherd lays down his life for the sheep' (John 10.11). The distinctive mark of the good shepherd is sacrifice. In sharp contrast to him is the 'hireling' – the paid servant who only does the job for what he can get out of it. 'He is no shepherd and the sheep are not his. Then the wolf harries the flock and scatters the sheep. The man runs away because he is a hireling and cares nothing for the sheep' (vv. 12,13, NEB). Because he cares nothing he is not prepared to make any sacrifice for the sheep. But Jesus cares. He cared enough for the sheep to lay down his life for them – and did so willingly, under the constraint of nothing but his love (vv. 17,18).

To return to the hymn: as we go through the dark valleys of life – however dark, however long – not only is Jesus the Good Shepherd beside us with his rod and staff. His cross, the shining emblem of redeeming love, is just ahead of us at every step, and as we venture into the unknown we need fear no evil.

III

Now the scene changes. A new imagery is introduced. The good Shepherd becomes the gracious Host. 'Thou preparest a table before me in the presence of mine enemies: thou anointest my head with oil; my cup runneth over.'

> Thou spread'st a table in my sight,
> Thy unction grace bestoweth;
> And O what transport of delight
> From thy pure chalice floweth!

As a good High Churchman Sir Henry Baker gives the psalmist's words a sacramental meaning. *Thou spread'st a table in my sight* – and of course it is the Lord's table that is spread. We are present at the eucharistic feast. The bread and wine are prepared, and Jesus as the Host invites us to draw near with faith and receive the sacrament to our comfort. But what is it we receive in the sacrament? Simply bread and wine? There is something more: *thy unction grace bestoweth*; and in understanding what that means we must remember that while 'unction' is literally anointing with oil (as in the psalm), it has in scripture a symbolical value. In 1 John 2.20, 27 it appears to be a symbol of the Holy Spirit. We may take it that the point the hymn is making here is that the sacrament is more than an outward and visible sign. By the unction of the Holy Spirit it becomes an inward and spiritual grace. In receiving by faith the bread and wine we partake of the body and blood of Christ. He is to us the Bread of life, as he is also the true Vine; *and O what transport of delight from thy pure chalice floweth!*

So to the final stanza and the end of the psalm: 'Surely goodness and mercy shall follow me all the days of my life: and I will dwell in the house of the Lord for ever.'

> And so through all the length of days
> Thy goodness faileth never;
> Good Shepherd, may I sing thy praise
> Within thy house for ever.

The hymn keeps close to the psalm in the first part of this verse. *Through all the length of days*, however many or few they may be, the Lord's *goodness faileth never*. Such is the immediate prospect. But what beyond that, when 'the days of my life' on earth are finished? Here there is a change. The psalm ends with an affirmation: 'I will dwell in the house of the Lord for ever.' The hymn concludes with a prayer: *Good Shepherd, may I sing thy praise within thy house for ever.* There is also another change, small but significant. The psalmist speaks of 'dwelling' in God's house; the Christian poet prays that he may worship there. He takes up the New Testament teaching about heaven as a place of praise and song. He wants to blend his voice with the celestial choir and sing the praises of Jesus without end.

In the minds of most church people the hymn is wedded to the tune J. B. Dykes composed for it, *Dominus regit me* (the

Latin title of Psalm 23) which first appeared in the 1868 appendix to *Hymns Ancient and Modern*. An attractive alternative is *St Columba*, an ancient Irish melody adopted by *EH* in 1906 when copyright difficulties prevented the use of Dykes's tune.

39

GRATITUDE

When all thy mercies, O my God

UNLIKE THE majority of men who wrote our hymns, the essayist Joseph Addison was a layman, though he only narrowly escaped becoming a clergyman. Born in 1672, he was the son of a parson (later Dean of Lincoln) and studied at Oxford with a view to ordination. While his natural inclination was towards literary pursuits, he felt it his duty to abandon this ambition in order to serve the Church. In his early manhood he wrote:

> I leave the arts of poetry and verse
> To them that practise them with more success;
> Of greater truths I'll now propose to tell,
> And so at once, dear friend and muse, farewell.

However, influential friends persuaded him that the Church's ministry was not his calling and urged him to devote his life to literature and politics. By the beginning of the eighteenth century he had not only attained high office in the affairs of State but had also become a distinguished man of letters. He had close associations with the *Spectator*, and to that journal he regularly contributed essays and poems. Which brings us to the origin of our hymn.

I

In the *Spectator* for August 9, 1712 there appeared an article from Addison's pen on the subject of Gratitude, in which he wrote:

> There is not a more pleasing exercise of the mind than gratitude. It is accompanied by such an inward satisfaction, that the duty is sufficiently rewarded by the performance. If gratitude is due from man to man, how much more from man to his Maker! Every blessing we enjoy, by what means soever it may be derived upon us, is the gift of him who is the great Author of good, and Father of mercies.

Following the essay was a poem of thirteen verses illustrating the theme and expressing gratitude to God for all the blessings of this life. It is from that poem that our hymn is taken. Two other of Addison's poems which have found their way into our hymn books and which first appeared in the *Spectator* are 'The Lord my pasture shall prepare' (a free paraphrase of the 23rd Psalm) and 'The spacious firmament on high', which is based on Psalm 19.

We must recognize that 'When all thy mercies' was written as a poem, not as a hymn. That accounts for its length. In using it as a hymn to be sung in church we are obliged to shorten it and make a selection of the original stanzas. In some hymnals as many as eight are printed. Most are content with a modest six (as *AMR* 177 and *EH* 511).

This creates something of a problem. In many cases the shortening of a hymn does not matter and is often desirable. But in the case of this particular hymn the cutting out of verses, though necessary, is unfortunate in that it spoils the scheme which Addison had in mind. His poem follows a clear and orderly pattern. It gives thanks to God for his mercies throughout the whole course of life, in all its varying circumstances, from beginning to end. The theme is summed up in the stanza beginning

299

Through every period of my life
Thy goodness I'll pursue.

This is the purpose of the entire work: to look in turn at each
period of life and express gratitude accordingly. To select
certain stanzas and omit others obscures the pattern and
breaks the sequence. In our study of the hymn we shall take
note of all that Addison wrote and supply the stanzas which
are missing from our hymnals.

II

The first stanza is by way of introduction and opens up the
theme:

When all thy mercies, O my God,
My rising soul surveys,
Transported with the view, I'm lost
In wonder, love, and praise.

All thy mercies – those three words strike the keynote of the
poem. From first to last Addison is occupied with those divine
mercies, recalling them, counting them, naming them in turn.
What he says here is that his *rising soul surveys* them. One
writer somewhat oddly suggests that the mention of the 'rising
soul' indicates that this was intended to be a morning act of
praise, to be used on waking from sleep. It shows how easily
words can be misunderstood. In the morning it is the body
that rises, not the soul. The idea Addison had in mind was that
of the soul rising up to take, as it were, a bird's eye view of
life's blessings under the good hand of God; and when that is
done the result is rapture. *Transported with the view, I'm lost
in wonder, love, and praise.* If those last words seem to have a
particularly familiar ring, it is because Charles Wesley borrowed them and used them as the closing line of his 'Love
divine, all loves excelling'.

The next three stanzas are missing from most hymn books.
The second verse of the poem is:

> O how should words with equal warmth
>   The gratitude declare
> That glows within my ravished heart?
>   But thou canst read it there.

What the poet is saying here is that *words* alone are inadequate to express *the gratitude that glows* within the heart — *my ravished heart*, he calls it, for he is enraptured with joy. The apostle Peter refers to a 'joy unspeakable', and certainly there are times when language fails us: we feel more than we can utter. But God can read our hearts and interpret their deepest feelings.

In counting his blessings Addison begins not with birth but before birth:

> Thy providence my life sustained,
>   And all my wants redrest,
> When in the silent womb I lay,
>   And hung upon the breast.

It is good to think about the mystery of life's origin, and its conception and growth *in the silent womb*. There are some words in Psalm 139 which echo the mood of this stanza: 'Thou didst form my inward parts, thou didst knit me together in my mother's womb. I will praise thee, for I am wonderfully made' (vv. 13, 14). For the psalmist, contemplation of God's work in the creation of each human life is a theme for adoration. As Alexander Maclaren comments, 'Every man carries in his own body reason for reverent gratitude.'

The next two stanzas deal with the years of infancy and earliest childhood, and can be taken together.

> To all my weak complaints and cries
>   Thy mercy lent an ear,
> Ere yet my feeble thoughts had learnt
>   To form themselves in prayer.

> Unnumbered comforts to my soul
>   Thy tender care bestowed,
> Before my infant heart conceived
>   From whom those comforts flowed.

To Addison, our *weak complaints and cries* in infancy are our prayers – answered under God by our parents. It was in fact their *tender care* which bestowed on us those *unnumbered comforts* to which the hymn refers; but the poet sees, behind the human agency, the hand of divine providence.

These two stanzas compel us to reflect upon those earliest phases of life of which we have no conscious recollection: the years of childhood when we were wholly dependent on what others did for us. Psychology constantly stresses the importance of those formative years when our characters were slowly being shaped. We can never be too grateful to God for parents who not only cared for our bodily needs but also prayed for us, taught us, and trained us in the ways of godliness.

Childhood passes into adolescence:

> When in the slippery paths of youth
> With heedless steps I ran,
> Thine arm unseen conveyed me safe
> And led me up to man.

Now we are reminded of our teens and *the slippery paths of youth*. The expression is a quaint one; but let us make no mistake, the paths of youth *are* slippery and beset by all manner of dangers and temptations. Modern life has not rendered that any less true than it was in Addison's day. If young people are not to slip up and fall by the way, they need all the guidance and help they can receive from parents, teachers and friends, as well as from the specialist agencies.

Not only in youth but in later years as well life has its perils:

> Through hidden dangers, toils and deaths
> It gently cleared my way,
> And through the pleasing snares of vice,
> More to be feared than they.

The *It* at the beginning of line 2 is *thine arm unseen* mentioned in the previous stanza. Both verses have the same subject. The arm of the Lord is our protection amidst all the *hidden dangers* of life's journey: dangers none the less real for their being unknown and unseen. Equally real, and *more to be feared than they*, are the dangers of a moral character, *the pleasing snares of vice* from which no one is immune. So here in this stanza, as in the General Thanksgiving, we return thanks to God for our 'preservation'.

Illness is another of life's hazards, and therefore health is another theme for gratitude:

> When worn with sickness, oft hast thou
> With health renewed my face;
> And when in sins and sorrows sunk,
> Revived my soul with grace.

Health means wholeness, and accordingly this stanza treats body and soul together. Few of us who have lived any length of years have never been *worn with sickness*. Probably it has happened to us many times. Possibly at one time or another we have passed through illness of a serious nature. Therefore we have good cause to offer thanks to God for *health renewed*. Nor do we thank him less for coming to our aid in our hours of deep spiritual need, lifting us up from our *sins and sorrows* and graciously ministering his pardon and comfort to our souls.

III

Now we turn to the brighter side of the picture:

> Thy bounteous hand with worldly bliss
> Has made my cup run o'er,
> And in a kind and faithful friend
> Has doubled all my store.

By *worldly bliss* we are to understand the good things of this life with which God richly furnishes us for our enjoyment (1 Timothy 6.17). Such things as home and family life, literature and music, the faculties of sight and hearing, the beauty of the natural world – these are probably what the poet had in mind. And there is one blessing which he rightly singles out for special mention, *a kind and faithful friend*; for true friendship is one of life's most precious gifts. All these good things we

303

receive as from our Father's *bounteous hand* with grateful hearts.

And what more? The list is unending:

> Ten thousand thousand precious gifts
> My daily thanks employ,
> Nor is the least a cheerful heart
> That tastes those gifts with joy.

The gifts of God are beyond our reckoning – *ten thousand thousand* in number. The psalmist exhorts us to 'forget not all his benefits' (Psalm 103.2); but in fact we cannot remember even a fraction of the many blessings a loving Father lavishes upon us day by day. Therefore we must offer him *our daily thanks.* Not the least of those blessings is *a cheerful heart,* for it enables us to appreciate God's bounty, to receive his *gifts with joy*, and to face life in a spirit of true gratitude. So we can say:

> Through every period of my life
> Thy goodness I'll pursue,
> And after death in distant worlds
> The glorious theme renew.

Through every period of my life: this, as we said at the beginning, and now have seen, is the key-phrase of the hymn. Its grand design is to trace the *goodness* of God in all life's varied circumstances and to make it a constant theme for thanksgiving. Nor will our thanksgiving finish when life itself ends. *After death, in distant worlds the glorious theme* will be renewed.

Death is not a subject to be avoided by the Christian believer. He is prepared to think about it, not morbidly but realistically, as the final episode of life's total experience:

> When nature fails, and day and night
> Divide thy works no more,
> My ever-grateful heart, O Lord,
> Thy mercy shall adore.

What Addison is saying here is, When my health and strength at last fail, and my days on earth are done, still *my ever-grateful heart* will be lifted up to God in adoration for his mercy. Isaac Watts, who was a contemporary of Addison's, wrote a hymn expressing the same spirit of faith, beginning, 'I'll praise my Maker while I've breath' (*CP* 8). It was a hymn greatly beloved by John Wesley, who during the night before he died attempted to repeat the first verse.

So much for death. And what after death?

> Through all eternity to thee
> A joyful song I'll raise;
> For O, eternity's too short
> To utter all thy praise!

The stanza makes a splendid finish to a splendid hymn, which spans the whole of our existence. It begins before our birth. It ends beyond our death. In life and death, in youth and old age, in sickness and in health, in prosperity and adversity, in this world and the next, we never cease to sing *a joyful song* to God's praise. And even *eternity's too short* to utter the whole of it!

40

PILGRIM SONG

Who would true valour see

ALTHOUGH BUNYAN's celebrated Pilgrim Song was written just on three hundred years ago, it did not find its way into our hymn books until the beginning of this century, when it appeared in a modified form in the *English Hymnal*, 1906. Before that time some hesitation appears to have been felt regarding its suitability for Christian worship. There was also the difficulty of finding a tune to fit the unusual metre. This latter problem was resolved by Dr R. Vaughan Williams, the musical editor of *EH*. The story goes that in 1904 he heard a ploughman from the village of Monks Gate, near Horsham, singing an old Sussex folk-song. The words were commonplace but the tune was distinctive, and it occurred to him that he could adapt it to suit Bunyan's lines. He did this and named the tune *Monks Gate*.

So much for the tune. But what about the words? Percy Dearmer, the general editor of *EH*, was not happy about printing the song exactly as Bunyan wrote it. He thought the opening lines struck the wrong note for a hymn, and he also jibbed at 'hobgoblin nor foul fiend' in the last stanza; so he prepared a revised version of the song for inclusion in the hymnal. In this form it also appeared in *Songs of Praise*, 1926, of which Dr Dearmer was also editor. Admittedly the revision was skilfully carried out and has something to commend it. The fact remains, however, that later hymnals, almost without exception, have preferred to adhere to Bunyan's original wording, and this is what we shall do in the present study.

I

The first thing to be said about the song is that Bunyan certainly did not write it with a view to its being used as a hymn in Christian worship. In his day 'hymns' in the ordinary sense of the word were not sung in churches or chapels. Nothing but the metrical psalms were considered proper for this purpose. Bunyan wrote the lines as a poem to fit into the second edition (1686) of his *Pilgrim's Progress*, part two – the part which tells of the pilgrimage of Christiana and her four boys. On her journey in company with Greatheart she met Valiant-for-Truth, 'a man with his sword drawn, and his face all bloody', for he had just been engaged in a long and bitter fight with three assailants. Questioned by Greatheart, he told how he had left his native town of Darkland at the behest of Mr Tell-true and had become a pilgrim. After describing the many adversities he had encountered and overcome along the way, he concluded his story by saying, 'I believed, and therefore came out, got into the way, fought all that set themselves against me, and, by believing, am come to this place.'

At this point in the narrative Bunyan inserted the Pilgrim Song. It is important to note that the song is not put into the mouth of Valiant-for-Truth, as though he were boasting of his valour and holding himself up as an example to all and sundry. The words are not his but Bunyan's. Before proceeding with his story the author is here directing the reader to 'come hither' and take a good look at Valiant if he wishes to see a picture of a courageous and victorious pilgrim. This is the purpose of the song. It sets before us an object lesson, not only for our admiration but for our emulation. 'Whose faith follow', Bunyan seems to say of Valiant, as did the writer to the Hebrews of others like him (Hebrews 13.7 AV).

307

The theme of the hymn is that of Bunyan's immortal allegory: the Christian life as a pilgrimage, a constant progress along the Way of Holiness 'from this world to that which is to come'. It is a sound biblical theme (see, e.g., 1 Peter 1.17, 2.11; Hebrews 11.13, 13.14) and the hymn-writers have not been slow to take it up. Neale's 'O happy band of pilgrims' is an obvious example. The theme is also found in 'Guide me, O thou great Jehovah',[1] 'Through the night of doubt and sorrow', and 'Children of the heavenly King'.

Bunyan's song has a character and quality of its own and is worth a close look. But in interpreting it we need to bear in mind the context from which it is taken and its close relation to the person of Valiant-for-Truth. This explains why it portrays the Christian pilgrimage in terms of hardship and conflict. To be a pilgrim is no easy-going affair. It calls for great resources of faith, courage and endurance. The song makes this abundantly clear.

The first stanza stresses the need for constancy in face of the discouraging circumstances to be encountered along the Way.

The second describes the strong and fearless spirit in which the pilgrim must meet and vanquish his foes.

The third points to the goal of the journey, the Life eternal which is the pilgrim's heavenly inheritance.

II

We accept Bunyan's invitation to look closely at the man who embodies the qualities of a true pilgrim.

> Who would true valour see,
>   Let him come hither;
> One here will constant be,
>   Come wind, come weather;
> There's no discouragement
> Shall make him once relent
> His first avowed intent
>   To be a pilgrim.

In his version of the song Percy Dearmer altered the first four lines because, as he put it, 'to ask the congregation of St Ignotus, Erewhon Park, to invite all to come and look at them, if they wished to see true valour, would have been difficult'. So he rewrote the lines:

> He who would valiant be
> 'Gainst all disaster,
> Let him in constancy
> Follow the Master.

Some may prefer this to the original lines in order to avoid misunderstanding; but once we are clear as to what Bunyan is about, and to whom he is pointing when he invites us to *come hither*, the difficulty is removed. *Here*, in Valiant-for-Truth, is *one* who *will constant be* – firm, resolute, immovable – *come wind, come weather*. Wind and weather represent the fluctuating and unpredictable circumstances of life's journey. The pilgrim must not retreat before the wind of adversity or be a fair-weather Christian. Come what may, he must press on and never give up.

There's no discouragement that will make him *once relent* of his purpose: *his first avowed intent to be a pilgrim*. But in fact this is not easy. Discouragements are plentiful and of many kinds – as Valiant knew only too well. He told Greatheart of how, when he set out on his journey, those at home had tried to dissuade him by warning him of the hardships he was likely to encounter, such as the Slough of Despond, the Hill Difficulty, the Valley of the Shadow of Death, and Doubting Castle.

> 'And did none of these things discourage you?' asked Greatheart.
> 'No,' replied Valiant, 'they seemed as mere nothings to me.'
> 'How came that about?'
> 'Why, I still believed what Mr Tell-true had said; and that carried me beyond them all.'
> 'Then,' said Greatheart, 'this was your victory, even your faith.'

The theme is continued and developed in the next stanza.

Whoso beset him round
With dismal stories,
Do but themselves confound;
His strength the more is.
No lion can him fright;
He'll with a giant fight,
But he will have the right
To be a pilgrim.

This stanza finds the pilgrim in the midst of conflict; but it reveals him also as a man of strong and fearless spirit as he faces his foes. Three sorts of opposition are specified. First, there are those who *beset him round with dismal stories* in an endeavour to make him lose heart and turn back. These are the discouragers, the sort of people to whom reference has been made in the previous stanza. Valiant, as we have seen, knew all about discouragement; but in the course of his pilgrimage he experienced not a little encouragement as well. There was the counsel given him by good Mr Tell-true at the outset. There was the comfort he derived from his trusty sword – 'a right Jerusalem blade'. There was the joy of meeting Christiana and her sons. There was the companionship of other pilgrims along the road. There was the memory of many mercies received, many triumphs won. So, far from losing heart, Valiant presses on his way with cheerful courage, and *his strength the more is.*

No lion can him fright. Here is another foe. In the Bible the lion is often the symbol of danger (e.g. Psalm 17.12; Isaiah 35.9). Bunyan made use of this symbol in the first part of his story when Christian came to the Palace Beautiful and was alarmed to see two lions guarding the Porter's lodge.

> Then he was afraid, for he thought that nothing but death was before him. But the porter at the lodge, whose name is Watchful, perceiving that Christian made a halt as if he would go back, cried unto him, saying, 'Is thy strength so small? Fear not the lions, for they are chained, and are placed there for trial of faith where it is, and for discovery of those who have none. Keep in the midst of the path, and no hurt shall come unto thee.'

Christian's fears were needless, and he went forward trembling but unharmed. Many of the 'lions' that frighten us along the pilgrim path are powerless to hurt us, for God is in command of the situation (*cf.* Daniel 6.22).

A third opponent is named: *He'll with a giant fight.* Bunyan was thinking probably of Giant Despair. Christian and Hopeful had encountered this fearsome foe when they strayed from the King's highway, and as a result they found themselves incarcerated in Doubting Castle. Despair, Doubt, Despondency are giants we all have to fight at times. But there are others as well. There are giants that confront us in our national life, and in our church life, as well as in our personal life – giants to be fought with high courage and strong faith if we too would *have the right to be a pilgrim.*

III

The final stanza looks onwards and upwards:

> Hobgoblin nor foul fiend
>   Can daunt his spirit:
> He knows he at the end
>   Shall life inherit.
> Then, fancies, fly away;
> He'll fear not what men say;
> He'll labour night and day
>   To be a pilgrim.

Hobgoblin nor foul fiend – what are we to make of that? Dr Dearmer, as we have noted, could not tolerate such language in a Christian hymn. Hence in his version he changed the first part of the verse to:

> Since, Lord, thou dost defend
>   Us with thy Spirit,
> We know we at the end
>   Shall life inherit.

'Hobgoblin' in particular was what bothered Dearmer. He complained that the word does not occur in the Bible, that it is found only twice in Shakespeare ('and then only in playful, fairy connections'), and that it had no serious religious associations in Bunyan's time any more than now. All this, of course, is true – and Bunyan would have agreed. He knew as well as Dr Dearmer that hobgoblins have no reality. They are nothing but a figment of the imagination. And *that*, in fact, is precisely why he introduced them into his narrative. Along with satyrs, fiends and dragons, they are part of the evil forces encountered by Pilgrim in the Valley of the Shadow of Death. Plainly the language is symbolical and nothing more. For Bunyan, 'hobgoblin' is simply a figure of speech. As G. R. Balleine remarks, 'He wanted a word that would suggest fears that have no foundation. Millions make themselves miserable with utterly baseless worries, fears that are every bit as absurd as fear of a hobgoblin.'[2]

Now we see why a pilgrim like Valiant allows neither 'hobgoblin nor foul fiend' to *daunt his spirit*. His robust faith overcomes these inventions of the mind and he bids such *fancies fly away*. He is not going to be deterred by religious make-believe any more than by public opinion: *He'll fear not what men say*. So labouring *night and day* he pursues his pilgrimage with good courage, for *he knows he at the end shall life inherit* – life eternal in the city of the King.

How it fared with Valiant-for-Truth 'at the end' is one of Bunyan's most famous pieces of writing. When the final call came for this brave pilgrim he summoned his friends and told them his departure was at hand.

> Then said he, 'I am going to my Father's; and though with great difficulty I am got thither, yet now I do not repent me of all the trouble I have been at to arrive where I am. My sword I give to him that shall succeed me in my pilgrimage, and my courage and skill to him that can get it. My marks and scars I carry with me, to be a witness for me that I have fought His battles who now will be my rewarder.'
>
> When the day that he must go hence was come, many accompanied him to the river side, into which as he went he said, 'Death, where is thy sting?' And as he went down deeper,

he said, 'Grave, where is thy victory?' So he passed over, and all the trumpets sounded for him on the other side.

NOTES

1 For this hymn see chapter 25.
2 *Sing with the Understanding*, p. 197.

BIBLIOGRAPHY

A Dictionary of Hymnology. Ed. John Julian (Murray), 1892; revised 1907.

Historical Companion to Hymns Ancient and Modern. Ed. Maurice Frost (Clowes), 1962.

Handbook to the Church Hymnary. Ed. James Moffatt (Oxford), 1927.

Songs of Praise Discussed. Ed. Percy Dearmer (Oxford), 1933.

The New Methodist Hymn Book Illustrated. Ed. John Telford (Epworth), 1934.

Companion to Congregational Praise. Ed. K. L. Parry (Independent Press), 1953.

The Baptist Church Hymn Book Companion. Ed. Hugh Martin (Psalms and Hymns Trust), 1962.

The English Hymn. Louis F. Benson (Hodder and Stoughton), 1915.

The Gospel in Hymns. Albert E. Bailey (Scribners, New York), 1950.

Hymns and Human Life. Erik Routley (Murray), 1952.

Hymns and the Faith. Erik Routley (Murray), 1955.

I'll Praise my Maker. Erik Routley (Independent Press), 1951.

Sing with the Understanding. G. R. Balleine (Independent Press), 1954.

The Hymns of Methodism. Henry Bett (Epworth), 1945.

The Hymns of Wesley and Watts. Bernard L. Manning (Epworth), 1942.

Hymns in Christian Worship. H. A. L. Jefferson (Rockliff), 1950.

The Church and the Hymn Writers. G. Currie Martin (Clarke), 1928.

English Hymns and Hymn Writers. Adam Fox (Collins), 1947.

They Wrote our Hymns. Hugh Martin (SCM Press), 1961.

Hymns and Worship. G. F. S. Gray (SPCK), 1961.

Famous Hymns and their Authors. F. A. Jones (Hodder and Stoughton), 1905.

Hymns and Hymn Makers. Duncan Campbell (Black), 1898.

INDEX OF AUTHORS AND TRANSLATORS

INDEX OF THE HYMNS